Sally
Meyers

LENA

LENA

by LENA HORNE and RICHARD SCHICKEL

1965
DOUBLEDAY & COMPANY, INC., GARDEN CITY, NEW YORK

FOR
Tom and Bill
Elois D.
Robert M.
Kitty D'A.
Ginette S.
Lillian and Maurice
Herbie B.

IF there be sorrow
       let it be
for things undone
       unrealized
              unattained
to these add one:
Love withheld . . .
. . . restrained

"If There Be Sorrow" by Mari Evans

LENA

CHAPTER ONE

I

I was born in a small Jewish lying-in hospital in Brooklyn, New York, on June 30, 1917. I've been told that the nurses exhibited me all over the place, terribly enthused and surprised about my copper color. Since my dad, whose fine copper glow I inherited, was hung up in a card game where he was earning the money to pay the hospital bill and did not appear until much later I'm convinced there was more sheer surprise than enthusiasm in the attitude of the nurses.

Both my mother and my grandmother, who accompanied her to the hospital, had very fair complexions (as had so many of the Negro families whom we knew); so those nurses just did not know they were Negroes. And given the time and the place it would never have occurred to the Horne ladies to say "Look out for a brown baby—we're colored folks." They—and especially my grandmother—knew who they were and they would simply have assumed that others knew too.

I sometimes think the pattern of my life was established on the very day I was born. My father was to continue to be far off-stage somewhere, pursuing his own interests. I was to be separated from him almost totally throughout my childhood and I was to be separated by forces largely beyond our control, from my mother for long periods of time —just as I was by those nurses that first day. Finally, most of my successes were to be the result of being exhibited, as I was that first day, as an oddity of color—a Negro woman, a Negro entertainer who didn't fit the picture of personality and performing style the white majority used to expect. How I hated those awful phrases they used to trot out to describe me! Who the hell wants to be a "chocolate chanteuse?"

And yet I have to admit there was a rough truth in this attitude toward me. I *was* different, for the experiences that formed me were different from those that formed most people. They were certainly different from those of the white people—that's true for any Negro. But they were also different from those of most Negroes.

You see, my family was regarded as one of the "First Families" of Brooklyn. This status derived from a great many things, color being only one of them.

My grandmother, Cora Calhoun Horne, was an ardent fighter for Negro causes, but even she, the direct issue of a slave-owner, never talked to me about the central issue of Negro history, which is slavery. She dismissed it, by force of will, I think, from her consciousness. And I realize now that I never learned anything, when I was a child, about who I was or what I was. Nobody in my family ever told me and I certainly never learned anything about my racial identity in school, because the only Negro ever mentioned in the history books was George Washington Carver, and he was too pure and good to believe. I did learn, however, that other races had backgrounds they looked upon with pride and I kept looking for some reason to feel the same way. Eventually, when "interested" people began to try to give me different "images" of myself, I came to realize that nobody (and certainly not yet myself) had any sound image to give a woman who stood between the two conventional ideas of Negro womanhood: the "good," quiet,

Negro woman who scrubbed and cooked and was a re-spectable servant—and the whore.

For me the problem of defining just what it meant to be a Negro was compounded because for many years I was to be virtually rootless in the world—a stranger in the white world, of course, for color must keep you forever a stranger there—but also a stranger in the world which most Negroes inhabit and with which they are forced, from birth, to come to terms. Neither world was ever to be totally mine because I would never stay long enough in either of them to acquire that intimate, bred-in-the-bones knowledge of them that comes from having roots so deep that you cannot see or even trace some of them.

The world into which I was born, the one which exerted the strongest pull on my personality, was a small, tight world, one which many people, white and Negro, are unaware existed early in this century. It was the world of the Negro middle class. Our family, I find, followed most of the patterns that sociologists—those few who have studied the so-called black bourgeoisie—have found were common to our class. We were isolated from the mainstream of Negro life, seeing a relatively narrow group of people. For example, I'm told it was characteristic of our class not to be Baptists or Methodists, which most Negroes were then. We were not. I was baptized, but not confirmed, in the Catholic faith; and my grandmother was interested in the Ethical Culture movement—she even had a scholarship named after her at the Brooklyn Ethical Culture School. We were a family of readers and playgoers and though we lived in the Bedford section of Brooklyn, now an infamous Negro ghetto, it was not then a predominately Negro neighborhood. It did not become so, I believe, until the subway came past, some years after I was born.

The house I lived in until I was six or seven, and to which I returned time and again as I grew up, belonged to my paternal grandparents. It was the first in a row of four brownstones on Chauncey Street. Two doors down was a "Boy's Welcome Hall," a youth center to which I can remember my Uncle Burke going to practice basketball. Next to it was a frame house occupied by an Irish family whom I didn't know very well, though I remember liking their front yard, which was much deeper than ours and had flowers. Then came our house, then the other three in our brownstone row and then a garage owned by a Scandinavian family. Their children were real towheads and seemed nice, although I was not allowed to play with them because the car grease could get you so dirty. Nevertheless, I was always instructed to be very polite to them. Across the street were three-story frame houses, mostly occupied by poor Irish people who were supposed to be the less privileged people of the neighborhood.

Our house was four stories and narrow, as most brownstones are. The thing I always remember first about it was the iron fence that separated our yard from the sidewalk and from the houses on either side. What the white picket fence was to some parts of America, the iron fence was to Brooklyn in those days. Painted shiny black, each spike topped by a neat, arrow-shaped point, I suppose those fences were supposed to tell the world, This is Ours; we have arrived at the point where there is property that must, at least symbolically, be marked off and protected. Anyway, you opened the gate in the fence, crossed a little patch of paved yard and then followed a walk around the left side of the house, went down a couple of steps and arrived at another bit of fancy iron work, the grille door to the basement. The front sitting room lay just beyond that door. I would come home from school (during the few times during my school years that I lived in this house) and take the key off the chain on which I always wore it around my neck and let myself in this door. Waiting for me on the kitchen table would be an apple and a Hershey bar. If the weather was good I would go out into the back yard and play under the cherry tree, by myself, until someone came home. I had a little table and chair out there and I would sit there quietly and read or just think. Sometimes I would take some clothes of my mother's or my grandmother's and play dress up. Every now and then I'd run to peer through the iron grille door to see if my Uncle Burke (the youngest of my grandmother's boys and a teen-ager then) had come home from school and had time to talk to me before he ran out again to play basketball or whatever.

II

When I was born, my parents were living together in this house, but by the time I was old enough to have any memories of it they had split up and left me there with my grandparents. I can only try to reconstruct what happened between them, but it must have been an odd match to begin with. How could a lovely, tender, indulged lady like my mother cope with a beautiful, young, wild, angry, northern nonconformist like my father? As I observed them in later years, the only thing I could see they had in common was good looks.

My mother was wildly in love with him. When she was carrying me she remembers touching him constantly, hoping this would make her baby come out a boy—and beautiful like him.

My father was the second of four sons. After him came Frank, who had already graduated from college and gone off to teach when I was born. Erroll, the oldest, was killed in World War I, and Burke, the youngest, I have already mentioned. At a very early age my father showed great independence, impatience with education and a desire to strike off on his own. When he was just a little boy—seven or eight years old—he sneaked off to Manhattan and got himself hired as a page boy at the Astor Hotel, where he remembers that one of his tasks was to carry the pug dogs belonging to rich ladies downstairs on pillows and then hand them to the ladies after they had been helped into their carriages and settled under their lap robes preparatory to taking their afternoon rides. How he managed to get the job at his tender age I'll never know, but he did and after a time proudly brought home his earnings to my grandmother—who promptly had a fit and snatched him back to Brooklyn.

It seems she continually had to take time off from her work with delinquent boys in Harlem to help the truant officer collect Daddy from various jobs and get him back to the classroom. He worked in order to get some "sucker" (his word) to do his homework rather than go to school. Part of his "income" also went to his little brothers to take his turn at dishwashing and the other chores. And how could my grandmother, who couldn't help but adore him, punish the beautiful son who smiled up at her and presented her with gifts he had bought himself for her?

But despite his knowledge of the power of money and the independence it bought, he found holding down a regular job, with hours to keep and bosses to heed, a drag. Also, he hated working for "the man." So, since the gambling spots in Harlem were the only place a Negro man could make quick money without holding the usual sort of job, "the other world" got him for good not long after his marriage to my mother. He had tried the working world, but it was not for him.

Now my mother was rather like one of those little Tennessee Williams white ladies—full of moonlight and magnolia dreams and nothing in her background had prepared her for him.

The dominant figure in her household had been her great-grandmother, Amélie Louise Ashton—tall, black, with long black hair, Senegalese. She died when I was two years old —and she was one hundred and three. Far in the past she had been a stewardess on a boat running from Marseilles around the coast of France and ultimately up the Seine to Paris. She was terribly proud of her Parisian French and utterly despised American Negroes. My mother does not know how she happened to come to America with a child (my mother's grandmother) or how they happened to settle in Atlanta. But the daughter, Louise, had three children and then died. Amélie brought the three of them North and my mother's mother, also named Louise, went to the only Negro teacher's training school in Brooklyn and after that she married a man named Cyrus Scottron, a Portuguese Negro from Springfield, Massachusetts.

My Granddaddy Cyrus' family intrigues me . . . my mother only recently told me that two members of it passed for white and were in show business. One of them was a fine, red-haired concert singer, another married a cowboy rope twirler and toured in vaudeville for years. Cyrus himself was the first Negro railway post office clerk. He was on the road from New York to Lord knows where and had to memorize the names of all the little towns and junctions along the way where the mail was dropped off. He wrote them all down on little cards and my mother claims she learned to read (place names, anyway) when she was four years old by helping him memorize the names of the towns on his route. He left home for good when my mother was eleven. Her mother taught school in Brooklyn, one of a handful of "first" Negro teachers in the public schools. Amélie ran the house—cooked, cleaned, ruled. When the family ran into trouble economically Amélie would go to her trunk and burrow around in it and come up with an ancient solid gold Senegalese coin with which to bail them out. She did not allow my mother to soil her hands, ruin her complexion or stuff her head with unladylike ideas. As to giving her any idea about the realities of Negro life, any idea of Negro history or problems, that was out of the question. She just drew herself up, asserted her African ego and said in exquisite French, "Those black, cowardly slaves."

In other words, my mother was not equipped to handle her husband, my father. And when she encountered Cora Calhoun Horne? *Voilà* . . . everything hit the fan.

The marriage must have ended when I was about three years old. My father simply lit out—working, I suppose—or gambling—his way westward. He sent money home to take care of my mother and me and to help out his mother. He has always been proud of the fact that he helped his brothers through school, and, just before she died, he gave my grandmother a round-the-world trip.

My mother stayed on with me in the house on Chauncey Street for a while, but she could not get along with my grandmother who was the kind of woman who tests people by being very hard on them. If they could not or would not stand up to her she immediately lost respect for them and then the testing spirit would turn to contempt. I learned quite early—but, of course, not quite this early—that the only way to get along with her was to break this chain of contempt. My mother could not learn that and she allowed herself to be driven out of the house.

III

That left four people at home—my grandparents, my Uncle Burke, and me. The others all offered me something. There was discipline from my grandmother, a little teasing and some jolly laughs with Uncle Burke before he ran out to join his friends in their activities, companionship on a grave and adult level from Granddad. And yet, we never meshed as a family unit. The house itself is the only thing that bound us all together, the only tangible I could touch which said "family" to me.

Looking back, I cannot remember my grandparents ever exchanging more than a formal, "Good Morning, Mrs. Horne, Good Morning, Mr. Horne." Other than that they did not speak. If they needed to communicate Uncle Burke would carry notes from one to the other. I see their relationship, in memory, rather like a theatrical company, with my granddad as the producer, paying the bills, Uncle Burke as the stage manager, and my grandmother—no one else—as the director.

Or, to break that metaphor, the absolute dictator. She was a tiny woman, with a very fair skin and gray-streaked hair. She wore round steel-rimmed spectacles. She had a short, straight nose, a straight, rather thin mouth, and a firm chin. She was very proud of her feet which were small and perfectly shaped and she always wore fabulous shoes. She was active in the Urban League and the NAACP, the Suffragette movement, and all kinds of social-work activity. Years later Paul Robeson, whom my grandmother helped to get a scholarship at Rutgers, told me that one of his vivid childhood memories was of Grandmother lecturing to gangs of loitering boys on Harlem street corners, telling them to break it up and be about something useful.

I have a clipping that was sent me in the summer of 1963. It is from the October 1919 issue of *The Branch Bulletin,* a publication of the NAACP. It is a picture of a grim, chubby child, wearing a white dress and high-topped white shoes and holding a rather wilted-looking rose. The caption reads: "This is a picture of one of the youngest members of the N.A.A.C.P. Her name is Lena Calhoun Horne and she lives in Brooklyn, N.Y. She paid the office a visit last month and seemed delighted with everything she saw, particularly the National Secretary and the telephones."

I don't remember the visit, but I'm sure it was my grandmother who took me, for of her many good works it was, naturally, the NAACP, along with the Urban League, that ranked highest in her interest. All through my adult life, no matter where my career has taken me, I have continued to encounter people who know my grandmother, if not in these early days of the NAACP, then in some other aspect of her life as a devoted clubwoman, doer of good deeds, and, I suppose—to put a negative connotation on it—as a practitioner of *noblesse oblige.* For she did have her own sure sense of who she was and of her place in the world, and she was not modest on either point.

The record of her activities may sound like that of one of those genteel middle-class club ladies in a Helen Hokinson cartoon. You will have to believe me that there was nothing genteel in her manner. There was, instead, a kind of polite ferocity. She was, after all, a Negro woman, which meant that there were problems to which she and her fellow workers had to devote themselves with a zeal, a passion that is quite beyond most women. For her these activities were something more than a way to fill, or kill, time. There was real work to be done.

And remember she was the daughter of a slave woman and the white man who owned her. If the name Calhoun strikes a chord, it is because I hear she was of the family of John C. Calhoun, the famous apologist for slavery in pre-Civil War days. As my father summed it up, rather inelegantly, recently: "She was the get of the lousiest sons of bitches in the South and she was determined to rise above it."

In short, I know now that there was more to my grandmother than might have met the eye. I know now that her class and her generation were right about many things, particularly in their ideas of what Negro aspirations should be and how they should achieve them. She did valuable work and she was herself a woman of great if forbidding character. She was no social climber in the ordinary sense and I don't think she engaged herself in a single fatuous moment in her entire life.

But that did not make her any easier to live with. I may not remember the visit to the NAACP office, but I have vivid memories of accompanying her to the meetings of the other organizations to which she belonged. I was always the only child there, sitting quietly, listening because I knew I would be questioned later about what I had heard. I must have been a pain and something of a prig to another, more relaxed sort of kid. But I was learning to "speak up like a little adult" in order to earn one brisk sign of approval from Grandmother.

I was nearly always with adults in Brooklyn. My association with children was limited to just a few in the neighborhood who met with Grandmother's approval. I was not allowed to play with the white children or with any children at all whose speech or deportment were not admirable in her eyes. When I was old enough to go to the Ethical Culture School (on my grandmother's scholarship) I was expected to leave school immediately at the end of the day and not to see my schoolmates until the next morning. My grandmother did not believe in idle chitchat for herself or for anyone else. Her conversation with me was always of an instructive nature: "Do as I say, do as I do! Don't cringe! Don't sulk! Stand straight! Speak clearly! Use your brains! Don't cry! Sit still in public! Be polite to those who are less fortunate!" That was not to denote those with less money. In fact that didn't impress her at all.

Things like house cleaning, cooking, making beds, or, for that matter, a broody little mother with a baby, did not constitute what she thought a suitable challenge to a

woman (they tell me house servants never were much good
for hard physical labor). She had a Spartan appetite,
further dulled, I'm sure, by the tea and cakes that accompanied meetings and fund-raising affairs. So the kitchen of
the house, which was my favorite room, rarely glowed
with the heat of great meals being prepared.

But she did have a taste for classic Southern cooking.
She thought—and I agree—that the gods had a great deal
to do with the creation of okra, the divine food. She liked
it fresh cooked, not too soft, served in a bowl with butter,
salt, and pepper on top. She also liked clabber (which is
something like yogurt), cool and lightly sugared, oysters
and clams, kale and mustard (if someone else would wash
and cook the greens).

So my grandmother did not fit the classic pattern of the
Negro matriarchy. Things like cooking, cleaning, and house-
keeping, etc., didn't seem to her a challenge for a woman
with brains. So we—my uncle and Granddaddy and I—often
shifted for ourselves as far as the amenities were concerned.
Mornings, for example, my grandfather would get up first
and make his own breakfast. In winter, before going off to
work, he would start the furnace, which was in the basement, so that by the time I came down for breakfast it
would be warm and cozy. The milk bottles, left outside
by the milkman, would be thawing, the icy cream having
expanded and pushed the cap off the top. Uncle Burke
would give me my oatmeal and then I would go off to
school.

My grandfather was, I think, a lonely man. I've learned
some about his background. He actually seems to have gone
to college in Indiana. One brother was a first Negro sheriff
of incredible strength in a small Indiana county and another
brother was dynamited and killed because his successful
trading on a Mississippi river boat angered the white com-

petition. Meanwhile, Granddaddy became a teacher. He seems to have arrived in Atlanta, met the three C's—Cora, Alice, and Lena Calhoun—famous belles of the South I gather—and eloped with Cora, a great beauty "who never fastened her own shoes until she was sixteen." He edited two Negro newspapers, *The Freeman* and *The Bee*, in Indiana.

He was the dreamer and the intellectual; she a very real lady from a very unrealistic system. Together they determined to go North, to raise their children in a freer atmosphere. Granddaddy got a job as a teacher in New York City. But in a little while he lost the position— His right of seniority had been ignored and a white man given the job. He promptly sued the city. It was a test case and he won—but his job was not restored. My Uncle Burke says that my great-aunt Lena's husband, Dr. Frank Smith, who was principal of Pearl High School in Nashville and certainly couldn't have been very rich, helped them whenever he could.

Granddaddy became an inspector in the fire department, which was a job that did not fully occupy his mind. He spoke six languages, he was interested in the arts; and even then a Negro who was more interested in them than in sports (Jack Johnson, the boxer, was a great hero to Negroes then) or in the more serious side of Negro development, as exemplified by George Washington Carver or Booker T. Washington, was considered something of an oddity. My grandmother was inclined to take a somewhat strained attitude of grudging acceptance toward actors and artists. They were "different," perhaps even a little bit peculiar, and they did not figure in her discussions of advancement through knowledge and social service (perhaps my ambivalence toward show business dates to these days).

So he took me as his companion and confidante. He was beautiful to my eyes. To me he looked like the picture version of Little Eva's father in the illustrations in my edition of *Uncle Tom's Cabin*, with his gray mustache, gray hair, beautiful sad blue eyes. He had a gentle voice and a dignified manner and there was always a lovely smell in the room from his Havana cigars. On Saturday mornings he would take me to the museums in Brooklyn and New York, or to the Bronx Zoo, the Aquarium, Grant's Tomb. Then we would go to lunch at the Automat and then, perhaps, to a matinee. I remember seeing the *Nutcracker Suite* danced at the Brooklyn Academy of Music, Eva Le Gallienne in *Peter Pan*. And I remember seeing three or four movies in a single afternoon. At home he would play Bert Williams records for me or talk about Ira Aldrich, the great Negro Shakespearean actor, or Florence Mills, the Negro singer who was then making a great success for herself in Europe.

Sundays I remember were spent in the front room on the ground floor. I see Grandfather in his leather chair, the phonograph turned on, playing Verdi, The New York *Times* strewn around the room, coffee cups and the remains of the breakfast Danish scattered here and there, a haze of cigar smoke spreading through the room. I would be on the floor in front of the bookcase, looking at the pictures in books. Even before I went to school I had been taught some of the little words in the books and could read simple things.

My grandmother's Sundays were usually spent in bed, sitting upright, reading, having a little tea and zwieback perhaps. It seemed as if she used the day to collect her strength for the coming week of activities. At suppertime Granddaddy would take me by the hand and we would walk down Chauncey Street to the delicatessen on Reid Avenue, where we would buy potato salad, cold cuts, baked beans, some kosher dills, anything we didn't have to cook. Then we would walk home, my grandfather nodding in his grave, dignified way to the neighbors, spread our feast on the kitchen table and go! This was not just a Sunday event, but one that occurred several times a week as well.

On Sunday after dinner I was expected to report to my grandmother's room to say good night. I would say what I had been reading. I would be asked if I had clean clothes for the next day, told to stop biting my nails and then say my Catholic prayers. My grandmother practiced no religion herself but she believed any properly brought up young lady should have religious training. Only when this had been accomplished to her satisfaction would I be dismissed to go to bed in the little room next to hers where I slept.

It was a strange life. I did not pay too much attention to the lack of communication between the adults in the house, because my Uncle Burke was the intermediary and because of him I was not often very conscious of the strain between them.

As for my absent parents, I must say I missed them. My mother was never mentioned but I had a tiny picture that I would look at and kiss. My father sent occasional letters and picture postcards and beautiful clothes and toys, and my grandmother would show me the postmarks, explaining that this was the name of the place my father was now.

One time, out of a clear blue sky, he sent Grandmother a player piano, one pedal of which I was permitted to pump away at when we played it. At Christmastime there would be more lavish presents from him. I remember a fur coat that seemed very elegant to me and once a very large Mama doll. It was an Effanbee brand doll, a very famous name of the time, much prized by little girls.

My mother, however, found it difficult to communicate with me directly. I'm sure her position must have been intolerable, so she finally resorted to a subterfuge to spirit me away from the house on Chauncey Street and into a life that was far different from any I had known there.

IV

When my mother left my grandmother's house she went on the stage. Naturally she did, because a beautiful Negro woman who wasn't trained and didn't want to be a prostitute had no other choice. I know now she romanticized the life of the actor, and since she was an attractive woman with a fine singing voice, she was a useful addition to an acting company. And, of course, there were those mysterious relatives on her father's side who were in show business. The only trouble was that there were virtually no opportunities for Negro actors in those days—not that there have ever been many possibilities for them. She got her first job with the Lafayette Players, probably the best known —perhaps the only—Negro stock company on the East Coast. The company played three cities—New York, Philadelphia, and Washington, in rotation. Its repertory consisted mainly of well-known melodramas originally created for the white theater, but the company included such well-known Negro stars as Rose McClendon and Edna Thomas. From the time I was one until I was five I was sneaked in by various cousins to peep through the curtain at my mother.

I have only the vaguest memories of my mother during this period. I do know that I visited her occasionally and that I made my theatrical debut on one of those visits. In Philadelphia I was the young child in the sickbed in one of the scenes of the melodrama, *Madame X*. I enjoyed the excitement of backstage and I still run into people who remember my mother—and even me—from those days. The thing I remember best was the huge fireplace that was a feature of the set for *Way Down East*. The children of the people in the company could sit behind it and peer carefully out through the opening to watch the action on stage.

I don't remember feeling particularly bereft when I had to leave my mother and return to Brooklyn, because the visits were too brief. The Brooklyn house was coming, I suppose, to symbolize normalcy and stability to me. I felt I belonged there and all through my life—until my father finally sold it a few years ago—the existence of that house, the knowledge that it was there, unchanged, was a comfort to me.

One time I remember being called over to her gate by Elsie Williams, who was a special friend of my mother and who lived in the third brownstone in our row. Elsie said, "Your mother's here and she wants to see you. But you mustn't tell anyone." So I went in and my mother was waiting and she talked and talked. I remember her promising that we would be together soon. I just stared at her—she was so beautiful to me.

I suppose that visit prepared me to accept without question her next secretive approach to me—which had rather more serious consequences. I was playing in front of the house. Everyone else was gone and I had dressed up in some elegant clothes of my grandmother's, the way little girls do, when a relative, Cousin Augusta, suddenly appeared. She said I was to come with her, that my mother was in New York and sick and wanted to see me. I went inside, got into my own clothes, and rejoined her.

I don't know exactly where she took me, but I think it must have been somewhere in uptown Manhattan. I wasn't frightened. I was simply thrilled to see my mother, that's all. We came to an apartment belonging to some friends of my mother's and I found her there in bed, sick. She said we were going to take a trip together and that we were to be together from then on. She said she had to get me away from my grandmother's because she knew my father was going to kidnap me from there.

I guess I accepted this explanation, which seemed very glamorous to me. After all, it was my own mother who offered it and I had no reason to doubt it. The trouble was that I was to hear that explanation time after time throughout my childhood, until it lost all its force. Until I was in my early teens I was never to spend more than a few months with my mother at any single time. There was never enough theatrical work for her and since she had no special training of any sort she was always having to pack up and move on, looking for something she could do. Every time she moved, I would be placed in the home of some friend or relative, or sometimes just with someone who could use the few dollars of support money which my mother tried to send them.

In nearly all of these places, I was the outsider just beginning to understand and see family relationships. As soon as I would become adjusted, my mother would turn up—sometimes quite dramatically in the middle of the night—and say, "Your father is coming to take you away from me and I can't let him do that." Off we would go again, and I'd find myself in some new group being careful to be good and trying to ingratiate myself and learn what they expected of me, or at least learning to stay out of the way. The thing I learned best was how to be secret because that's how I got along most easily.

Of course, the truth was that my father never had any intention of kidnaping me. He had ended up in Seattle and was doing very well at whatever he was doing and certainly had no time or ability to take care of a little girl. He had kept in touch with me and had sent me presents and support money when I lived in Brooklyn. There was no mention of kidnaping, or even of any intention of having me visit him.

Years later, my mother told me there was no such threat. She said she had received a letter from my father's second wife, telling her he had no designs on me and that he would, in fact, support me so long as I stayed with my grandmother. The odd thing was I believe that both my parents wanted the same thing for me—a stable environment.

The need to pay for it, perhaps even to save up to create a place where we could eventually be together, was, ironically, the thing that drove her to search so far and wide for work, compelling her to leave me so often. On the other hand, my father refused to help support me unless I was in his mother's home which was his idea of a stable place.

But the simple truth was that my mother just didn't want my father—or my father's family—to have me. And so she was prepared to go through all these difficulties to prevent that happening. It's easy for me to understand now—the marriage had not worked out and my grandmother had, in effect, been too strong for her. My mother must have been terribly resentful and unhappy, especially when my grandparents had the normal comforts of life whereas most of mother's life she had nothing but hard-scrabble. Also she had the unrealistic idea that she could become a star on the stage, a generation before any Negro woman could do that.

But that did not make things any easier for the child who was me. I so often wished I was back with my grandparents where I was someone who belonged in the family, in the neighborhood and not simply someone known as the strange kid who lived at So-and-so's house.

But all this was still in the future. For the moment, I was simply excited to be with my mother and to be taking a trip with her.

We left New York and went to Philadelphia almost immediately. We stayed there for about a month and then set out for Miami, where my mother had the promise of work. My mother was ill with rheumatism and a fever. We had a berth on the Pullman car to Washington, but when the train pulled out of Washington we had to move into a coach at the front of the train behind the engine. That was my introduction to Jim Crow.

My mother was in agony. Each jolt of the train seemed to cause her excruciating pain. I didn't know what to do for her. I was scared for her and scared for myself going so far from home and knowing no one. But if that trip was my introduction to Jim Crow, it was also my introduction to the kindliness of my people. I remember two or three stout, dark women in our car cuddling me in their laps and rocking me to sleep. They gave me food out of their baskets and sang to me when I was restless and let me play with their children. They also did everything they could to make my mother more comfortable.

Miami, when we got there, seemed to me nothing more than an extension of the misery of the train ride. I do not, thank God, remember a great deal about it, just impressions.

We had a little frame house on First Avenue. It had just two or three rooms and latticework decorating the porch. I can remember sitting there and watching the trains go by—they ran right down the center of the street. And I remember having to take camomile all the time—terrible, bitter-tasting stuff everyone used to take for malaria. I remember too, the contemptuous familiarity of the white people when they waited on us in stores—I had never seen anything like that in New York. And I remember that my shoes always hurt me because Negroes were not allowed to try on shoes before they bought them. My strongest sense memory is the nighttime smell when the men came in their wagons to collect from the privies in the back of the houses.

It was in Miami that I learned about what I realize now is corruption. The cops called everyone in the Negro section by their last name and they would simply walk in and look around to see what they could hustle. A lot of the people were making home-brew or running a little game—something like that—so there would be shakedowns. And they would get drunk and beat up Negro people on Saturday night. The sounds of corruption all around me were many and varied.

I have hated and feared cops ever since those days in Miami when I was six years old. Years later, the FBI came to interview me about a friend of mine they suspected of running dope, and when those polite, well-dressed college men entered my living room all I could see were the tight faces of those Miami cops of my childhood.

But most of all, I remember my mother's cries of pain. And doctors coming in the middle of the night and needles being given. She was terribly sick and we were strangers in a strange town. It was during this period that I was beaten for the first time. Some woman, whose name I don't remember, whose very presence is vague to me (and menacing, still) took care of me sometimes. And she demanded strict obedience. The slightest noise caused my mother pain, she said, so she beat me whenever I forgot myself in the trivial ways that a small child will. And that, too hastened my education. Because after that, wherever I lived, however far away my mother was, I was obsessed with the idea that I had to be good, that my mother must never hear anything bad about me. That woman in Miami had beaten the notion into me very thoroughly.

In some ways school was a relief from the pain and the tension in that little house on First Avenue. But it was also a far cry from education at the Ethical Culture School in Brooklyn. It was a one-room affair—five grades, one teacher. I was put ahead a grade when I entered it and that did not endear me to my schoolmates. They knew who I was. Sure, I was that little smart-aleck, fresh, yellow kid from up North. I might be smart enough to skip grades at first but I was too dumb to keep my damned mouth shut, wasn't I?

I paid my dues in that school. I paid them to kids who might not be able to read, but who could do everything else better than I could. I learned to change my accent and I learned to play ring games instead of play-acting by myself. I learned to duck and I learned to play politics so I wouldn't get thrown in the dirt and be punished when I got home for ruining my clothes. Most important of all, I learned to bury Lena Calhoun Horne, my grandmother's little lady, in a corner of my brain. She was no use to me now. My mother did not even know who she was. To her I was just her little Lena, her baby whom she had got back at last.

CHAPTER TWO

I

No one was directing or editing my life during the years I spent in other people's houses all over the South, but a mood certainly was established in my mind. It was a mood of loneliness and self-protectiveness, broken occasionally by the hope that somehow I might finally be allowed to settle down in one place permanently—and occasionally, by some act of kindness or cruelty that stands out from the gray tones of the background.

There is an awful sameness about living with strangers and being a stranger yourself all the time. I find it almost impossible to remember the sequence of the houses I lived in and the people who took care of me. Nor is it possible to remember exactly how long I stayed in a particular place. The best I can hope to do is re-create a little of the feeling of what it was like to be me in the years I spent in the South.

One should remember, too, that this period was frequently broken by trips back to Brooklyn, where I got some of my schooling and where my image of a home that was truly mine would be renewed. In a way those trips back home were the cruelest thing of all, occurring just in time to sharpen my awareness of what had been mine and to freshen the contrast between it and whatever place I was returned to.

After a few months with my mother in Miami, I was placed with a family in Jacksonville, Florida. I remember almost nothing about them, except that they were both very jolly people. The woman was brown and very fat and she used to let me play the player piano, which she kept out on a very pleasant sun porch.

The important memory of Jacksonville was of the lynching. My mother had come up to visit me and there was a tent show playing just outside town and the grown-ups decided to go see it. These people I was staying with were show folks, too, I think, and they knew some of the people in the cast. At that time in the South there were a great many traveling tent shows, white and Negro, and I think this one was probably playing one of the classic comedies of the tent circuit, *Silas Green from New Orleans*, which is a variation on the theme of the city slicker who gets outslicked by the rubes he starts out to con.

Anyway, they decided I ought to be introduced to theater and we all piled into a car and set out for the tent located somewhere outside Jax. Suddenly along the road a Negro man flagged us down and told us to turn around. He said, "There's going to be a lynching. Turn around." We did so and as we raced home, the grown people were discussing, over my head, what could have triggered the lynching. We never really found out, but any kind of trivial excuse would have done it. The tent shows were always fair game for the mobs. What I remember clearly was the surge of fear that was almost palpable in our car, and the sudden, shocking change in my mother's mood from one of holiday to one of terror. It was the first time I had ever experienced fear like that. I was to learn more about it in the South as I grew older.

Often, since I became a professional entertainer, I have thought of those Negroes in that show, who must have so desperately wanted to act, to entertain, that they were will-

ing to work in a form of show business in which the threat
of sudden violence and even death was one of the conditions of employment. I don't believe I have ever had that
kind of passion for my art.

I did not stay long in Jacksonville after that. I believe
I spent a short period in Birmingham, and another in Brooklyn. The next place I remember with any clarity was a town
in southern Ohio; I lived in a big white house where I had
a room of my own, the first I had had outside of Brooklyn.
The house belonged to a doctor and his wife. They had two
children with whom I never did make friends. The person
in that family I remember with fondness was a maiden aunt
who lived with them. I used to read late into the night from
the crack of light under the door—to stave off sleep because
I had terrible nightmares. Even so, the bad dreams would
come and when I'd wake up, crying and scared, she would
be there and she would let me come into her bed with her.

She took me to a play, the first one I had seen since leaving New York. It probably wasn't the best possible choice,
given my mental state. It was called *The Ghost Train*. It
was about a train no one could see but which you could
hear most vividly. There would be the sound of the train
coming close and then all sorts of crimes and murders
would be committed and then it would disappear as mysteriously as it had arrived. To me both the play and the act
of going to the theater were very thrilling—worth the nightmares that followed.

My mother took me away from there after a time and the
place she took me to could not have been more of a contrast. She took me to Macon, Georgia, to a little two-room
house that stood on brick pilings in a little alley. Spick-and-
span it was, a wooden frame house just like nine or ten
others that shared that alleyway. There were communal
toilets, and big black iron pots in which to make soap and

do wash, in the center of the backyard. Inside the house the walls were covered with newspaper. There was a brick fireplace where we baked cornbread. On Saturday nights we put a big tub in front of the fireplace and took our baths. In the kitchen there was a huge, old-fashioned wood stove.

The house was owned by two women—a great-grand-mother, who must have been over ninety, and her daughter, who must have been my grandmother's age—though it was hard to tell; she was an ageless kind of woman. There were two children, grandchildren of the younger woman. I slept in a cot at the foot of the older woman's feather bed, which she shared with the younger grandchild, a little boy younger than me. The younger woman and her granddaughter slept in the kitchen in a trundle bed.

The old lady was very thin and strong and spry. She took snuff and dipped it with a willow twig. She made fruitcakes at holidays, to sell in the stores downtown, and we children helped her. She was wonderful to me. I developed rickets at this time, and I was in great pain. She had a home remedy for them. She wrapped my legs in brown paper soaked in vinegar and she would sit up with me until somehow that remedy had drawn off the pain and I could sleep.

Her daughter went out every morning to work in the "white folks'" kitchen. I remember the way they said "white folks"—with a very special intonation. And I remember the contrast between what we ate and the leavings she would bring home to us on a tin pie plate from the kitchens where she worked. The things we ate—and I learned to love—were white meal cornbread, huge baking powder biscuits, sweet potatoes baked in ashes, neckbones, and, on Sunday, chicken fricasseed with dumplings and greens. What she'd bring home to us was, by contrast, very fancy-seeming, though it was probably nothing more than asparagus or spinach or, occasionally, a leftover piece of pie. But that plate was always fascinating, because it always contained things we would never have seen otherwise.

I was happy there. The old lady would read the Bible to us, or maybe just tell Bible stories to us—Joseph and the children of Israel and Moses in the bulrushes. I suppose they were Baptists, though I have no memory of ever being taken to church. I do remember being taken downtown on Saturday afternoons, though.

The only man connected with this household was an old gentleman, a cousin, who lived in one of the houses farther back in the alley. On Saturdays he did the heavy shopping for us, over in the white section, on the main street which was called Cherry Street. Usually he would treat us to something like a hamburger and a Nehi. The crackers in their overalls and their big soft, floppy hats would joke with him, call him "uncle" and they'd tug our hair and tease us a little. I suppose I was afraid of them, or at least wary of them, as you learn to be with white people. But it wasn't the kind of fear I had learned in Miami when the cops came around, or that night on the way to the tent show. With these people you knew that if you followed certain patterns of behavior, if you fitted their idea of what a good Negro kid was, you would be all right.

So, Macon was not a bad place for me. I even had a little academic triumph there, that has stayed with me for some reason. I went to a school that was actually bigger and better than the one in Miami. One day the teacher came in, somewhat upset. She said Florence Mills had died and asked if any of us knew who she was. Well, none of the other kids had ever heard of her, but of course my grandfather had told me about her when he had told me about the theater and about the great Negro performers. So I was able to have my little victory.

But the most important thing I learned there was how good people could be. Those women with whom I lived were not self-righteous, but they were godly-good, hard-working Negro women, getting along like so many of them, without a man's help. These women never struck me or were unkind to me about the fact that the money was sometimes late in coming from my mother. They were kind to me in every way. In fact I've always said the only people who ever sent me to bed without my supper were the people who could best afford to give me supper in the first place.

II

I looked up one day when I was playing in front of their little house and there was my Uncle Frank. I had seen him once or twice before, but I really recognized him from his pictures. He said, "I've come to take you to Fort Valley with me." And so I left the little house in the alley and found myself in a new home.

Uncle Frank is a remarkable man. Like all his brothers—except my father—he was a college graduate and he had left Brooklyn when I was just a baby and had gone to Chicago to study optometry with my great-uncle. Then he had decided that what he really wanted to do was teach. He also published some poetry and, in the early Roosevelt years, he was a member of what was called "The Black Cabinet," a Negro advisory committee, semi-official in character. He was a slender man, with auburn hair, blue eyes, and a clear, ironic speaking voice—rather like Leslie Howard's, I thought. He was always a brilliant man and in later years he was head of racial relations in housing.

When he came to get me, he was teaching in Fort Valley, Georgia, about thirty miles from Macon. Apparently my mother had got in touch with him and asked him to look after me. He had always been kind to her and I guess he was the one member of my father's family she totally liked.

Even though I had learned to feel close to the people in Macon, I was very happy to go with Uncle Frank, because he was family.

He taught English and was Dean of Students at Fort Valley High and Industrial. It was then something like a junior college. That is, you got a high school diploma there and then did a little post-graduate work, enough to enable you to teach in the Negro schools in the state, or work a farm. There were and are a lot of schools like this for Negroes in the South.

The school was strung out along a dirt road just outside of town. The first building you came to was the president's house; it stood well back from the road and to me it was impressive, large and white, and I remember it as having pillars, but I wouldn't swear to it. As far as I knew only the most privileged teachers ever visited it and I never did see the inside of it. Beyond it, down the road, there was a main academic building, a large assembly hall, a girl's dormitory, a dining hall. On the same ground there was a Carnegie Library, an agricultural building, the boys' dormitory, and a peach cannery. Fort Valley was at the center of the Georgia peach region and part of the tuition program was working in the cannery.

Besides the academic courses the boys were taught to plow and to plant; the girls learned cooking and handicrafts. It was an intensely practical kind of an education. The white townspeople were very proud of their Negro school. It was the main showplace of Fort Valley, the place where young Negro people were being taught so that they might go forth and teach others. The students in the school did not mingle in any way with the townspeople. Almost the only time we saw the people of Fort Valley was when they came out to be shown how nicely the young people were progressing.

They also used to come out to hear the choir sing. The

school had what was at that time a famous choir. On Sundays the whole campus went to church services, and some of the Negroes from town would come to them, too, mostly to hear the choir.

But the year's big event was Founder's Day. The whole school was spruced up and the barbecue pits would be dug two days in advance. And the most vivid memory to me is the smell of that good food being cooked all day. Especially in the first year, I was hungry all the time. That's one thing, apparently, that all boarding schools, white and Negro, rich and poor, have in common. Many years later, when my daughter was in a fine Quaker school, I remember her complaining about the food just the way I had done down there. As you can imagine, the diet leaned very heavily on peaches as a staple—a pretty odd staple. Of course, no one complained about the food to the white trustees when they came around on Founder's Day. In fact, the kids weren't allowed to have any contact with the trustees. The trustees were guided around in groups by members of the faculty and then they got to eat all that barbecued food. If you have read Ralph Ellison's great novel, *Invisible Man,* you have a very good idea of what the school was like and even what the atmosphere was like on Founder's Day, though we never had any breakdown in protocol such as Ellison describes.

I can't pretend that I understood very clearly the nature of the duplicity my uncle and the others were forced to practice at Fort Valley. Or cared about it. For me, it was one of the good times of my life. I realize now that I spent a great deal of my childhood living in the company of adults and that I paid more attention than most kids to their conversations. During my sojourns with strangers I had to. I had to know exactly what they were saying so I would not make mistakes and thus make my mother get bad reports about me and worry. Listening for cues and clues,

I learned to keep my mouth shut, and I learned to be afraid. The biggest stretch of peace I had in this period was in Fort Valley. There were no overheard conversations about my mother or what the white lady said in her kitchen, or the sounds of pain and fear from the beatings of Negroes. Instead, I was introduced to the intellectual concerns of the Negro teacher.

My first year in Fort Valley I lived in a girl's dormitory with my uncle's fiancée, Frankie Bunn. I had never experienced anything like dormitory life and for a lonely child it was exciting to be around older girls with their talk of boys and dates and cosmetics, and that, too, was good for me.

Saturday afternoon in the dorm there would be a great getting-together down in the basement. There would be hair-washing and hair-straightening, because that was the evening the boys could come over from their dormitory to call on the girls. I wanted so much to join in, even though I was much younger. So some of the girls straightened my hair. I was scolded severely for it and told, rather haughtily, that I didn't have to do that to my hair, and forbidden to try it again.

I suppose it seems a small point, but to me it seemed a denial of my right to share a group activity with my associates. For in school here, as in other Southern schools, I was set apart by my color and my Northern accent.

I did not go to my uncle's school. I was too young. I attended a little Rosenwald-endowed school across the road. There, as elsewhere, my speech was made fun of, my color was made fun of and I was often called a little yellow bastard because I had no visible, immediate family. I was always being asked why I was so light, why my uncle was so light. To some Negroes light color is far from being a status symbol; in fact, it's quite the opposite. It is evidence that your lineage has been corrupted by the white people. It was an irony. On the one hand much money was spent on hair-straighteners and skin-lighteners, on the other you were put down for being naturally closer to the prevailing ideal of beauty.

I did not know whether I was supposed to be proud of my color or ashamed of it. One thing I did observe, though. There were some very light-skinned children who went to school with me. Their father was the most prosperous Negro farmer around there, so as members of a first family no one ever called them bastard. Perhaps what I learned from that was that the exact shade of your color was unimportant so long as you could offer evidence of respectability of your family connections. Most of my childhood I could not, and that is one thing that made the question of identity so important, except when I was home in Brooklyn.

In Brooklyn, my grandparents knew precisely who they were, they were unchangeable. Each of them always presented the same face to all comers. Questions about the exact nuances of color were irrelevant to them. They had no interest in a man's background; they cared only about who he was now, what he had made of himself. And they assumed that was all anyone would ask about themselves. My uncles tell me I am more like my grandmother than like anyone else in the family, but I was not enough like her in those days not to be bothered by questions about my "yaller" color or by the taunt of "bastard." I vacillated between a poor imitation of my grandmother's self-control and arrogance and simple, frightened withdrawal. I was a changeling, presenting different faces to different people and, to this day, I am two or three people. I can hear myself sometimes even now changing accents from one group to another. I hear it happening and still I go ahead and do it. It's a pattern I cannot totally break.

But I cannot blame that on Fort Valley. It was the one place I was often not afraid to be myself, because I did have one tie—my uncle.

I went back to Brooklyn to spend the summer after my first school year at Fort Valley and by the time I returned to Fort Valley my uncle and Frankie Bunn were married and had a little house off the campus. This was an even better year. In Brooklyn my father sent me another fur coat —a little muskrat one—and when I returned to Fort Valley I had a little room of my own in my uncle's house. I guess it also doubled as my uncle's library because it was filled with books, which only made it seem even warmer and cozier to me. We had a wonderful kitchen; best of all, I got all I wanted to eat, which was a vast improvement over life in the dormitory.

On weekends Frankie and my uncle usually entertained other faculty members at their house. I can still remember the uncanny clarity of the corn liquor as the bottle was dug up from its cool hiding place in the backyard. And I can remember lying in my little room, lights out, the door slightly ajar, listening to them talk about "Mr. Charlie" (in this case the trustees), what northern Negroes (which most of them were) thought about the South and southern Negroes, and what adjustments they had made when they came South to work. And more—they spoke of lynchings, of politics and poetry and history, of the YMCA and of the NAACP, too. I listened to these conversations with a different ear. These were things I did not have to learn in order to keep a roof over my head. These seemed to me like stories from a history book, and my uncle seemed to me the most friendly and beautiful man I'd seen since I left my granddaddy.

That second year my father came to visit with us. He had been in a very serious auto accident up North and he came South for the warm weather and to rest. This was the first time I spent any time with him; I had been too young to know him before he left home. He had come to seem a very romantic figure to me. His pictures had shown him to be an extremely handsome man, and because of his travels and his occupation an air of mystery had been added to my thoughts about him.

He arrived in a very long, black car—easily the most expensive one in Fort Valley—he always drove Pierce Arrows or LaSalles—and that reinforced my romantic image of him. He kept the car in a garage in town and all the white people—the crackers—came to stare at it.

My father is tall and has this beautiful coppery skin, the heritage of a great-grandmother who was a Blackfoot Indian. To me, his features have always resembled those of the young Fredric March as he appeared in movies like *Death Takes a Holiday*. My mother claims the thing she loved best about him was his nose, which is strong and straight and rather Roman in shape. In any case, he was famously handsome, as I discovered in later years when he would come to visit me and act as my escort for nights on the town.

My father is a very crusty, very salty, very independent man. And I was unprepared for that when I met him in Fort Valley. The only male I knew at all well was my Uncle Frank, and he had a much gentler nature than my father. He had a marvelous, wry sense of humor, very complex but very subtle. My father's style could not be more opposite. He's blunt and cynical and he talks very tough. He was and is full of maxims like "Trust no bush that quivers" and "Ask for no mercy and give less." Those are not just words to him; he lives by them. I was, to say the least, unprepared for him. He had never had to pull a humility face, even with a cop. He just paid him off and was done with him. He was and is impatient with less direct approaches to authority.

The thing I remember best about that visit was his attitude about education. He was the only one of the Horne brothers who had not gone to college. Yet he had helped pay for all his brothers' higher education, so he tended to be rather sarcastic about higher education. (But my Uncle Frank was less of a snob about having gone to college than my father was about not having gone.)

As a result, I think my father had a need to show off his natural talent for mathematics while he was in my uncle's house, because he undertook to drill me in arithmetic. He was very stern and frightening about it, and sometimes my gentle uncle would have to come and rescue me when my father pressed me too hard and I became upset. Of course, when I didn't know the answer I would put on a great show of agony, screwing up my face and twisting my hands to show how hard I was concentrating, trying to remember. Then my father would say: "Don't play to the gallery." Or he'd accuse me of hiding my fingers behind my back to count on them surreptitiously. I was never very good at arithmetic and my father's impatience didn't help me. As a result I have, to this day, a mental block about figures, which served me ill when I was beginning my career.

My father stayed a month or two, then departed to resume the life that was so very different from any I had observed either in Brooklyn or in the South. Was I disappointed in him? Had I expected him to be more of a conventional father? I suppose I would have liked that. But as I have grown older I have come to understand him better because I have come to better understand the world that made him.

The summer after my father's visit I stayed in Fort Valley after school closed. It's the only rural summer I ever had and I can remember kicking along the dusty Georgia back roads and I remember the thick skins of the muscadine grapes that I raided from the vineyards near the school.

That idyll ended when suddenly my mother was heard from again. I don't know how she managed it, but with a friend of hers named Lucille, she had bought a house in

Atlanta. She wrote me first, very happily, saying, "At last we'll be together, with a roof over our heads, a home of our own." A little later she and her friend appeared for a sort of preliminary visit before taking me away for good.

III

A bad thing happened to me almost immediately. My mother's friend had a relative living in Fort Valley. I suppose he was an uncle of hers, but I'm not certain. He was a fat, elderly man who had a big house, or anyway, so it seemed to me. My mother and I had a bedroom together with a big feather bed we shared. I remember a huge back yard with locust trees growing in it, and chewing on the long brown branches. And I remember watermelons kept in a big tin tub under the porch where it was cool. And mosquito netting—the first time I had slept under it. And the dirty old man who owned it all.

I guess from time immemorial little girls have had to run away from dirty old men. At first I didn't run. I didn't know what to do. Somehow you know what he's trying to do is wrong. All you know is that if somebody touches you it's bad. Back in Macon, those good women had told me and told me: "Don't be a bad girl. Don't be a bad girl. Don't let a little boy touch you." But you haven't been told whether you're to blame or it's the other person's fault. Also this was a man whose hospitality my mother was accepting.

And I couldn't go to my mother. For one thing, I was afraid of her friend. For another, I was afraid for myself, afraid the whole hateful business would be misinterpreted and made to seem my fault. So I just resolved to be careful and not get caught alone with him. And mostly I was lucky and did not get caught by him. But I've remembered him always and hated him always. The most terrible thing was that even when I finally moved to Atlanta I was taken back to visit him one more time. And still I didn't talk to her about it.

The inability to talk to my mother, which had begun in Miami, grew worse here. It's an inability that persists to this day, but it had its most serious consequences almost immediately.

We had hardly settled into the house in Atlanta when my mother and her friend had to leave. They had found some kind of work somewhere else. So my mother hired a man and wife to look after me and keep house.

The house was a large red brick house on West Hunter Street, in a solid, middle-class Negro neighborhood. We had a front yard and a back yard and a sun porch. I remember a player piano and a dining room with a fancy sideboard and plenty of cut glass. And I remember a large, warm kitchen. It was there that I read *Little Women*. My mother had sent it to me for Christmas and I remember reading it over and over again.

But the housekeeper was a strange, sick woman. She made an extraordinarily rigid program for me. I would come home from school and dust and do my other chores. And then she would come along, put on a white glove, and run her fingers over the places I had worked on and if she found any dust I had missed or a dish that wasn't as clean as it should be, she would mark down a mental black mark against me. Then on Wednesday night and Saturday night, after I had undressed for my bath, I would be punished for all my transgressions of the previous days. She would cut switches from the trees and come to me and I would stand, wet and naked, and be beaten. Every minute of every day I would be dreading those punishment nights and I would know, well in advance, exactly how bad it would be. And I could anticipate the humiliation that would inevitably be mine.

This woman never said I was bad. She just said she would make sure that I wouldn't be. "You're not going to be like show folk," she would say.

Once again, I was unable to tell my mother what was going on. I knew how hard she worked to get this place and hire this woman, and to tell her that it was the worst treatment I had ever had seemed too cruel. I had already learned to protect my mother from unhappiness and from the pressure of responsibility for me. She returned to Atlanta several times that year to visit me and I never told her what was happening.

Two things saved me. One was school. This was in a relatively good neighborhood and the people who lived there were more urban. I remember I was less often called "yaller" there than I was in the small towns. And they placed considerable value on their schools; the junior high school, Booker T. Washington Junior High, where I had some classes, was a good one. I ran into the first really inspirational teachers I had in the South, excepting the wonderful lady, Mrs. Walden, who taught crafts at Fort Valley and who let me come to her classes even though I was not technically enrolled in the school. In Atlanta, the teacher's name was Thelma Rivers. With her sister, who was also a teacher, she opened my eyes to all kinds of wonders. But the thing I remember best about school in Atlanta was the Hayes drugstore on the corner near it. They served the best hot dogs in the world with sauerkraut and chopped onions and chili sauce. They only cost five cents.

The other good thing was the railroad. It ran right behind our house. I could see the trains going by and when I did I was reminded that I had some place to go. I suppose my immediate thoughts were of New York and the life I had known back there. But there was more to it than that. Whenever I see a movie that has a scene in which the country people are looking wistfully at a train, I immedi-

ately understand their emotions, for I felt them that year
in Atlanta. The train is your link with the outer world.
The train reminded me that I could go to New York if only
I could get away.

And I did. My mother finally heard from the neighbors
about my mistreatment. They had apparently heard my
cries when I was being beaten. She sent the housekeeper
away and then she came to me and cried and asked, "Why
didn't you tell me? Why did I have to hear from other
people?"

I don't think I answered her. I had no answer. How could
I explain that we had, through the years of separation, become strangers?

Shortly thereafter my mother lost the house—somehow
she was cheated out of it—and I left the South for the last
time and returned again to my grandmother's house in
Brooklyn. The fact that I went back to live, not simply to
visit, was evidence that my mother had given up the hope
of gaining recognition for herself, and with it, financial stability. Now, I think, she finally accepted the fact that her
attempts to take sole responsibility for me were doomed to
failure.

CHAPTER THREE

I

When I returned to the house on Chauncey Street, I joined battle with my grandmother in a monumental running fight. The subject under discussion was my mother. It was not that my grandmother disliked her, it was just that she had no respect for her. By my grandmother's standards she had no guts.

On the other hand, I had already begun to adopt this protective attitude toward my mother, trying to shield her from the harsher realities of the life that I seemed to recognize more clearly than she. Now I extended this protectiveness to include an active defense of her and her reputation with my grandmother. It was a kind of tournament in which I carried my mother's colors against my grandmother. It was not easy. My grandmother laughed at my mother, particularly at her fears about kidnaping. Her laughter was hard to fight, but I tried.

And in trying I strengthened myself—which may have been her intention in the first place. If I didn't feel particularly warm toward my grandmother, at least I was not intimidated by her. I respected her and, at least unconsciously, wanted this respect to be returned. Fighting with her, trying to win her respect, drew me out of the self-protective shell I had created around myself during the years in the South. Instead of retreating inside it when trouble threatened I came out to meet it; I was thinking of something more than just trying not to be hurt. This process was helped by the fact that in Brooklyn I was somebody. I was Lena Horne whose family lived on Chauncey Street and whose relatives lived in this place and that place and whose friends were known to be So-and-so and So-and-so.

My Uncle Burke, who was there in those years, says now that I am very like my grandmother. I didn't know that in scrapping with her I was coming to emulate her, and I certainly wasn't doing it consciously. But that is apparently what happened, and it was good.

I can't pretend that I totally changed. I'm still as likely to go into that shell as I am to come out fighting. This is particularly true when I perform. I developed a certain kind of guile and toughness, a way of isolating myself from the audience. It is a means of not letting them get to you, not letting them see that they can hurt you. I suppose isolation of this kind is really just a form of disguised hostility. The image I have chosen to give them is of a woman they can't reach. And it has worked, not because I am artful, but because they are usually so busy comparing me to their preconceived images of what a Negro woman should be like, and so busy being surprised that I did not seem to fit it, that they never seem to notice they are not getting *me*—someone they can touch and hurt—but just a singer. I'm sure that the isolation I wrap around myself when I perform has its roots in this childhood when isolation was sometimes my only defense.

On the other hand, the part of me that responds to causes or to injustices, or issues fighting statements on all kinds of issues, that part of me is the creation of my proud, activist grandmother, who never seemed to be afraid of anything.

I am glad I had that year with her, because very soon

I was to have need of what she had tried to teach me about pride and strength. When I was thirteen or fourteen, after I had lived with her for a year, she died quite suddenly. Most of our family suffers from chronic bronchial asthma. I'll never forget the sound of those attacks coming on in the middle of the night. It's the most terrible thing. Finally there came an attack which my grandmother could not fight off. When she died, whatever had kept my grandfather going also died. Two or three months later he, too, was dead. My Uncle Burke and I stayed on in the house. But I remember how gloomy it was. My uncle was too young to take care of me and continue with his schooling, so I was sent to stay with Mrs. Laura Rollock.

She was an old friend of the family, very active in the Urban League and the NAACP and she was a wonderful person—a marvelous cook, a scrupulous housekeeper and a loving woman, warm and jolly. She had an apartment on the top floor of a brownstone. I had a room of my own and a little radio of my own, too. The best thing about it was that Mrs. Rollock would let me have club meetings at the house with my friends.

I had never had many friends in the South—just the two kids who had lived in that house with me in Macon. The business of being a high "yaller" and on top of that being the dean's niece in Fort Valley had prevented me from making friends there. But back in Brooklyn I had taken up once again with girls at school and with the daughters of the families who were in my grandparents' set. I had known them before going South, but then the trouble was that my grandmother's dislike of idle social gatherings, those that didn't have as their goal raising money for or planning some good work, had affected these relationships. She would not let me entertain my friends. Since these were the first ones I had it was terribly important for me to be able to be their hostess for meetings of the Peter Pan Club or, when we were a little older, the Junior Debs. When I was at Mrs. Rollock's she would put on collations that were the equal of anyone's, and I could hold my head up socially.

She also encouraged me in dramatics. My Uncle Burke remembers that I was always dressing up in adult clothes at this time and acting out little plays, based on my reading, all by myself. I got together with a little group of girls and fellows and we wrote a play—I don't remember what it was all about—and gave it at the Urban League. All I remember about it was a fabulous dress that Mrs. Rollock made for me.

Then there was the dancing school. Mrs. Rollock sent me to Anna Jones' Dancing School, and a group of us won some kind of local award and there was a great to-do about us in the Negro press in Brooklyn, so we were hired to play a week at the Harlem Opera House. We did what was loosely termed a ballet. It was rather exotically costumed and we all waved our arms around very artistically—rather as I imagine Isadora Duncan's troupe did—while the band played *Stormy Weather*, which was the big hit from the Cotton Club show of that year. The Harlem Opera House was just down the block from the Apollo and was, at the time, at least as famous. They had a professional chorus line and the girls in it were very nice to us. One of them gave me my first lesson in stage make-up. We were hardly competition for them—I guess we'd been hired as a joke— but it was a great adventure for me.

So life was, at last, very pleasant for me. I had a home in which I was not a stranger, and I had friends and I was going to good, solid New York schools—P.S. 35 first, and then Girls High—and for the first time I felt secure in myself. I knew who I was and where I belonged.

And then a letter came from my mother. She had been working in Cuba and she had met a man and they were married and we were all going to be together again in New

York. She told me how lonely she had been and how much
this man loved her and how he would take care of both of
us and be a father to me.

I had a terrible sinking feeling when I read that letter.
I was happy, I didn't want to change anything at all, and
I didn't want to leave Mrs. Rollock's. We both cried when
my mother came to get me. And then I met my stepfather.

He was a white man. He spoke English with a very heavy
Spanish accent. And I knew there was going to be trouble.

II

My stepfather's name was Miguel Rodriguez, known as
"Mike." He was a fierce little man, who loved my mother
with a kind of protective fervor I had never seen. He was
also a tremendously decent man, very industrious and eager
to work, yet unable to find it, partly because his English was
very bad and partly because this was 1932–33, the depths
of the depression. It was the first time the depression had
any direct effect on me and consequently the first attention
I paid to it.

I did not pay very much attention to it, because our personal difficulties blotted out everything else. Mike and my
mother and I tried to live at first in Brooklyn. That was
when I first heard the whispers, "Lena's mother is married
to some white man." And I'm sure my mother was snubbed
by the people who had known her before her southern
odyssey, partly because of her marriage, partly because the
years of her absence were a mystery to others and mystery
meant suspicion and a certain amount of polite ostracism.
This was my first introduction to the prejudice of the Negro against the white. It can be as intense as its reverse,
particularly if a white man is married to a Negro woman,

and especially if the man is as exotic as Mike seemed to most people.

I don't believe I resented Mike as a replacement for my father. I remained, as always, absolutely fascinated by my father and the glamour and excitement that surrounded his life, but as I was never able to picture my father and mother as man and wife, I never missed him as a father figure. The only strain I felt was hiding my fascination with him from my mother.

No, the real trouble was that Mike, simply by his presence, caused me to be uprooted again, just as I was settling into a life that I liked. The atmosphere toward us in Brooklyn was highly unpleasant, so we moved to the Bronx. It was a section in which a great many European-born whites, many of them Jews, lived. I went to a public school there for a while. But the accents were strange and the style of life was strange and I did not make friends at school or in the neighborhood. I tried to maintain contact with my friends in Brooklyn, but the distance was too great and inevitably we saw less and less of one another, and I could find no new group to replace them. I started slipping back beneath my shell.

Our family unit was now a mixed one, which meant we had no place among either Negroes or whites. On top of that Mike was a very angry man. He turned his fury on me if I did anything at all to upset my mother. Worse, he could not understand why Negroes did not fight back more violently against discrimination, which meant that we were, in effect, living with a white man, who, however much he loved my mother and me as individuals, could not conceal his contempt for our race. I'm sure these tensions were heightened by his inability to find a job, which must have increased his background anxiety to almost intolerable levels.

In short, the return of my mother with Mike tore apart

the tenuous, newly-woven fabric of my life—school, friends, pleasant surroundings all disappeared. We lived on groceries supplied by relief organizations, and it became clear that the family's chief asset was me, that I would have to go to work.

That was all right with me. By this time we had moved from the Bronx to a tenement in Harlem where my stepfather, of course, was more deeply resentful than ever. I had grown increasingly disenchanted with the school in the Bronx and was ready to go to work or do anything to get away from the tensions at home. Ever since coming back from the South I had been listening to the broadcasts from the Cotton Club, featuring the bands of Cab Calloway and Duke Ellington. So when my mother, through friends, arranged an audition for me there, I was ready to go along with it. By this time I had lost touch with my Brooklyn friends, and Mike's misery was creating a great deal of anxiety in our home. For the first time in my life I specifically blamed color for our troubles. Up until then the things I suffered I suffered because of the rather ill-defined (in my mind, anyway), bad luck that had been visited on my mother. But Mike's presence made me focus my resentments on color, or should I say the color line, that was now suddenly so confused in our family. In any case, I thought that if only I could make a little money I might earn a little more respect in the family. I even think, now, that I may have been trying to win away from Mike the love my mother was giving him. So the Cotton Club held no terrors for me. I would as soon go to work there as continue what I was doing, though I do not know what made me or my mother think I would be of any value to the club.

I could carry a tune, but I could hardly have been called a singer; I could, thanks to Anna Jones, dance a little, but I could hardly be called a dancer. I was tall and skinny and I had very little going for me except a pretty face and

long, long hair that framed it rather nicely. Also, I was young
—about sixteen—and despite the sundry vicissitudes of my
life, very, very innocent. As it turned out, this was all that
was needed.

The audition was nothing to worry about. The joint was
controlled by Owney Madden's gang but it was managed
by a man named Herman Stark, who was your typical stout,
cigar-chewing manager. The audition came during the rehearsal period for the new show, the one which was to
follow *Stormy Weather*, in which Ethel Waters had been
such a big hit singing Harold Arlen's great song. She was
due to leave and the star of the next show was to be Ada
Ward, the great blues singer. Stark was auditioning some
new specialty numbers and also looking for some girls as
replacements in the chorus. I was wearing a simple cotton
dress and I came out and did a little time step, which was
about all I could manage at the time, and sang a few bars
of some song or other and I was hired.

The thing I remember best about the audition was that a
girl about my age, Winnie Johnson, was also hired. Winnie
is now married to a physician, and, like me, she came from
a good family that was having trouble making ends meet
during the depression. My mother accompanied me to the
audition, and her mother had to bring her little brother and
sister along, not being able to afford a baby-sitter.

My going to work in the club caused quite a stir in the
Negro press, to which my grandmother and her good works
were well known. It caused more than a little stir in bour-
geois Brooklyn, where respectable girls were not supposed
to go to work in Harlem nightclubs known to be owned by
white hoodlums, or any other hoodlums for that matter.

Actually, there was nothing to worry about. My very
youth protected me. I was jail bait and no one ever made a
pass at me or suggested I go out with one of the customers,
which happened all the time to the older girls. The owners

apparently figured that any kind of fooling around with underage girls was the quickest way to lose their license.

I was also protected in another way. On my way into the club I was always being stopped by Negro men who were friends of my father's—gamblers, people who were in numbers, or who had the binocular concessions at a track, or were partners in some syndicate. They were people who knew their way around the fringe world I was now inhabiting. They would say things like, "We're friends of your father's and we've known you since you were a baby." They formed a sort of underground protective association for me. And I have no doubt they were effective. They were known to Madden's people and important enough to them to actually get into the club, which never admitted ordinary Negro people. Whenever there was some important sporting event in town you always knew it at the club. They would be given side booths, near the kitchen. They were big spenders and sharp dressers and drove the biggest cars. And my father was one of them. He would appear occasionally at the club to see the show and then we would have a little conversation at the foot of the steps backstage afterward. He, too, would tell me to get in touch if there was ever any trouble, or if I needed anything. Also, it was quite thrilling to me to hear about the glamorous reputation my father had with the older girls in the chorus.

Beyond this informal protection I was formally guarded by my mother, who came to work with me nearly every night and sat in the dressing room until I was finished. As far as boys were concerned, I was as eager for dates and fun as any teen-ager. I don't know just how I expected to work boys into a schedule that involved seven nights of work—until 3 A.M. at the earliest—or even where I expected to meet any kids of my own age, since I had quit school. Nevertheless my mother lectured and lectured me on being a "good" girl. By the time my mother and I separated I was thoroughly confused on the subject of sex. I was conscious of the paradox of exhibiting myself in skimpy costumes, of existing in a highly charged sexual atmosphere, and yet being constantly reminded, in the strictest terms, of the value of virtue. I remember thinking that if it were such a precious thing I had certainly been placed in the wrong atmosphere for its preservation. The most galling thing was being prevented, as much as possible, from association with the older girls. Most of them were very nice, but they naturally resented the special air my mother created around me, and that led some of them to think that I thought I was better than they were. In short, I was once again an outsider.

It was all so unnecessary. Cab Calloway's band was on the bill and on my first day at the club I remember I was sitting on a railing, waiting for rehearsal to start, when he glanced at me, did a double take and said, "My God, it's the little squirt from Brooklyn." He and his band had been featured at some sort of charity affair in Brooklyn a little while before and some of us Junior Debs had been hostesses on that occasion and, naturally, had spent a lot of time hanging around the band. This encounter at the club was the beginning of a good friendship—we worked together on and off for years—and he would offer me all the protection I needed, not to mention *realistic* guidance on how to behave.

The Cotton Club was a remarkable institution, as were two or three other Harlem clubs—Smalls and Connie's Inn among them—that had gotten their start as speakeasies during prohibition and had become fashionable places for the downtown white crowd to visit. It was on the corner of Lenox Avenue and 142nd Street, on the east side of the avenue, one flight up over the Douglas Theater. The room itself was very large, shaped in the classic cabaret manner as a horseshoe, with the audience seated on two levels.

Some of the tables surrounded the dance floor in front of the tiny proscenium stage, some of them were a couple of steps higher on a raised area in the back. There were booths around all the walls and as many tiny tables as they could cram in on the floor. They could probably seat seven or eight hundred people for a show.

Working conditions were terrible. There was only one ladies' room, and the people in the show were discouraged from using it—it was for the customers. There was practically no room backstage. Cab had a little dressing room under the stairs that led up to the crowded chorus girls' room. The stars had little private accommodations just offstage. We did three shows a night—8:30, 11:30, and 2 A.M., seven nights a week, and we were paid $25 a week. On top of that we were frequently obliged to take the show downtown and play a week in one of the vaudeville houses, in addition to our regular schedule, and then too, we were expected to play smokers and conventions—anything some politician or local big shot asked the owners to do, with no extra pay. As I said, I assume the older girls were expected to entertain important people when the boss asked them to. It was a grueling life and I suppose in my case it violated the child-labor laws as well as the truancy laws. The latter were circumvented by an understanding officer who dutifully called on my mother every week and dutifully wrote down her response—that I was "missing"—and never went looking for me. He apparently could not bring himself to force me to return to school, knowing that I was the principal support of that household.

At sixteen, I was inexhaustible, and if I did not see the Cotton Club as a steppingstone to a much larger career, and if there were a good many distasteful aspects to life in the club, I was still enough of a stage-struck kid to take some pride and pleasure in associating with the great talents who played the club.

By the time I arrived, the Cotton Club had seen its great days, although I, of course, was not aware of it at the time. It had begun, like so many nightclubs, as a speakeasy during prohibition days, as one of the principal outlets for "Madden's No. 1" beer, manufactured in his own plant. The club also served "the real stuff" at prices roughly comparable to what a drink costs in New York today. Madden was never much in evidence at the club, but his top henchman, "Big Frenchy"—his real name was George DeMange —spent a good deal of time there. I suppose his presence was an added "kick" for the crowd. It was a group that spent most of its time looking for kicks.

Other things were responsible for the popularity of the Cotton Club. One of the most important was that it was one of the few after-hours spots offering entertainment so late at night that the show business crowd could catch a show there after their own work was done. The club also encouraged them to come up on Sunday night and take over the entertainment themselves at a special early show. So it was a place that was "in" with all the right people. I have read that Lady Mountbatten once declared it "the aristocrat of Harlem," and the club carefully nurtured that image.

I arrived at the club in the fall of 1933, after the depression was well under way. It had severely inhibited the downtown crowd's search for pleasure. In any case, the club folded only four years later, after trying a desperation move down to the Broadway area, closer to its audience.

Besides this, the people who had created the Cotton Club shows in the early days had left. The first producer had been a very sweet man named Lew Leslie, who enters my own story a little later on, and his leading songwriters were the team of Dorothy Fields and Jimmy McHugh. They had departed, and the guiding production genius who replaced Lew was a dancer turned choreographer, named Dan

Healy. He too had left by the time I had come to work at the club. But he had left his mark on the shows. He had worked in book musicals on Broadway, in the *Ziegfeld Follies*, as well as in clubs. He liked fast-paced, rather long shows—one and a half to two hours—and he may have been the first director to introduce elaborate scenery and lighting effects into nightclub shows. As productions, they would probably seem absurd by modern standards, but they compared with the best, black or white, of the time, and they contained wonderful songs, many of them after 1930 written by Harold Arlen and Ted Koehler. And there is no question that they lived up to the somewhat patronizing line in one of the club's brochures, which promised "the cream of sepia talent, the greatest array of Creole stars ever assembled, supported by a chorus of bronze beauties." Hot dog!

Nostalgia has not played anyone false about the Cotton Club shows. They were wonderful. But for the employees, it was an exploitative system on several levels. The club got great talent very cheap, because there were so few places for great Negro performers to work. Duke Ellington, for example, was known throughout the musical world as the greatest jazz composer ever, but the white audience was convinced that Paul Whiteman and Isham Jones were the last word in jazz. So for many years Duke had to sell his songs and arrangements to a white publisher for far less than he deserved. There were few places for Duke except Europe or some joint like the Cotton Club. The same thing was true of a great actor like Juano Hernandez, who appeared in the second show I was in, doing a kind of fake voodoo incantation, with drums and dancing, that just thrilled the audiences silly—they figured it was a real taste of the jungle. Juano was marvelous in this act, as he is in anything, but I'm sure he wished he was doing something different with his talent. He had to wait a decade to get the chance. This was true of most of the people who played the Cotton Club.

That was one kind of exploitation, or maybe that's the wrong word. The guys who ran the Cotton Club didn't invent the system—they just took advantage of it. They were also very clever at exploiting Negro stereotypes, of catering to them in order to bring in the white people. That made it hard for people who didn't fit the stereotypes to get work there in the first place. For instance, Cab's band left just before the second show I was in and they had to find a new band. Now the Calloway group was a fine, wonderfully precise organization full of wonderful musicians like Benny Paine, who played the piano. But by this time Cab's band was a known quantity, it was "Negro" to the uninitiated, though actually it was pure Cab Calloway. So they were auditioning this new band, and it was Jimmie Lunceford's. I didn't know anything about anything in those days, but standing around listening I could tell this was something new and very different. And I could sense the excitement of the other performers around me. But the white owners were highly dubious—they didn't have any inkling of what they were hearing. It was a young band, a band that did a lot of singing, and which had got its training playing in the Negro colleges in the South. For it, the Cotton Club could mean the beginning of huge success. First of all, there were the twice-weekly "TC" (transcontinental) radio broadcasts, featuring the bands that played the club; second there was the tie-up with the Loew's theaters around New York, which meant good exposure in the city. They finally got the job, and, of course, they made their reputation and in the process contributed a great deal to the development of an audience for swing. All the bands that developed themselves at the club—Duke's, Cab's, Lucky Millinder's, Claude Hopkins'—went through the same process—taking the low pay in order to establish themselves, working for owners who didn't know what they had until after the bands had left.

I suppose it is possible to say that the bands and the performers who used the club as a jumping-off place for their careers were exploiting as much as they were exploited; that, on balance, the club contributed a great deal to the development of their talents and to the development of an audience for those talents.

But those of us on the lower levels were in no position to appreciate such subtleties. All we knew was that we were underpaid and overworked in the most miserable conditions. I've heard the club was famous for its cooking—especially for the chicken Mexican—for its Chinese dishes, and for the fried chicken the downtowners liked to order when they came up for the 2 A.M. show. We rarely got any of it. In fact, the only meals I can remember at the club came after the whole show had been up to Sing Sing to entertain the prisoners—that meal at the club was free and there were seconds. I always looked forward to that bus trip up the Hudson.

But perhaps the most galling thing was that the club was owned by whites—(white ownership of businesses is still one of the sorest of the many sore points in Harlem today)—who based their business on giving their white brethren a thrilling peek at the "exotic" world of the Negro, but refused to allow Negroes into their club as paying customers. There were bouncers at the door to keep out Negroes. Even the parents of the kids from the show couldn't get in. They were allowed to sit in the booth near the kitchen door when we did our final dress rehearsals.

As for the "exotic," wonderful, rhythmic, happy-go-lucky quality of our lives, that was a real joke. Especially for my family. We lived in a typical, roach-infested tenement, that thanks to the superintendent and my stepfather—and no thanks to the slumlord—was superficially neat and clean, its halls and walls treated to constant whitewashings. My salary didn't go far and we used to get those big bags of groceries from relief—containing flour and red or black beans and salt pork and whatever cheap vegetable—maybe cabbage—was in season. My stepfather was a wonderful cook, frequenting the inexpensive Spanish groceries in the neighborhood to get the spices that raised this stuff very often from the level of the edible to the delicious. I remember the girls at the club used to get mad at me for coming to work smelling of the garlic Mike used so liberally. I don't blame them—in that crowded, awful backstage I must have been a menace.

Exotic me—I got home no earlier than 4 A.M., ate breakfast with my mother and fell asleep on the living-room couch, hoping I could sleep the day away, grateful if we didn't have to play matinees downtown or some benefit show. If we didn't, I'd move into my mother and stepfather's room to sleep as long as I could on the only proper bed we owned. Of course, if any of us were late for or missed a show or rehearsal, our pay was docked; and there were penalties for all kinds of minor rule infractions while on the club premises. And to this system I was, I discovered, bound by an inflexible, virtually lifetime contract, that my mother had signed in her eagerness to get me a job. I have no idea if it was an enforceable contract. I'm sure the owners counted on their employees' inability to pay for lawyers and court costs to test them. They were also not above using a little muscle to keep you in line should you grow restless at the club.

I was too young to be any sort of troublemaker. This was my first working contact with the white world, and it was easy to heed the advice my mother and stepfather and everyone else kept pounding into me—"Don't let them near you." Considering the conditions at the club, nothing could have been simpler. My longest contact with any of the white owners or their hood friends was to say "Good evening," or "How do you do."

If I can't share in the general nostalgia for the Cotton Club as an institution, I can certainly share in the nostalgia for the shows and their stars. The first show I was in was not one of the big hit shows. But even so, Cab was there and the blues singer, Leithia Hill, and Ada Ward, who was a famous singer of the time. There was also undoubtedly a male baritone with a powerful voice, someone like George Dewey Washington, doing spirituals; and surely one of the great tap dancers, who were always featured in these shows; and, of course, the comics—great ones like Miller and Lisle. The thing I remember best was a fan dance we did. The club very frequently built its shows around whatever the dance craze of the moment was, and the dance everyone was talking about that year was the fan dance, because Sally Rand had made it famous out at the Chicago World's Fair. So, of course, we had to do it. We weren't quite as naked as Miss Rand, but we were pretty close—my costume consisted of approximately three feathers. We did a semi-tap-semi-jazz kind of step, choreographed by our captain, Elida Webb. Then there were some tall show-girl types who just walked around and looked pretty, in the Ziegfeld tradition. In this show, they got to carry the biggest fans. The big production numbers at the Cotton Club were probably no funnier than the big numbers in the Ziegfeld and George White shows, or those huge, gaudy things Busby Berkeley was doing in the movie musicals at that time. But ours were, perhaps, a little sillier than the rest, considering the crowded stage and floor where we had to put these huge numbers. Then, too, there was the rich irony of doing these expensive, expansive numbers in the middle of Harlem. One that I remember as particularly ironic was a thing about sailing to Europe and the boys in the show carried out eight or ten deck chairs in which we reclined to sing the number. Considering who we were and where we were, it must have seemed pretty silly (and I'm sure a lot of people came there just to get a laugh out of our pretensions).

My second show at the Cotton Club was more successful than the first. It was the last one for which Arlen and Koehler did the songs. In it I got what I suppose must be classed as my first big break in show business, though nothing much came of it. The show starred Adelaide Hall, who was a very important star. To understand her career you have to understand a little bit about the history of Negro show business in the twenties and early thirties.

Generally speaking, you made your reputation abroad in those days. Josephine Baker is the most famous example of this, but there were others. Noble Sissle, the bandleader, who comes into my own story a little later, had made a reputation in Europe before the war, accompanying Vernon and Irene Castle on their triumphant tours. His association with the Castles made him famous, and when he came back to the United States, he and Eubie Blake wrote a famous show called *Shuffle Along*, which was probably the first all-Negro musical show ever to play a legitimate theater. It was all very down-home, with a lot of talk about pickaninnies and watermelon and a song about the "dear old bandana days" and what-have-you. Noble would have been shocked to think he was perpetuating a racial stereotype. As far as he was concerned, this *was* Negro life that white people wanted to see. Which is the trouble with stereotypes—you end up being trapped by them. Anyway, *Shuffle Along* was a sensation. Lew Leslie picked up the idea and did a series of *Blackbird* revues. If Ziegfeld glorified the American girl, Lew glorified the Afro-American girl and two of the girls he glorified the most were Flo Mills and Adelaide Hall. Adelaide starred in one of the editions of the show he took to Europe, and it was said that the Prince of Wales had pursued her. In any case, she was the darling of that set. Eventually she married a West Indian who was a British subject and she stayed on over there and got work. So when she came to the Cotton Club, she was in the position of being the local girl who had made good, and there was tremendous interest in her.

Her first number was "Primitive Prima Donna" and she was dressed to the nines in gorgeous satins and laces. Then gradually, the sexiness, the wild quality began to emerge until, by the end, she was indeed, a primitive prima donna. She was great in the number, and it was just what the audiences seemed to like. She also did a great number called "Ill Wind" that Frank Sinatra still likes to sing.

There was another song in that show that has also become a standard, "As Long as I Live." It was done by Avon Long, who, of course, went on to become a famous dancer. Avon was another Negro who didn't fit any of the accepted notions about Negro performers, and about whom the Cotton Club owners were very dubious. The tradition in the club was for what I have since heard called "eccentric dancers," of whom Jigsaw Jackson and Earl "Snake Hips" Tucker were famous examples—at least among the *cognoscenti*. Certainly the club favored the more spectacular, contortionistic, exhibitionistic sort of dancer. It fitted with the image they wanted to present and which led them to, at first, dub Duke's band as "The Jungle Band." But Avon was different. His style was a smooth, gliding, almost balletic movement, but featuring a distinct jazz beat. It was subtle and individual without calling attention to its individuality. Anyway, he got to do the Arlen song—"As Long as I Live." He needed a partner and I was chosen. It was the first time I ever had a featured spot in a show. It was therefore probably the first time it ever occurred to my mother that the Cotton Club might be more than just a job—that there might be a career in show business for me.

If the thought ever occurred to me, it was only a fleeting one. I was preoccupied with other problems. The most important of these had to do with my mother and stepfather. As I've said, Mike was violently protective of my mother, and he expected the hoods I was working for to treat her like a lady. They were not about to do so, and that led to a lot of tension around the club. As for the Negro men around the club, they had no respect for Mike. To them, he was just an interloper who had married one of their women and who had no understanding of their problems. They took plenty from the white men they had to work for and were not very receptive to my stepfather's ideas of how to earn the respect of the white man, which mostly had to do with standing up to him very forcefully. I tried to buffer for both Mike and my mother, feeling the different pressures that were exerted on them and also feeling the anguish each of them felt.

Besides that, I was subject to pressure from both of them. Mike's was the easiest to deal with. He simply would not tolerate anything that seemed to upset my mother. If I tried to do anything on my own, not including her, she would get upset and then Mike would tax me with a whole string of questions: "Where did you go, what did you say, who were you with?" I'm sure I resented him as an intruder and I certainly resented his somewhat oversimplified way of dealing with the problems of our existence. My mother was a more serious problem, for not long after I got my chance to do the specialty with Avon, she decided that I was going to be a star.

It came about this way: We were doing a week in a theater with the Claude Hopkins band and he had a boy singer with the band—not one of the club regulars—and he needed someone to do a duet with him. Now I could carry a tune and I had very good diction—just a natural endowment, that diction—and so I was chosen to do the duet.

It was "Cocktails for Two." Suddenly there I was, singing and sort of dancing around with this boy. The older club girls were beginning to very strongly resent the way I seemed always to be pushed into the spotlight. Besides which, I was something of a fraud. I knew nothing about projecting my voice in a large theater and nothing about taking care of it properly. By the third show of the day I was so hoarse I couldn't finish the number. Which pleased everyone—even me—except my mother.

The result was that I started having voice lessons. I really don't know if they did me any good—probably not. We couldn't afford a fine teacher and it was to be several years before I learned anything about the technical side of singing. I do know that the lessons were a heavy economic strain on us, cutting seriously into the $25 a week I was bringing home from the club.

But my mother was now in the grip of a dream, which was that I would succeed in show business where she had failed. I had not realized how desperately she had wanted to make it until she turned her full attention to me. She turned into the typical stage mother of lore and legend— my dreamy, impractical, rather defeated mother.

I did not object too strenuously. Several times in my Cotton Club days I had tried to re-establish myself with my Brooklyn friends, paying the club's fines in order to skip a show and attend one of their functions. But I was a complete stranger there. I wore make-up and they did not; my world was that of show business and theirs was that of boys and dates and parties and school. Since the only life I wanted was one like theirs, and since there now appeared to be no hope of my having anything like it, I went passively along with my mother's plans. I could think of nothing better, although I shared none of her confidence or her determination.

My mother saw a little ray of hope in 1934 when I got a

job on Broadway. It was a thing called *Dance with Your
Gods* and I was listed in the program as "A Quadroon Girl."
The play starred Rex Ingram and Georgette Harvey and it
was, so far as I can remember, a silly thing about a white
Southern boy who believes he's under the spell of voodoo.
He goes to a witch doctor and she agrees to transfer his
curse to someone he names. He gives her what he thinks is
an imaginary name, but it actually turns out to be the name
of a distinguished old New Orleans family that has lost its
money but not its pride. He rushes off to warn them, which
enrages the witch doctor who puts a curse on him, whereupon he attacks the girl of the family and carries her off as
his voodoo bride. What I did was play the living effigy of
the white daughter in the voodoo ceremony. All I remember
about the part is that the girl I played was supposed to have
been convent-bred (don't ask me how she got mixed up in
voodoo). I was required to speak a few lines and to do some
native-type dancing when the hex was put on me.

I think maybe Juano Hernandez mentioned me to the
agent originally. He was one of the few people at the club
whom my mother liked—they spoke Spanish together. I do
know there was terrible difficulty in getting the Cotton Club
to let me do the show. I've since been told that the producer of the show, Lawrence Schwab, had to get the head
of the Broadway mob to intercede with Owney Madden's
people in order to get me. They worked out an arrangement by which I was allowed to skip the first show at the
Cotton Club in order to do my work in *Gods*. But I had to
rush uptown and work the late shows at the club.

That was my Broadway debut. Big deal! The show was
a flop and didn't run more than a couple of weeks. My
mother's hopes for an overnight success were dashed because no one paid any attention to me, though the director
kept insisting that he could develop me into a dramatic

PHOTO BY RICHARD AVEDON

1

Cora Calhoun.

This is my grandmother's father, I'm told.

My uncle Frank—my first crush.

My father as a pageboy at the Plaza.

My beautiful grandfather
Edwin Horne.

Cora and Edwin Horne.

This is the first time the black
man voted the Democratic
ticket.

My great-aunt Adele, and my
maternal grandmother Louise
Amelie.

My great-aunt Lena Calhoun and her family.

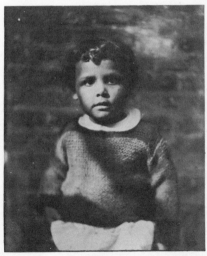

Me, very young.

My father's brother Erroll,
a lieutenant in World War I.

actress if he only had had the chance to work with me longer.

After that, however, my mother and my stepfather became more determined than ever to get me away from the club for good. They pleaded and cajoled to no avail. At first the bosses kept promising that they would eventually break me into one of the shows as a singer, but that was just a put-on. They had no intention of doing so. I was sucker bait as well as jail bait—young and pretty and innocent—an aid to bringing in the customers and probably more valuable to them in that role than I could ever be as a singer.

Finally, Mike went up to the club after hours and put my case to the bosses a little too forcefully. He had fought against some dictator in Cuba and he wasn't afraid of a few hoods. Some of their boys followed him out into the street and beat him up very severely. Next day, one of the bosses came to me and said: "Who do you think you are? You know you can't work anywhere but here." After that it became much more urgent for me to get out of there in a hurry. Flournoy Miller of the comedy team of Miller and Lisle came to our rescue with an idea. He had no love of the system—a lot of his best material was stolen by white comedy teams in those days—and he said to us: "Noble Sissle was the first man to put lovely Negro women on stage and he can help you." It was through him, I believe, that my mother got in touch with Sissle, who was then playing in Philadelphia. A meeting was arranged and, without telling anyone, my mother and I went down to Philadelphia for an audition. The one song I knew which they had an arrangement for was "Dinner for One, Please James." I did it and I got hired. We returned briefly to New York and then we all literally ran away—Mother, Mike, and me—to go on the road with Sissle. When I think that really great singers like Ella Fitzgerald were singing with competing bands like

Chick Webb's I don't see why Noble wanted me. I couldn't sing jazz and I couldn't sing blues. All I could do was carry a simple tune simply. Perhaps he just wanted to do a good turn for somebody. He had a fiddle section and his arrangements were rather sedate. But he featured Sidney Bechet, the clarinetist, and he had a great male singer named Billy Banks. Billy had a very high voice producing a tone something like that the Ink Spots were to make famous a little later.

The biggest thrill about being with Sissle's band was the dress he bought me. The day before I was due to open he took my mother and me to Wanamaker's to get it. What was thrilling to me was its sophistication—I'm sure the Brooklyn mothers would have been scandalized to see me in it. It was made of black tulle with a wide over-skirt and a slim skirt under it. It had puffed sleeves of see-through net.

My song was the one with which I had auditioned. We made a little production out of it. Billy Banks put on a white waiter's coat and carried a napkin over his arm and seated me at a little spotlighted table. There was a microphone hidden in the flower pot on the table, which shows how much I knew about voice projection in those days.

III

The Sissle band or, to give it its full and proper name, Noble Sissle's Society Orchestra, spent most of its time on the road. Its nominal headquarters was New York, and occasionally we would circle back there for a few days, but mostly we lived catch-as-catch-can on the road. And the road was hell. It's not very pleasant for any band—the overnight jumps by bus to make the next date, the bad food and lousy hotels. But it was much worse for a Negro band. In

1935–36 when I was with Sissle, the few good hotels we could afford were barred to us and we usually stayed in some little rooming house in the Negro section, which posed a special problem for me. My mother and stepfather traveled with me and Mike was only grudgingly welcome in those places. The only reason we got in at all was that Noble had such a good name in the community. Wherever we went it seemed we would have a meeting with the leaders of the local NAACP and perhaps be interviewed by the local Negro press. We represented quality. We were not a typical Negro band. That is to say we didn't have any of those dope-using, drunken, horrible Negro people of popular lore in our band. We didn't even play that decadent jazz.

As a result, the band frequently varied its schedule of out-of-the-way roadhouses and casinos and summer gardens by playing for the parties of rich white people, who were under the impression that we were a very swinging outfit. None of us knew it, but we really had very little future as a band. Once swing really became popular, once the great Negro bands like Duke Ellington's received the acceptance they deserved, we would probably have wound up as the Lester Lanin of the Negro world.

Of course, none of us saw this at the time—least of all my mother. I was kind of cute, so I kept getting good writeups, and that convinced my mother that she had a future star on her hands. Just where she thought I was going from there, I never inquired. I was just a band singer, and the really good bands all had better ones. There was absolutely no hope of my doing a single act in the clubs. All I could see for me, realistically, was an endless road trip stretching endlessly ahead of me.

I didn't mind the work. Noble devised a little revue-like show that we used in the theaters, and before I went on the road he taught me some routines that were fun to do.

Besides the "Dinner for One, Please James" song that I did with Billy Banks, I also did a number with Noble himself to open the show. It was a thing with telephones. He'd be in one spotlight holding one, and I'd be in another, also with a phone. He'd sing "Hello." And I'd sing "Hello, I've just called up to . . ." And he'd sing "I've just called up to say goodnight." Two lovers you see, making the same phone call simultaneously. Very romantic—but Noble was a romantic at heart. Then the band would play a lot of numbers, and then I'd do my specialty. Before going out on the first tour Noble had sent me to New York to learn a special dance routine. It was psuedo-Eleanor Powell. I wore slim, crepe trousers and a sequined tail coat just like a man's, except it was cut very low in the back and had short sleeves. And I wore a top hat. The band had a special lyric about how I was their little sister and they sang while I danced. I liked doing that dance, I felt confident about it in a way that I never did, at that time, about my singing. Of course, I learned a good many of the popular songs as they appeared, and when we were playing a dance—not doing a show—I had to sing more than I did in our regular shows.

Billy and I had uniforms like the band's. I wore a red jacket with an ascot at the neck and instead of the white flannel pants the men had, I wore pants cut rather like culottes, with bell bottoms. We were supposed to sit on little chairs in front of the orchestra and sort of bounce and keep time with the music, as if we were really swinging. Then one or the other of us would get up and do a chorus or two of whatever they were playing.

I never did any up-tempo things. I did ballads like "Old Fashioned Love" or "I Want to Be Kissed," or "Blue Moon." I couldn't sing any songs of real emotional stature and, on the other hand, I couldn't do the little wispy, sweet songs in the manner of Helen Morgan or of Florence Mills, who was the one Noble really wanted me to try to imitate. I

tended to be more interested in the lyric than the music—
that's what decided whether I liked a song or not. Then,
too, I was very impressed by the movie musicals just then,
so if a song came from a movie score I was likely to think
more favorably of it. We also did songs from Noble's *Shuffle Along* like "I'm Just Wild About Harry." I suppose they
were expected of him. They were written by Eubie Blake
and they were fine songs.

My state of mind was this: I was still very neutral in my
feelings about myself in show business. I looked upon what
I was doing simply as a job, though this may just have
been my way of dealing with my mother's unrealistic enthusiasm about my possibilities in the business. I certainly
had no sense of vocation about singing, as yet. I didn't like
touring at all, but then no one could. The thing that bugged
me incessantly and caused me to withdraw into myself as
much as I could, was the strain that developed between
my family and the men in the band.

The musicians were as kind to me as they could be. They
could not, of course, protect me from the world—they had
plenty of trouble simply protecting themselves from the
cruelty you encounter as a Negro who is also leading a
gypsy's life in a profession that is not particularly respectable
in the eyes of many people. But tension quickly developed
between them and my stepfather.

The first incident I remember occurred early in the tour,
in Boston. It was the first time I experienced a thing that
was to recur frequently, both with the Sissle band and in
my own later career. That was the business of being "the
first Negro to" . . . play a certain hotel or club, or whatever. We were the first Negro orchestra to play the roof of
the Ritz-Carlton. Which was swell, except we had to come
in through the kitchen door. Now Noble was a man full of
fine speeches. He always said things like, "Remember, you're
a lady. If you want to be treated like a lady you must act

like one." He was also always insisting that "We'll show
them. We'll show them that we know how to protect our
women." But somehow his concept of what a lady was and
the things they must be protected from did not seem realistic. He knew that ladies do not enter a joint through the
back door but we had to. In Noble's defense I must say
that no one else thought in any other terms in those days.
It's too bad the next generation would describe this attitude
as "Uncle Tom." Noble and people like him did the best
they could.

My stepfather, however, kept demanding more than they
could give. He pointed out that there was a considerable
gap between Noble's pretensions about the dignity of Negro
womanhood and the discriminatory practices he let go without protest. In pointing this out, Mike, as usual, let his
anger get the better of him and there was a terrible scene,
the worst I can remember up to that time.

"You talk about being ladies and my wife and my daughter have to come in the back door," he said and he gibbered
wildly at Sissle in Spanish. Now it is a characteristic of
Spanish men that if they cannot absolutely rule the destinies
of their women, if they cannot to some degree protect them
from the harshness of the world, then they go right up the
pole. It's the surest way to threaten their masculinity. So
that exacerbated Mike's feelings; he wasn't fighting only
for justice, he was also fighting for his image of himself
as a man. He got hysterical—and we went right on coming
in through the back door.

You have to be taught to be second class; you're not
born that way. But the slanting process is so subtle that
you frequently don't realize how you're being slanted until
very late in the game. The paradox of our desire for dignity
and the slights and insults and second-class treatment we
accepted as a matter of course, as something that seemed
to be preordained, was never made clear to me until I met

Paul Robeson a few years later. He felt the same way as my stepfather—that it was useless to prate on about dignity and the progress we were making until we had ceased to accept the small indignities constantly heaped upon us because they were a part of the way things had always been.

The difference between Paul and Mike, however, was huge. Paul was a Negro. He had the right to speak as he did, for he experienced these things himself. Mike was a white man and had no right to talk, especially since he was just along for the ride on our bus, contributing nothing and always able to simply walk away from the problems if they got too much for him.

The men in the band hated him. They knew he was right and they hated him for being right. But somehow you could never get it through his thick skull that at that time that was the way things had to be. It was easy for him to have contempt for Negro men for not defending their rights and their women, for not acting more like men, but he had no gut-knowledge of what it was like to be a Negro man. Sometimes I wanted to plead with him to be more tactful. Sometimes I wanted to pick him up and shake him and say, "Goddamit, if you don't do it the way they do you'll get lynched or you won't be able to work or even get food." I never really did escape the memory of that lynching in Jacksonville and how easy it is for a gang of toughs to work over Negro men who are traveling and have no friends to protect them in strange towns.

With my stepfather on that bus I always felt as if I was sitting with a gun that was loaded and cocked and ready to go off. Then, too, I felt exposed, I felt as if the whole world was being made privy to the secrets of my family's emotional life, the problems we had together.

And there was another thing. When you're traveling like that you are always miserable—the prejudice, the living conditions, they all work on you. So everybody's mood is always bad. But after a while you settle into a kind of rhythm, an acceptance of the way things are. Once that's established, you find the life bearable. The only thing that can throw you is the unexpected. Even if someone does something nice for you it upsets you because it's unexpected; even if you solve a problem before the time you had allowed yourself to worry it, you get thrown. It's an odd thing. You would think it would be the good things that you'd live for, that would make a tour like that bearable. You'd even think that the bad things would at least excite you and interest you. But you wrap the monotony and the misery around you like a blanket, and you pray no one will yank the covers off.

My stepfather was a constant threat to that mood. Just his presence, even when he wasn't stirring things up, made everyone uncomfortable. And it made me especially so. I was still being overprotected. For one thing, my voice was often in bad shape so everyone was always hovering over me, telling me to rest, offering advice on the care and feeding of it. No one had thought to link the voice troubles I had with the chronic bronchial condition that our whole family suffered. I was this delicate flower over which people kept huddling ineffectually. And then there were all those musicians I was supposed to stay away from, and the people who always hang around bandstands that I mustn't look twice at. All this increased my sense of separateness. It also increased my need for a "normal" life, whatever that might be.

Once or twice on the tour I tried to establish contact with the middle-class world. In Boston, during the stay at the Ritz-Carlton, I took a day off and went, with my mother, to a summer camp outside of town, where some of my friends from Brooklyn were staying. I arrived wearing a pink linen dress and high heels which I dared not get dirty. They were all wearing sneakers and blue jeans and I couldn't participate with them in any activities. All I could do was concentrate on keeping my good dress clean and preventing my hairdo from getting ruined. I even had to worry about getting a mosquito bite that might detract from my glamour on stage. The girls were very nice to me, and I loved seeing them again, but I felt stiff and awkward and, for me, the meeting was tinged with sadness.

I was luckier when things were a little more casual. Noble's band was very popular with the Negro middle class; they thought he was a credit to their image. So we were frequently invited to someone's house after the show or dance and treated to a lovely spread of some sort. I think I developed a crush on someone in every town we played. They were all very nice boys, the sons of doctors and lawyers and leading merchants. I was never allowed to go off with them anywhere. But we would get to hold hands in a corner or out on a porch for a minute.

The incident I remember best occurred in one of the large towns in Indiana. The larger share of our touring was done in towns along the New York Central right-of-way. All those towns had large Negro populations—initially, I suppose, because the men had been able to find work on the railroad; they had formed the nucleus of the Negro population. In some of those towns, incidentally, the Negroes and the Jews lived side by side in one large, rather friendly ghetto, and on Sunday, when the Jewish delicatessens were open, people would come from all over town to shop in those sections. Anyway, in one of them, probably Indianapolis, my mother let me go off with some of our host's friends to swim in the local Negro swimming pool. As I recall, it was owned by one of the large Negro life insurance companies, one of those firms that had been formed because for many years the white insurance companies simply would not insure Negroes. There was a big, good-looking kind of crazy guy there—not the sort my mother would have approved— who apparently had seen me perform. He saw me dabbling my toe in the water—I couldn't swim very well—and he gave this big shout of recognition and yelled to everybody:

"Hey, you sons-of-bitches, get out of that pool and let this pretty lady have it to herself."

I was terribly embarrassed, but terribly flattered too. I don't think very many people climbed out of the pool, but I loved the feeling that a boy could just respond in a natural, healthy way to my presence and that I was free to respond simply as a girl.

There weren't many incidents like that, though. The feeling I remember best was that of being in prison. I resented the lack of trust my mother and stepfather appeared to have in me, the constant implication that if I wasn't watched every minute I'd run wild and go completely to hell morally. Sure I had a normal, girlish urge to have dates with fellas, but more important I had an urge to be trusted by my family. Why couldn't they see that I was trustworthy? Why couldn't they see that on the few times I did get a chance to have a date their attitude took all the fun out of it? I would know in advance that I couldn't possibly have any fun because of all the anxiety with which they surrounded the occasion. A perfectly healthy interest in the opposite sex was being twisted by them into something it was not; and at the same time, I was being asked to exhibit myself and to say to the audience, "Look at me. Don't you want me?"

I began to dream of marriage, partly as an escape from the grind of the tour, but mostly as a way to have some kind of personal freedom. You had to be married in order to go to bed with someone. Since I was denied the usual adolescent experiences of this forbidden thing—sex, love, maybe just simple natural affection between a man and a woman, whatever that was—it was no wonder this desire started to grow in me. It was the only way I could think of to legitimize my desires.

Meantime, the tour rolled along. In Terre Haute, we could not get into a hotel, so we spent the night on the grounds of a Clyde Beatty circus that was also playing there, awakened periodically by the howling of the animals. At around the same time, Sissle finally suggested that my stepfather leave the tour—the dissension he was causing had reached an unbearable level. My mother stayed on with me, and it must have been bad for her. After all those lonely years she had finally met a man who cared deeply for her, who got into trouble, really, because his feelings for her were so strong, and now she was forcibly separated from him.

But then something happened which must have taken her mind off her troubles. We had a date in Cincinnati, at a dance hall called the Moonlight Gardens—it was in a park on a lagoon where you could rent canoes, and there was, I remember, a huge Ferris wheel. The band had arrived ahead of Sissle, who was driving there in his own car with his white manager. A day or two before we were supposed to start our engagement we received a phone call from a little place called Delaware, Ohio. There had been a crackup and Noble was in the hospital. He asked my mother and me and some of the guys from the band to come see him as quickly as we could. We piled into a car and drove down.

When I walked into his room the first thing he said to me was, "Sister, you've got to take charge of the band." (In his band, all the girl singers were always called "Sister.")

"You're out of your mind," I said. "Take charge doing what?"

"I want you to get out there in front of it and conduct it."

"You're kidding," I said.

"You've got to," he said. "I'm going to be in this hospital

for at least a month. We cannot afford to lose this engagement—we'll all be out of work."

It was to be a long engagement and if we were not able to
fill it the band would probably break up. The musicians
could not afford to sit around for a month without pay. I
suggested he let Billy Banks lead the band, but he said,
"No, you're cuter."

Meantime, my mother was chiming in, all excited, saying,
"She can do it, she can do it."

One of Noble's lawyers was there and he applied the
clincher. "The park people are willing to give us two nights
to see if it'll work out."

I couldn't refuse. The next day there were ads in the
paper. "The Noble Sissle Orchestra, directed by Helena
Horne." Noble had never liked the name Lena—it wasn't romantic sounding. I'd never really liked it either, so he came
up with this classy stage name, Helena, with the second
syllable drawn out in what we both thought was a very
hoity-toity way.

So, on opening night, I led the band. I had his baton—a
long, stupid thing—and I had always been able to move
around on stage, and the people just stood there and stared
up at me. I guess they had never seen anything like it before.
I announced the numbers and did my songs and waved
that big stick. At least I didn't interfere with the quality
of the band's playing. They followed the first saxophone
just as they always did.

It worked out fine. The papers all reported the next day
that there was a good band out at Moonlight Gardens and
Noble called from the hospital and said, "I knew you could
do it, Sister," and the *Amsterdam News* and the Pittsburgh
Courier sent their local representatives around to interview
me, so Noble actually got some publicity breaks out of
the whole business. Besides my personal "first" the engagement was also a "first" for the band—we were the first Negro

orchestra to play the Moonlight Gardens, which even for our engagement still did not allow Negroes to buy tickets.

I have one other vivid memory of our stay at the Moonlight Gardens. That is the night of the first Joe Louis-Max Schmeling fight. Until that night I had no idea of the strength of my identification with Joe Louis.

We had the radio on behind the bandstand and during the breaks we crowded around it to hear the fight. I was near hysteria toward the end of the fight when he was being so badly beaten and some of the men in the band were crying. I think we felt this defeat so deeply because we were, at the time, virtually being exhibited as freaks. The police kept patrolling around so there wouldn't be any incidents (by which they meant Negroes trying to get in to hear us play) and the men in the band could not even go to the toilet because it was reserved for the white men. Joe was the one invincible Negro, the one who stood up to the white man and beat him down with his fists. He in a sense carried so many of our hopes, maybe even dreams of vengeance. But this night he became just another Negro getting beaten by a white man—or so it seemed to that little group in Cincinnati. My mother was furious with me for getting hysterical. "How dare you?" she screamed. "You have a performance. The show must go on. Why, you don't even know this man."

"I don't care, I don't care," I yelled back. "He belongs to us." She just did not understand the personal involvement. For that matter, neither could I have explained my reactions.

She was wrong about one thing though. I had seen Joe. My father had come into town one time when I was still at the Cotton Club and without my mother's knowing it, had taken me out to Pompton Lakes, New Jersey, to visit Joe's training camp. Carl Van Vechten, the writer and photographer, had been there that day and had made some portraits of me. But, typically, my mother knew nothing of this. It is not that we wanted to be sneaky about it. We just didn't want unnecessary trouble. I suppose the incident is as good a symbol as any of our whole relationship.

CHAPTER FOUR

I

I had been in touch with my father in a seemingly casual way while I was on tour and then when we came to Cleveland he decided to drive up from Pittsburgh to see me. He had been established for years there, running a small hotel, the Belmont, with a small gambling room back of a restaurant which he always called "The Bucket of Blood." The chief game that was always running was skin. He was already involved in the very lucrative numbers business, too. Numbers are a poor man's preoccupation. You can buy a number for a few cents and you may strike it rich. It's not likely, but it is a hope, and in the Negro ghetto it is about the only hope you can afford.

Anyway he drove up to Cleveland and asked my mother to let me come to Pittsburgh for a visit. After the Cleveland stand, the band was due for a short lay-off and I think my mother saw that I needed a little let-out, a little loosening of the chain for a few days. Besides, it would give her a chance to go to New York and be with Mike. My father prevailed upon her and I begged and she surprised me by saying "yes." So after the engagement was finished I was put on a train with somebody from the band and went to Pittsburgh.

I stayed in my father's hotel, and got to know my step-mother for the first time. We had an odd relationship. She was, in many ways, a very charming woman, who found it easy to attract people to her. Besides that, she was very shrewd with money and she managed my father's affairs.

The first few days in Pittsburgh were very exciting for me. I just wanted release at this point and my father determined I was going to have fun. So he was my escort and he took me to the little after-hour joints. People would come up to us and ask him, "Is that your sister?" or they'd tell us how beautiful we looked together and that made me very proud.

Now when my father had driven up to Cleveland to see me he had brought a young friend of his along. His name was Louis Jones, the son of a minister, a graduate of West Virginia State College, a very polished, polite young man —very different from the kind of men I had been around. My father came to know him because he sometimes sat in on the card games at the hotel or at a club they both belonged to.

I thought he was the nicest thing in the world. He treated me with respect, and he was as different as he could be from the men I had been around, the married musicians or the ones who were always dying to get some chick into bed—but were scared of me—and the old lechers who ran the places where I'd worked. I don't know if he really respected me, but he seemed to. He was charming, polite, and not someone my mother could dismiss by calling him a musician. Louis was also respectable. I'm sure he seemed to me the perfect incarnation of the whole so-called normal world that had so attracted me for such a long time.

In short, I liked him from the beginning in Cleveland, and I began to like him even more in Pittsburgh. By the time I had to leave to rejoin my mother in New York I had a very big crush on him and I was determined, since there was a place for me with my father in Pittsburgh, to wangle a little time from my mother to stay in Pittsburgh so I could be around my father and Louis a little longer.

When I returned to my mother and told her about Louis, her first response was: "How could Teddy let this happen?" I explained that my father had nothing to do with it, and didn't even know I was seriously interested in Louis. As a matter of fact, he was against the romance. He genuinely liked him as a man's man, but he did not think he was the right person for his daughter. If he had known me better he would have also known that I was absolutely wrong for Louis. But my father believed that people should mold their own decisions. He took the line that I was a grown woman who would have to make my own mistakes and my own happiness, too. The only trouble was that I was not all a grown woman at that time. I wasn't quite nineteen years old, and, because of the life I had led, I had less maturity of judgment than a lot of nineteen-year-olds. I know now that my father hoped I would eventually lose interest in Louis.

My mother called my father and asked a lot of questions. He disclaimed knowledge of the whole affair and also told her the decision was up to me. Her next move was to take me around to see Sissle. In brief, our dialogue went like this:

He said, "You can't do it, you're going to have a career in the theater."

And I said: "I don't want it. I want to be like normal folks."

He had no contractual hold on me, so that was that. Whereupon, my mother became ill. When she wanted to be, my mother could become an intense, high-tempered person. In essence, this was the same kind of crisis that every parent has with his teen-age children, but it was heightened by the fact that the fifty or sixty dollars a week that Sissle paid me was the most important money coming into the family. At least that's what I thought at the time.

I ended the discussion by saying, "I'm going back to Pittsburgh and stay for a while and make up my mind. And then I'm going to marry Louis." Which, of course shows that my mind was already made up.

As I look back on it, I was going into this marriage for all the wrong reasons. I was getting married because I thought it would set me free which, for all the virtues of that institution, it cannot do. I was simply using marriage —and I'm afraid Louis—to run away from a life I did not like. I often wonder now why people, when they must run away from some bad situation, must run *to* something else. Why can't we be strong enough to run away just to be alone for a while?

I also realize now that I could have been talked out of that marriage. To put it bluntly, I was still a virgin and one of the reasons marriage was so attractive to me was that I was desperately eager to know the physical side of love. If someone had simply told me to go to bed with Louis, or with some other nice boy, a great deal of the pressure that simple curiosity can generate would have been dissipated. I remember thinking that, "If I could only get pregnant, then they'd have to let me get married." I was so confused that no simple answer would have worked for me. Except, perhaps, one. I now think my father could have charmed me out of marriage. At that time he was infinitely more glamorous to me than that young man. If he had said, "Look, you need a little rest, why don't you just hole up here with us and have some fun," I might have been distracted long enough to see that the marriage would not work out. But my father, with that fierce belief of his in the individual's right to independence, to make his own decisions, would have none of it. In the few weeks before the marriage in Pittsburgh the only people who tried to talk me out of it were a couple of guys from Jimmy Lunceford's band who happened to be passing through. But they only repeated the familiar argument that I was too young to really know my own mind. I wasn't having any of that.

Though I enjoyed being with my father, I began to realize that a certain amount of unconscious and perhaps unjustified resentment had built up in me over the years when we had been separated. I couldn't help but think that he had only come back into my life after the hardest years were past, after I had learned to survive on my own and when my need for him was not as desperate as it had once been.

So Louis and I continued our courtship and, in a few weeks, decided to marry. We went to New York together to make one last try to get my mother's blessing. Also I had to pick up my belongings and to see if she was going to be all right financially. My stepfather had a little job of some sort but it wasn't bringing in much money. I remember telling her that after we got married and Louis started his new job that we'd help them out all we could.

That made Mike angry. "Don't you worry about your mother. I'm her husband and I'll take care of her."

My mother chose to play the whole scene tragically. "It's the end of your life," she said.

But one thing I thought I knew: that the life they were talking about was not really my life. It was only a dream of theirs—a never-never land where some day I would be a star and rich and famous. I simply could not share that dream. There was no place for me, anywhere, it seemed. So I went with Louis.

II

We were married in the preacher's living room. My father and stepmother were there, and Louis' family. I wore a black dress. I wore a black dress for both my marriages. We went to the home of Paul Jones, one of Louis' brothers, after the ceremony. It was in the Herron Hill section and we lived there the first weeks of our marriage. We lived in one of the rooms.

The next morning Louis got up early and went to the store. He bought eggs and flour and syrup and other staples. Then he woke me up and said: "Okay, cook breakfast."

"I don't know how," I said. "What'll I do?" I had never cooked in my life. By the time I was old enough to start learning, my mother had been intent on protecting my appearance and wouldn't let me near the rough work of a kitchen.

My husband was reasonably understanding. He said: "I'll show you, and I'll help you at first."

He did, and thank God, he liked what was called "plain cooking"—biscuits and homemade bread and pork chops and deep-dish apple pie—things that were easy for me to learn to do.

I felt—I still feel—a little sorry for my first husband. He was some nine years older than me and I'm sure he found me flighty—which may have been pleasing at first—but which could not last long. A Negro man needs more, expects more, from his wife than other men do.

A Negro woman, no matter what their age or background or understanding of the problem, has to be terribly strong. They cannot relax, they cannot simply be loving wives waiting for the man of the house to come home from work. They have to be spiritual sponges, absorbing the racially inflicted hurts of their men. Yet at the same time they have to give him courage, make him know that it is worth going on, worth going back day after day to the humiliations and discouragements of trying to make it in the white man's world. It isn't easy to be a sponge *and* an inspiration. It doesn't leave enough room for simple love to develop. You both become victims of the system you're trying to fight. The strain on a marriage is incredible. And I had not expected such a

strain. Quite the opposite. I had looked for marriage to re-
lieve the strains I felt. I hoped Louis would be a more mature individual than he turned out to be. I felt I needed
protection and inspiration just as much as he did. So, very
simply, neither of us could fill the other's needs. If I had
had real strength and maturity perhaps the marriage would
have had a better chance. But it was in trouble almost from
the beginning.

Louis had two special strikes against him—he was a college man and he was a minister's son. Both led him to expect more of the world than it was prepared to give a Negro—any Negro—then or, for that matter, now. He was an
intelligent and sensitive man, but he could not get work in
which he could fully utilize his intelligence or his education.
The best he could get was a job in the county coroner's
office, registering and filing papers. The job was a pay-off
for the faithful work he and his brothers had performed for
the local Democratic machine. He was not grateful for it,
though I'm sure people in those depression times told him
he ought to be. But why should he be grateful for a job
that was beneath his capabilities? Despite the lack of a
really suitable reward he continued to work hard for the
party throughout our marriage, campaigning, joining this
and that faction. He saw that his only chance to move up-
ward was through faithful ward heeling. But this meant he
was away from home many evenings and I, the young and
naïve bride, was not very understanding. Since I knew nothing about the machinations of politics I could not understand what he hoped to get out of all this extracurricular
work. All I knew was that I wanted him at home with me
in the evening. I had, after all, married in order to have
the home life, stable and protective, that I had never known
before.

How being a minister's son hurt him is a little more difficult to explain. I have made a little, informal survey of

life in the Negro church, and I've come to believe that in former times for most ministers and their families it was a trap, or maybe a cocoon, psychologically speaking. This is changing now, with the church becoming the heart of the protest movement, acting as the conscience of the community. But when I was young, there was nothing at all militant about the church. The people used it as a refuge, if not from life, then certainly from the white man. It was a pacifier. And it was also the one place where the white man never, never interfered with the lives of Negroes. He could trust the minister to keep them happy, and, in turn, the church made the white man happy. It assuaged his guilt to see the happy, docile Negroes going to church on Sunday, apparently content with their lot.

It also contributed in great part toward the Negro matriarchy, which had the largest stake in community stability. As a result the ministers, and their sons, generally came to be rather spoiled, and to have a certain contempt for the people who spoiled them and who in turn, were so easily exploited by them.

Practically speaking, it worked like this: The ladies of the church came in and cleaned for them and were always inviting them over for a good homecooked meal. They saw to it that the minister had the best house and that he drove the best car and that he had as many amenities as he thought he needed. The minister, the minister's sons, they saw that women are the ones that made all this happen and as a result they had a sense of how easy it was to exploit women and a definite expectation that women should be their servants. Put crudely, the result to me was an attitude that the world owed you a living and that the women were the ones who should be the chief instruments of providing that living. But it was very easy to have contempt for women who do this work. It sounds noble when you talk about it in the abstract. But when you are a man, living intimately with these facts, it is easy to be contemptuous first of the mentality that willingly accepts such conditions of life, then of the values which seems to motivate that mentality of all women, whether they are part of the system or not.

In my own case I know I was dumb; I didn't know what was expected of me in my new life, I had had no experience that could help me. I didn't mind having to wash clothes or cook or clean house. But I did very deeply mind being treated as if I had no wits at all. I minded not being made privy to our financial status (not a very good one) but then being asked to be the one to stave off creditors. Most of all, I minded that, once again, change for me merely meant the substitution of one form of brainwashing for another. First my mother had substituted her special kind of thinking for that of my grandmother. Now Louis was substituting his kind of control for that of my mother. I think I was especially conscious of this issue at this stage of my life. It had been a great psychological shock for me to leave my mother and her thoughts of my "career." Now it seemed to me that Louis was systematically applying himself to put down this new-found, and to me precious, independence.

I did have a temper, though. And I fought back. He wanted to live well and he didn't want to have to work where some cracker, who wasn't as smart or as attractive as he, was his boss. But a lot of Negro men have had to suffer this, and I unfortunately put him down for what seemed his inability to conform. What really shriveled me was the way he tried to escape our problems. It's an irony, but as true as anything in this world; when you're poor you need, in a deep, aching kind of way, luxuries. You need them, psychologically, as you never do when you're well off. Their absence is a continual reminder of your state in life. I could understand and sympathize with this need for possessions. But in the course of growing up often in poor homes, I had developed a horror of being in debt. I retain it to this day. It's not a matter of saving—I've never been any good at putting money aside. It is, simply, a pride in paying your debts quickly (maybe I inherited from my father the gambler's sense of honor about settling your debts quickly). It is also, perhaps, something that is embedded quite deeply in the Negro's subconscious. Being a minister's son was probably very bad for Louis. He had been brought up believing something most Negroes can't believe—that someone would take care of him. He had the most sublime faith in everything working out all right. "I have to keep up appearances," he would say, and all I could do was wonder who was going to pay for our appearances. Usually it was my father.

Besides these problems there was, more seriously, the problem of communication. It colored our life at almost every moment. I served food and drinks to his political cronies who were mostly unsuccessful and therefore hungry, but I was never allowed into their discussions and Louis never talked to me about his political plans or hopes. I can't even remember now what offices he ran for himself, what campaigns he took part in. I was told of vague promises that never seemed to be kept, and I was told of "bad luck" that had robbed him of something he wanted. But I never knew the details. So, in the deepest sense, I was never able to share his life, for I was shut out of the things that were most important to him.

I do not believe the marriage would have lasted as long as it did had it not been for my real affection for Louis' father, his brothers, and his sisters. They were extraordinarily kind to me, and I never got the feeling from them that I sometimes got from Louis, that he had married beneath himself. They did their best to make a place for me in their family and to patch up the difficulties between Louis and me as they arose.

More important, however, I got pregnant just a couple of months after we were married. Once I was sure I was going to have a baby there could be no question of an immediate separation. We moved from my brother-in-law's house to a rooming house and then to a little home of our own. I concentrated as best I could on becoming a satisfactory wife.

Gail was born in December, 1937. My husband and my stepmother accompanied me to the hospital, and my doctor, who had attended me throughout the pregnancy, a great guy named Buster Cornelius, met us there. Of course, I was terrified when they put me in the wheelchair and started to take me upstairs to the delivery room. Louis was allowed to come up with me, but as we started off Buster startled me by saying: "So long and take it easy and I'll look in on you tomorrow."

"Where are you going?" I asked.

"You'll be all right," he kept saying. "You'll be all right."

And that's when I learned that Negro doctors could not work in this hospital. They could bring their patients there, but they were not, themselves, allowed to practice within its walls.

I froze. For two days I would not let that baby come down. I remember the high, barred sides of the bed I was in, and through the pain I was conscious of strange, white faces peering at me and of people I did not know giving me injections to ease the pain. I was twenty years old, and except for the rickets I had as a child I had never been sick and I had never had much to do with doctors and certainly not with hospitals. So I was scared to begin with and without my own doctor there I was terrified. And lonely beyond description. I think this is perhaps the cruelest act of prejudice that was ever visited upon me personally.

It was two days before my daughter, Gail, was born. And we were segregated. About a half-dozen Negro mothers were kept in a little ward away from the white maternity cases. And our children were kept in a small room right next to us. As if in unconscious protest to all this I found I could not nurse my Gail. And for days I heard what I was certain were her cries of hunger—and perhaps anger at me—in the nursery. I'm sure they fed her bottles, that she was not, in fact, hungry. But I could not escape the feeling that, right at the start, I had failed her.

They at least allowed my doctor to visit me after it was all over. The first thing I said was: "I'll never forgive you."

And he said: "Oh, baby, I didn't know you didn't know. I thought everyone knew."

And once again, I was conscious of the fact that, for all my wanderings, for all the instability of my childhood, I was still terribly innocent in many ways. Or maybe just damned stupid. I had been sheltered from the cruel, middle-class brands of racial prejudice. The Negro middle class that I knew in Brooklyn just did not encounter it very often, because they had managed to insulate themselves so well, creating a self-contained world that did not bring them into conflict with the white middle class. As for life in the South, it was so far removed from middle-class existence that the little niceties of prejudice never presented themselves as live problems requiring solution. When you are right down to nitty-gritty, as you are in the South, you just have your babies on the kitchen table. The question of whether your doctor will be allowed into a hospital never came up, because the question of your going to the hospital never came up.

Physically, I was healthy, and I recovered quickly from my ordeal. So did Gail. We moved into our first house right after she was born. It was a little stucco place, also in the Herron Hill section, with a living room, dining room and kitchen downstairs, two bedrooms upstairs. Louis' sister came to live with us and help out with the baby and be my friend.

Gail could not have been more than four months old when I received a call from Harold Gumm, who was an agent in New York. He had remembered me from my days at the Cotton Club and now he was rounding up talent for a little quickie Negro musical that was about to be shot in Hollywood. It was called *The Duke Is Tops*, starring Ralph Cooper who had been an emcee at the Apollo Theater. It was being produced by some shoestring independents, the Popkin Brothers, and they wanted me for a part. The shooting schedule was only ten days. Louis and I needed money, but it never occurred to me to leave my baby. Gumm kept calling so we had a big family conference. Louis said, "Maybe you can buy a few things you want." And I thought, "Maybe I'll be able to pay some bills." But still we hesitated. I don't think either of us thought that my going back into show business, even for such a short stay, was a symbolic announcement that our marriage was not working out. It was the need for money that finally decided the issue for me.

Louis immediately insisted that I must look like a star, so we went into debt for a fancy outfit and I climbed on a plane—my first one—and took off for Hollywood, which I had never seen. The plane was grounded somewhere in Arizona and I continued on by train. It was not a good omen, and neither was Ralph Cooper's greeting at the station. He remembered me as a skinny little teen-ager. But I had put on weight, having the baby, and he was disappointed at the way I looked, though I've seen stills from the picture and I must say that if I wasn't exactly svelte I did manage to look presentable.

Making the picture was no fun. First of all, there was trouble about money. The producers apparently had not completed their financing before starting up and they were paying off in promises of what we would make later, when the picture went into release. There is nothing that depresses

theatrical people as much as a situation of this kind. I
called home to tell Louis about it and his immediate reaction was that I should walk out on the picture. He started
making calls to Harold Gumm, trying to get my money.
Later, when I told him the plot of the picture he became
even more adamant about my leaving.

I suppose he was right, though the picture seemed in-
nocuous enough to me. The plot had Ralph Cooper and me
as a husband and wife working in show business. Our careers kept colliding and we kept splitting up and reconciling
throughout the picture. Finally he decides to sacrifice his
career for mine and we live happily ever after. It was certainly not an important picture and the plot was just an
excuse to string a lot of song-and-dance numbers together.
I had a couple of numbers to do, including one called "I
Know You Remember" that a couple of critics eventually singled out as the best in the picture.

Louis and I had a terrible fight "long distance" when I
called to tell him there were money problems. He knew
nothing about the protocol of show business, which demands
that you not walk out, especially when walking out could
cost other people their jobs—people who were just as hard-
pressed as I was.

Anyway, the picture was to be finished in such a short
time that the argument seemed rather academic to me.
Whether I stayed or walked out would not change the date
of my arrival in Pittsburgh by more than a few days. We
finished on time and I went home—the only good memory
of my first stay in Hollywood being that of the wonderful
woman at whose house I stayed. She was Lillian Randolph,
a character actress who gained her greatest fame playing
Beulah, the maid, on "The Great Gildersleeve" radio program for many years. She was the best sort of woman, who
afforded me stability and human warmth at a time when
I desperately needed them. It was while doing this picture

that I also met Phil Moore, who arranged the songs for it
and was later to be my pianist and arranger, and also Marie
Bryant, who was to become a best friend.

The picture, even when it was finished, continued to
cause me trouble. I never did receive my full salary, but
worse than the embarrassment of being made a fool of financially, was the scene when the picture was premiered in
Pittsburgh. There was to be a special showing for the benefit of the NAACP and as the local girl featured in it I was
expected to attend. And I wanted to. But Louis refused to
let me go. I don't know what he was trying to prove, except
the fact that he was master in his own house and that my
activities were dependent upon his permission. Beyond that,
he had a great deal of contempt for show business and show
people. His attitude—at least as I read it—was always that
he had rescued me from a life of sin. Then, too, there was a
strong and not always unattractive streak of rebelliousness
in him. He liked to refuse to do what important people
wanted him to do. This premiere involved important people,
and by forbidding me to attend he demonstrated that we
were not at their beck and call. Still, it seemed a petty point
to me.

III

We had no sooner lived through the movie crisis than we
faced another, more profound one. Partly it was because,
shortly thereafter, Harold Gumm called again. This time he
wanted me as the ingenue in Lew Leslie's *Blackbirds of
1939*. Harold said the job was mine if I wanted it. It was a
small part and there was no need for an audition. This was
in the fall of 1938 and our life together was getting more
and more strained. I never thought that Louis therefore
would let me take this new job, but to my amazement he

told Gumm, "Okay," and proceeded to discuss business details with him.

As I have already said, Lew Leslie was one of the pioneers of the all-Negro show. Several of his earlier *Blackbirds* revues had been tremendous hits, and now he was reviving the form after an absence of some years. He had gathered a great cast for this one. The Hall Johnson Choir was featured, along with Dusty Fletcher (who later had a famous hit record, "Open the Door, Richard") and Kate Hall, who had a fabulous voice, and a very handsome young actor named Bobby Evans, who is a distant cousin of mine by marriage, and a great comic named Bigmeat Dewey Markham. It was a marvelous group.

Lew Leslie was, of course, the discoverer and producer of Florence Mills, the great singing star of the twenties, the one whose name I had heard for the first time from my grandfather and whom I had been the only one to identify in that little school in the South years before. Sometimes, after rehearsal, Lew would sit backstage and tell me stories about his travels with Florence Mills, and tears would come to his eyes as he talked. Working with her had been the greatest thing in his life, and I believe he was always trying to find someone like her and in that way, to recapture the best part of his past.

Almost from the first rehearsal he thought he detected something of Florence Mills in me. "You know, the English made her their star. I must take you to England."

"Why will the English like me?" I asked.

"Because you have talent and you're a lady," he said.

"Well, if I have talent why do I have to be Florence Mills talented?"

He had no answer for that, but he did answer in his own way my question about why Paris had not responded to her. "Because she was not glamorous," he said.

It was not until I started playing in England and France

that I discovered my own answers to these questions. Florence and Josephine Baker were, roughly, contemporaries. Jo, with her fabulous body and her extroverted personality (even then what freedom!) appealed to Paris in a way Florence Mills never could. With all their "civilization" the French adored the lions and tigers, beautiful extravagant creatures, that reminded them of the jungle, and Jo must have seemed to them a fabulous child of nature. Florence Mills, on the other hand, I like to think, must have been a little like Judy Garland, a waif they could cry over and pity sometimes, perhaps feel a little superior to, but also kindly toward.

Since I had so little of the great extrovert or the child of nature about me, Leslie patiently tried to fit the mold of Florence over me.

He described her to me. She had been tiny, with small bones, enormous eyes and skinny legs. Her voice was high and sweet and pure. Her most famous number was one in which she appeared dressed like a little boy in a checked shirt and little, cut-up denim overalls with straps over the shoulders. She carried a bandanna-wrapped bundle suspended at the end of a stick and sang: "I'm a little blackbird, looking for a bluebird."

Well, I did resemble her in one way—I had skinny legs. But when Lew would say, "Lena, be tender" and I'd see his eyes fill with tears as he remembered her, I would only feel inadequate. The tears I rarely shed in real life had always been the tears of sheer anger, and I had long ago learned from my grandmother that crying was not admirable and would get me nowhere. When I tried to be tender and appealing all that came out was coyness. So we dropped that sort of number and I was more successful in another of her numbers—"Shine."

So there I was, neither Jo nor Flo—but who? Lew insisted on out-and-out hard work, which is the foundation

that the whole thing has to build on. I think he was the first
person to introduce me to that interesting notion. He really
stood in the back row and shouted "Louder, sing louder"
and "All right, try it again," just like the impresarios in those
backstage movie musicals (my mother had taken me to a
lot of them, particularly during a period when she was sure
I could be the next Eleanor Powell). As a result, I began
to feel more and more like the little girl Miss Powell or
Ruby Keeler always played—the chorine who was suddenly
thrust into the spotlight in order to save the show.

By the time we took the show to Boston I had several
numbers: "Thursday," which was part of a comedy sketch
with Dewey Markham and Bobby Evans, all about the
maid's night out; "Name It and It's Yours" (both of these
with Bobby); "You're So Indifferent" (a lament), and something called "Shake Your Bluesies with Dancing Shoesies."
I can't remember now if any of these songs were by Johnny
Mercer, but I do know that *Blackbirds* was the first Broadway show to which he contributed lyrics.

Lew also had me sing in the big choral number that included bits and pieces from "St. James Infirmary" and other
dramatic songs. Kate Hall, who was the star singer, encouraged me to use my innate sense of the dramatic and
she taught me to use that sense of drama as I sang. Thanks
to her, I did not do too badly in the choral number.

But the most important thing about *Blackbirds* was Lew
Leslie. He was the first man I ever worked for who did not
act like a boss. He and his brother were old-fashioned Jewish people with that traditionally strong Jewish sense of
family, and they drew me into their life. They had trouble
raising money for the show, as everyone did at that time,
and they couldn't pay us our agreed-upon salaries. But they
always saw to it that we had money for our food and rent
(I had brought Gail and a family friend, who acted as
babysitter and chaperon, with me from Pittsburgh).

More important, Lew and his family came into my life at a time when I had begun to recognize that being a mother did not automatically turn me into a strong woman, and my pride—or whatever it was that had kept me from being at the mercy of others—was badly shaken. I know Lew helped me to develop a new kind of strength. He made me feel that if I failed I would only be failing myself —not him or my mother or my husband or any of the other people I had been trying so hard to please all my life.

He never played the "great white father" as so many other liberal white impresarios tried to do with me in later years. He never put me down because I couldn't sing the blues or wasn't dark enough or primitive enough. Sure, he tried to make me into Florence Mills, but when that didn't work out, he bent all his efforts toward helping me to make a style of my own. Sometimes at rehearsal I would get completely involved in this process, dizzy, carried away with a great excitement, almost outside myself. I had never experienced this in show business before.

I believe Lew really felt he had made a contribution to the theater by presenting Negro talent in what he called a "high-class" way, and he took pride in that.

Nearly every night I would join Lew and his former wife, Belle Baker, and his brother and other people from the show for dinner. They introduced me to Jewish cooking. We always went to a little place on the Lower East Side, and I got to know the people who ran it. I would have their special dishes—flank steak with garlic and tomato pickles, and maybe eggplant with chicken fat.

I loved it so, and I felt comfortable with these people. For the first time I began to feel that there could be some dignity in show business. I began to understand that it was actually possible to make a life—a stable, loving, reasonable kind of life—while working in the theater. For the first time

I was beginning to feel like a strong person who could cope with responsibilities.

It was a discovery of great importance to me. It did not break up my marriage, but it was to make the break possible when the time came. During the rehearsal period I was in constant touch with Louis back in Pittsburgh. He took the same attitude toward this show that he had taken toward the movie. He thought I should quit because I was not receiving my full salary. Before, I had stayed because of loyalty to the tradition of not walking out on a project that was in trouble. This time, the added factor was my growing sense of responsibility and strength. And also there were people in the show who hadn't worked in years.

We took the show to Boston for tryouts. Lew firmly believed you should not read your notices—a practice I still largely follow—and so I don't know how we fared there, but I gather we were something less than a sensation. One nice thing happened to me, though. A bunch of Harvard boys had apparently become fans of mine when I had sung at the Ritz-Carlton with Sissle. They turned up on opening night and gave me a big, cheering "Yea, Lena" when I came on.

The show came back to New York in trouble. On the afternoon of the night we were to open there was doubt whether the curtain would go up. Lew apparently did not have enough cash to post the bond the theater demanded. The money was raised by Belle Baker, who pawned her jewelry, just hours before curtain time.

But even with all this trouble, Lew tried his best to keep me calm. He knew how scared I was with all the responsibility he had thrust on me. He had hired a dresser for me who had worked with Florence Mills and she talked to me about Florence, too, and tried to ease my tension and reassure me about how good I was going to be. I remember saying to her on opening night that I'd do the best I could.

Besides the simple tension that an opening always brings, I felt a high excitement, too. I felt, for the first time, that I was part of something, part of a community effort. It was something I had never felt before. And it was good.

Louis came up from Pittsburgh, and quickly brought me back to earth. He refused to let me attend the cast party after the show. That made everybody else feel bad. It made me furious.

The show got only so-so notices, though some of the critics were very kind to me, especially about my looks. One of them even said I was likely to see my name in lights. But the show only lasted eight nights on Broadway and then I returned with Gail to Pittsburgh, where I tried to put behind me the good feelings the whole experience had left with me. But Louis' refusal to let me go to that party, his whole attitude of negation toward me and my efforts as a wife, continued to rankle. Having appeared in a flop show, and sticking with it, didn't help me with him. Finally I decided to walk out.

IV

I went to my father and told him my decision. He said, "I don't want to have anything to do with breaking up a marriage."

"I don't want you to do anything," I said. "Can I just stay at your house for a couple of days until I decide what to do?"

"Well, you know, you can't," he said. "You've got a child."

"But I have to think."

What we compromised on was a family meeting. My father called Louis' sister, Marguerite, who had been living with us and who was frequently as furious with him as I was. She came and brought Louis' father, and they were loving and reasonable. We did have Gail, we were both young and had made mistakes, but that was to be expected at first. Wouldn't I try again?

I had no place to go. My father did not want to be a party to the divorce and I did not think I could live under the same roof with my stepmother. My mother and Mike had gone to Cuba, where they stayed until the end of World War II, and I would not have considered joining them anyway. So I went back to Louis.

It was wrong. Nothing really changed between us as a result of my threatened separation. Except that I almost immediately got pregnant again. I spared myself the misery of my previous confinement by going to a white doctor right from the start. But I was afraid for that baby, because I was convinced, by this time, that sooner or later our marriage would end for good and I did not know what might happen to that baby.

Teddy, my son, was born. It was an easy birth, physically. And Louis was very proud because this was the first male born into the Jones family in this generation. He said: "You're not going to get this boy. I'm going to take this boy away from you." He said it lightly but he felt it deeply. Later, he was to make good that promise. Over the years Teddy has been much closer to Louis than to me, and this alienation between us has been the great sadness of my later life.

At the time I did not believe this was more than the idle threat of a man who was, in his way, as hurt by the failure of our marriage as I was and who, I'm sure, has his own good case to present against me. I did not believe, at the time, that our bitterness would ever cut so deep that our children would be separated. I did not think much about the implication of Louis' words and shortly after Teddy was born I went back to singing regularly again—though on quite a different level from Lew Leslie's show.

It came about this way: My husband was a member of a bridge club, most of the other members of which were older and better established than we were. I did not feel comfortable with this group. I resented the money he lost to them, because they could afford their bridge losses and he couldn't. And I was embarrassed because I couldn't invite them to our home which was not as elaborate as theirs were and where, in any case, our budget did not permit me to serve such fine meals and whiskey as they did. Besides which, I had a block about gambling, inherited from my mother, and could not learn to play bridge. So I used to go to these parties and sit in the corner. But one woman was very kind to me. Her name was Charlotte Catlin and she used to play piano at very elegant white parties. She and I used to entertain ourselves while the card playing was going on at the club. One day she asked me if I'd like to go along and sing at some of these parties.

I had all sorts of excuses: "Louis will never let me . . . I don't have anything to wear."

But she said: "I'll ask Louis." I was relieved because by this time I was too timid to ask him anything.

She told him that these were very respectable parties, given by people like the Mellons and the Carnegies, and Louis decided that it would be all right for me to go with Charlotte. I was thinking only of the five or ten dollars a night that I could make, thinking it might help out with the groceries or free me from having to ask Louis for money for the little extras I wanted.

The people we worked for were charming. They were, after all, aristocrats and they were so well bred they didn't let us smell any condescension. Still, I could not get over the feeling that, to them, we were these charming Negro people who were ever so amusing to have entertain at their affairs.

The routine was this: We'd arrive after they had finished dinner and we would wait in a bedroom or an anteroom—

usually they were pretty little rooms and I would amuse myself by taking in the details of how the other half lived. Then we would do our songs. There was a hit number from one of the later Cotton Club shows called "Copper-Colored Gal" that they liked very much. And "Man I Love"—it seems I was always singing that—and also "Sunny Side of the Street" and maybe a few of the passing hits of the day. Afterward we were frequently given ice cream and cake and coffee, and everybody came up and said how good we were. We would say thank you and go home.

To me, this was not like going back into show business. There was nothing back-breaking about it, the way there had been at the Cotton Club or on the road with Sissle, or even bringing *Blackbirds* in. And it was good for me. My natural talent was in knowing what to do with a song. I could get to the heart of the matter in a lyric and put it across. Charlotte recognized that and helped me to develop this ability. Charlotte worked with me on those problems of strength and projection and it was not long before we had a very pleasant little act. Yes, pleasant is exactly the right word for it. We were not about to become stars overnight, but we did a very competent entertainment for that time and place.

The only other time I did much singing at parties was early in my second and longer Hollywood stay, and I must say that the situation in Pittsburgh was much less exploitative than it was out there. We did our modest business on a strictly cash-and-carry basis, whereas my singing at Hollywood functions was nearly always done as a favor—for the host or, at an even further removal from reality, as a favor for some friend of the host who was using me to do him a good turn. The Pittsburgh work was at least straight-forward, honest work.

Meantime, the situation between Louis and me continued to deteriorate. During the time I was carrying Teddy I had been so concerned over what might happen later to the children that I communicated my tension to Gail. As a tiny child she was very close to me, but now she began to seem withdrawn and she cried easily. It seemed to me that I had better make a plan for our escape. My father and stepmother had given me some money to pay for a wonderful woman who worked for me after Teddy's birth. I asked my stepmother if she would lend me enough money to buy me a ticket to New York and to live on until I could get a job. I also asked for money to continue the nurse's pay to take care of Teddy and Gail for a while. I planned to come back and get them once I was working.

I've said that I never felt I could be very close with my stepmother. But she was one of those women who were at their best when there was a crisis. She just said: "When do you want the money?"

"I don't know," I said. "I'd just like to feel it's there in case I need it in a hurry."

All she said was: "It'll be there."

And it was. The incident that triggered our final break-up occurred one night when Louis was packing for a political trip around the state. I had been upstairs with him, folding diapers while he filled his suitcase. I wandered downstairs for some reason and I found a shoe box hidden away behind the couch. I opened it and found a brand new pair of expensive, hand-made shoes he had just bought. I had just had a visit from some finance company trying to collect a bill, and these were an indulgence I knew we couldn't afford. Somehow, they suddenly seemed symbolic of all our troubles—the secrets between us, the endless fight about money.

I waited for Louis to come downstairs and when he appeared I said very quietly, "I think I'm going to go, too."

"Oh, you've said that before," he replied.

"Yes. Well, this time I mean it."

"Well, you'll come back," he said.

All this was very calmly stated, probably because both of us were very sure we knew what we were doing. He was certain I could not make the break and I was certain I could.

For the moment we left it that way. He went on his trip and I called up Mrs. Turner, the maid who had been helping out, and made arrangements for her to stay permanently at our house. Then I went to my father's place and asked for the money from my stepmother.

The next time I confronted Louis I told him that Mrs. Turner would be moving in the next day. He said that he had no money to pay her and was amazed when I told him it had all been taken care of.

"What are you going to do?" he asked.

"I don't know," I said, "but I know I can't stay here any more."

"You can't *do* anything," he snapped. "What are you going to do, go hoofing at the Cotton Club?"

I honestly did not know and it was no help at all when he added: "Just because a bunch of Pittsburgh socialites think you're cute, doesn't mean you can make it somewhere big."

I blew up. "I don't know. Maybe I'll have to eat a lot of crab. But at least it'll be a change of crab."

And then I started going over my grievances with him, one by one—the big ones and the little ones. There were so many of them, most of which I had never mentioned. I was not really inarticulate, it was just that I had had no one to talk to and I had learned to talk to myself, to figure things out in the course of long dialogues that took place inside my own head. Now everything I had been brooding about came tumbling out in a torrent of angry words.

The last thing Louis said was: "My God, how can one person have kept inside her what you have for so long?"

That was my failure in marriage. Maybe if I could have

brought forth all that I finally did, before it was too late, we might have had a chance. But all those years of secretiveness, of being afraid to complain, or even to call attention to myself, had had their effect on me. By the time I married Louis it was simply not in my nature to deal openly with people.

Two days later, I left Pittsburgh and headed for New York.

I wish I could say the break was a clean one. I said to him, "I'm coming back to get the children." And he said, "You can take Gail, but you'll never get Teddy."

CHAPTER FIVE

I

I got a room at the Theresa Hotel in Harlem—the place that got into the news a few years ago when it was the hotel Castro stayed in the time he visited the UN. It had always been the leading place for Negroes to stay in Harlem.

I immediately went to the Apollo Theater to see if I could find out where Noble Sissle was. I thought maybe I could get my old job with him back, or that at least he might know where I could look for work. He was out on tour and I discovered, incidentally, that there was no work for me at the Apollo, either. It was just as well, because I really did not want to go back to hoofing in a chorus line.

Then I called up Harold Gumm, the agent who had placed me in the movie and in *Blackbirds*. He told me to come downtown and see him—the first time I had ever gone out to see anyone about a job all by myself. I was scared, but I had gained a funny kind of confidence in the few days I had been in New York. Every time I walked through the Theresa lobby the sports were taking shots at me from every corner—the young, married lady mysteriously alone in the big city. It made me think that at least I was still a female.

But the fact that I did not seem to fit the prevailing racial stereotype *was* against me. At one of the little clubs we went to, the manager said to Harold: "She just isn't our idea of what a Negro entertainer should be like." Another manager said, "But she doesn't sing the blues." And a couple more seemed to imply something George White was at least honest enough to bring out into the open. He said I was crazy to try to make it as a Negro. "Don't say she's Negro, don't admit she's colored," he told Harold. "Let her learn a few Spanish songs, give her a Spanish name and I'll put her in."

By this time Harold was getting discouraged and, for that matter, so was I. "Well, you know, maybe there's something to it," he said after the interview with White.

"But I don't want to be Spanish," I said, and I got quite angry with Harold. At the time, I was thinking about not wanting to be like my stepfather, who was the only Spanish type I knew. But there were a couple of other factors, too. The first was that I had a horror of "passing." I didn't know anyone who respected that solution to the problem. I had relatives who could have taken that road and did not. It would have been a terrible thing for me to do. The family would never have got over it.

I realized there was very little hope that Harold would be able to cope with the situation that I faced, so I retreated back up to Harlem, to look for work there. A benefit was scheduled for the Apollo Theater and I agreed to sing a couple of songs on a program that featured some of the biggest Negro names.

I went around to the Apollo the afternoon before and found that Noble Sissle and his band were scheduled to appear and that they were rehearsing in the theater that very moment. I went in and Noble greeted me very warmly and was surprised to see me and even more surprised that I was going to be on the same program with him.

I said to him, very casually, "By the way, do you need a girl singer?"

He said, "Oh, I *am* sorry, but we have someone."

And I replied, "Oh, I'm sorry too," not letting him know that at that moment he seemed my very last hope.

Still, there was the benefit coming up. There was always a chance that something might come of that.

I don't know which band I sang with; three or four of them were playing that night. My stepmother had sent me a couple of very nice dresses from Pittsburgh to use for auditions. And I had some good songs to sing—"Yes, My Darling Daughter," of which Dinah Shore had made a hit recording at the time, "Good for Nothing Joe," which had been in a Cotton Club show I had been in, and something from a current Betty Grable movie, *Down Argentine Way*. If I say so myself, I went over okay that night and people apparently remembered me from the club and from Noble's band.

My goodness, there was a lot of talk around the Theresa lobby the next day. But I felt very depressed. Part of it was a let-down from the excitement of the night before and part of it was the result of not being hired by Sissle and plain fear for the future. That business of being asked to be either Spanish or more classically Negro in style had got to me. My entire life until then had been a succession of attempts by other people to give me what nowadays I suppose would be called "an image." But who was really me? The respectable middle-class Brooklyn girl, the rootless child, the band singer, the wife and mother, or maybe just a chick who would end up faking it as Spanish or as a blues shouter? I was still grabbing my identity on the fly.

This day I was just plain down. So I went off to a movie at the Victoria Theater on 116th Street. I was sitting there, not paying much attention to the picture, when Clarence Robinson came down the aisle, looking for me. He was a very sweet man and was the choreographer at the Apollo. When he saw me he grabbed me and said, "Come on, come on out."

So I followed him out to the lobby and he said: "Charlie

Barnet is up at the Windsor Theater in the Bronx. One of the people on the bill with him is sick. So why don't you go up there and see if you can get the job?"

"Don't be ridiculous," I said. "What would I do in that white band?" I think I had a few more excuses besides that.

"No, listen," he said. "Charlie's a great guy and he called the Apollo looking for someone and I thought of you, maybe."

So I climbed on a subway and went up to the Bronx to see Charlie. He took one look at me and said what I would later recognize as a typically Charlie thing to say: "*Wow, who are you?*"

I told him, and he told me he was just about to go on stage, but to wait around. When he was finished we went downstairs with the pianist and I did a couple of songs I had done at the Apollo the night before. When I had run through them Charlie just said: "You want to work in the next show?"

And that's how I started with Charlie's band. A couple of hours later I was on the stage, singing.

After work that night the first thing I did was to call my stepmother in Pittsburgh. "I've got a job," I said. "I'm going to go with a white orchestra. What do you think my father will say about that?"

She said she thought he would probably object. My family is just as prejudiced against white people as white people are against Negroes.

"I don't care," I said. "If I can finally get a job I don't care who it's with. Besides, I couldn't get one with anyone else, so I'm going to take it."

So she said, "Go ahead."

And I said, "I'm going to move out of the Theresa and as soon as I start drawing my salary I'll send you some money every week." I had my loan to pay back.

She just said, "Okay, but take your time."

The next day I took a nice room in the YWCA at 135th Street, just off Seventh Avenue. That was to be my home base for several months, though actually I spent most of my time out on the road with the band. I had a little radio there and it was the first time I heard an Artie Shaw recording of "Stardust," that I liked very much. I used to call up Stan the Milkman, who had the "Milkman's Matinee" program, and request that record all the time. It was a wonderful arrangement. I did not know at the time that the arranger was Lennie Hayton.

A week later I went out on the road with this band for the first time. The first place we played was Hartford, Connecticut, and Charlie had, as his star act, Elaine Barrie, the young girl who had married John Barrymore. She fancied herself an actress. She came out and cracked a few jokes with Charlie and then she'd do a scene or two with an actor who also traveled with her. It was pretty corny, but I didn't care.

Charlie was a big favorite with the Negro people because he played good and he had a great band. He had had a hit record, "Cherokee," and he had played the Apollo. That house is tough for any band—very critical—but it's twice as tough for a white band.

Personally, he had empathy in all kinds of situations. He was one of those people who just naturally blend in. He had come from a wealthy family and was in the band business simply because he loved it. He was a soft touch for anyone with a good story and as far as color was concerned, it just never came up. Around some of the men in the band I was made aware of our differences in color, but around Charlie it was never discussed. I just felt safe with him. I don't know if he knew it then—I don't think I was letting anyone know what I was thinking about in those days—but I thought he was a good man and after we got to know each other we became good friends.

As usual, there was a lot of crap for me on the road, but at least it was different from the kind I had shared with the Sissle orchestra. Then, we were all Negroes together and there was no question about where we stayed—it was a Negro hotel; or where we played—it was usually for Negroes, or, if we played for whites it was in a situation where we were well segregated. With Charlie, the problem was the surprise I caused. The band would be booked into some hotel and I'd turn up at the reservation desk. A lot of times there would be no Negroes allowed. There would be a discussion and sometimes the hotel man would back down, not wanting to lose the business of a big band—twenty, twenty-five rooms. Other times he wouldn't back down, so then Charlie and at least some of the boys would walk out and we would find a hotel that would take us all. The same thing would happen when we played college dances. Sometimes they would say they didn't want a Negro singer around. Then I would get the night off, but always with pay—because that's the kind of man Charlie is. Then sometimes it would be all right for me to sing but I couldn't stay on the stand with the boys. I'd have to wait somewhere else until it was time for my numbers. The guys would be great about that. If I had to sit outside in the bus they would come out and keep me company. Sometimes, though, I'd have to wait in the powder room, and nobody could visit me there. Except the little white broads who came in to use the facilities. Boy, did I get some odd looks when they came sweeping into the john and found me hanging around in there.

I think it was in those powder rooms that I developed my lifelong prejudice against middle-class white women. You never can totally explain a prejudice, but somehow it was the realization that these little girls were being protected by my being hidden from their sight and away from my friends in the band. No one seemed to think that maybe

This tired look is due to three
shows a night at the Cotton Club.

My lovely mother,
Edna Scottron Horne.

A Sunday on Jones Beach
with Mother.

Me and my dad. People were always
saying, "Hey, who is that sharp cat
you're with, Lena?"

L. Hayton and F. Astaire
rehearsing with L. Horne.

Ensenada, Mexico, with
Lennie, 1944.

I make a movie star entrance
at Great Lakes Naval Base.

First you sing for the officers
and then the "fellas."

Lennie and Luther Henderson at the Jazz Club, 1947.

Canada—first trip. I've just been told my opposition is Frankie Laine.

I'm godmother to the newest Horne, John Burke, Jr.

7

Lennie really thinks the singer obscures the arrangement.

The story of my life.

DRAWING BY VIRGIL PARTCH.

my sensitivity was being offended in the process. Of course, I have been able to set aside this prejudice occasionally, but my initial reaction to a nice pretty white woman is wariness.

I suppose Charlie was not what you would call a great crusader for civil rights. He just reacted correctly. Also he did what he reasonably could and, like Artie Shaw, who had Billie Holiday with him at about this same time, he was among the first to hire Negroes for his organization. He did not feel he could buck the entire system when he took the band South, so he left me behind; but he paid me for the whole period and, oddly enough, I went South on my own. My stepmother and I took a cruise down the Mississippi on a steamboat to New Orleans. At about the same time, I made a trip to Chicago to ask my cousin Edwina if she would come and live with me to look after the children, when I got them back and found a place for us. She agreed to do so, and I told Charlie that I was going to look for a job to keep me off the road so I could maintain a residence for the kids.

Finding a place was easy. My father had inherited the old house on Chauncey Street and I asked him to rent it to me. Getting my children back, getting a new job, and leaving Charlie's band was not so easy.

II

Not only did Charlie and his band provide an atmosphere in which I could exist as a human being, it was also good for me artistically. He was the first person I worked for who had special arrangements made for me, arrangements that were specially tailored to bring out my strong points and gloss over the weak ones. Until then, I had either been forced to fit myself to standard arrangements or to try to fit vocal roles that represented someone else's idea of how I should try to make myself sound. In short, Charlie's respect for the individual included respect for his natural talents, too. It grieved me to think about leaving after only six months.

I had the house and Edwina arrived from Chicago. I went to Pittsburgh to see what arrangements I could make with Louis. He simply refused to part with Teddy but I would not leave without Gail. I was terribly frightened for her, and I identified with her very, very strongly because she was a girl. Perhaps my need and my panic communicated itself to Louis, because he let me take her without a fight. Or maybe he thought it was simply fair that the female should belong to me. I accepted this for the time being and went back to New York with Gail, fully intending to make a second try to get Teddy a little later when, perhaps, I would have more money or at least a more stable position from which to bargain.

Back in New York I was lucky in my job hunting. Charlie and the band had an important date to play the Paramount and I was with them. Dinah Shore was the star of the show and I had to cut a couple of my numbers because she had first choice of material. Even so, a certain amount of attention was paid to me. I also had going for me a hit record—one of those special arrangements of Charlie's—called "Good for Nothing Joe." So I was in the strongest position I had ever been in when I started looking for work.

John Hammond was then a friend of Charlie's. He was young, but a prominent figure around the music business, an important contact point between whites and Negroes. He had managed Count Basie's first tour (during the course of which he brought Billie Holiday into the band) and now he was an A and R man with the firm for which we had recorded. John sent me to see Barney Josephson, who ran Café Society Uptown and Café Society Downtown.

Barney was also an important figure in the process, then just beginning, of melding Negro show business and white show business—previously mostly separate and unequal—together. He was the first white owner of important New York clubs to hire Negro talent; he did it very simply because he cared about talent and not about color. Pete Johnson and Billie and Hazel Scott and a lot of other talented Negroes got their first important club dates at one or the other of the Café Societies. So did white talents who were later to be important, among them Zero Mostel.

I almost lost my chance at the job because I was less conscious of the racial stereotypes than was Barney. Teddy Wilson's orchestra was playing at the club and Teddy was at the audition to accompany me. Not thinking, I asked Teddy if he knew "Sleepy Time Down South" and he said "sure" and I started right in. Barney stopped me after a few bars, asking, "Do you know what you're singing?"

I said, "What do you mean?"

And then he asked me if, as a Negro, I really thought life in the South was exactly as idyllic as the lyric of the song pictured them. I was startled by the question; I had never heard it asked before and I had never asked it of myself. The people I had lived with did not tell their children anything about the way white people mistreated them. They tried to get their kids into school and hoped they would never have to work in the white folks' kitchen the way they had to. I had, of course, never heard the question discussed during my middle-class interludes in Brooklyn, and in Harlem we had been so preoccupied by our particular brand of Northern-style misery that we thought little of the lot of the Southern Negro.

I may have suffered psychologically during certain periods of my life in the South, but I did not understand the social misery most Negroes are made to feel down there. That's not the kind of thing you can learn in a book. So all I thought was that "Sleepy Time" was a pretty song. Now, of course, Ray Charles sings the song and nobody thinks anything about it. I suppose everyone figures that Ray knows and they know that he knows. I would find it hard to do the song, even now. In my era, once all the implications of a song like that were made clear, we reacted very strongly—probably to make up for our previous lack of awareness.

Anyway, I sang "The Man I Love" for my audition and I got the job. When I finally opened at Café Society Downtown I did a song of Gertrude Lawrence's, "Jennie Made Her Mind Up," and a couple of songs of Billie Holiday's, among them "Fine and Mellow" and some of her other blues numbers. This was very shrewd show business on Barney's part. "It's almost satire to hear you sing the blues," he said to me. That's what I liked about Barney—he was always painfully honest.

Barney realized I had no deep knowledge of the quality of life that had created the blues in the first place. What did I really know about being mistreated, or working and slaving for my man? And I had been told by those people in Macon, Georgia, that those were only whorehouse songs.

You could say that I had never really heard the blues before; I had only overheard them, on a radio playing in the apartment next door or from someone singing on the same bill with me. But I had never really listened. The middle-class people in Brooklyn and Pittsburgh also did not think this kind of music was art. They thought it was dirty, an unpleasant reminder of their low origins. It's ironic that the people who taught me to appreciate the blues were the so-called white liberals. In the late thirties and early forties they discovered this music, and they were listening very hard to it.

Barney Josephson also helped in this process. He knew why I reacted as I frequently did—because he'd read it in a book. Since I had read no books about it, it must have given him a lot of pleasure to inform me when I was acting like a Negro. I was acting on instinct only, but any fool knows you can't rely on instinct all the time. One hopes to be in charge at all times. So when my dander would be aroused by some white women, Barney knew the history of that mutual antagonism. On the few occasions some white man was able to get near me and I jumped salty, Barney knew the history of what caused that and helped me to understand. That I was able to feel at home with the waiters, busboys, working folks was easy. Everybody backstage works like a dog for the customers. The only difference between them and the waiters at the Cotton Club was that they had a union and got a little more money, and since Barney didn't segregate their families in the audience I never felt that atmosphere of hating the boss that I was used to.

At the time Billie Holiday was singing at Kelly's Stable, not far from Café Society Downtown and because I was singing one of her songs, "Fine and Mellow," I dropped around to see her. I asked if she minded my using material that was really hers and I also wanted her opinion of my singing. She didn't care about the use of the song and she was complimentary about the way I sang. We took to dropping in on one another, very casually and from her, too, I learned something about a side of Negro life I had not been exposed to. Billie didn't lecture me—she didn't have to. Her whole life, the way she sang, made everything very plain. It was as if she were a living picture there for me to see something I had not seen clearly before. Her life was so tragic and so corrupted by other people—by white people and by her own people. There was no place for her to go, except, finally, into that little private world of dope. She was just too sensitive to survive. And such a gentle person. We never talked much about singing. The thing I remember talking to her about most were her dogs; her animals were really her only trusted friends. She was not, even then, as tough as I was; but she took a rather protective attitude toward me. If I was with a man she did not approve of, she would tell him off or she would draw me aside and lecture me. It was ironic, but it was also very touching.

Josh White was also singing in the clubs at that time and he introduced me to another kind of music—protest songs and sin songs. More important, he reinforced the notion I had gathered from Lew Leslie, that singing could be an art. Josh was a wonderfully sexy man and you used to have to beat your way through swarms of women just to say hello to him.

Paul Robeson was another person I met during the Café Society period who was to have an important influence on me. He was the first Negro person I met who enjoyed universal respect from everyone, white or black. He came into the club one night and the waiters and everyone came backstage to tell me he was out front. I sang and then he came back to my dressing room and he told me that he knew my family. He said my grandmother had helped him to get his scholarship to Rutgers where, I believe, he gained his first fame as a football player, not as an actor or singer. Over the next months I saw quite a bit of Paul and gradually a picture of my grandmother began to emerge which was quite different from the one I had gained as a child. Obviously, she had done a great deal to win the respect of people like Paul. It was very good of him to do this for me; I feel it helped me to develop a pride in myself and my background.

Paul used to tell me that we would never win through anger or bitterness but only through pride and a belief that our cause was just. He didn't tell me about being a Negro from a book. He was himself a good and kind man and it is a tragedy that the insanity of the witch-hunting days hounded him into exile and, I suppose, a bitterness he certainly did not have when I met him in 1940.

He used to tell me, half-jokingly, that I was too self-centered ever to be a very effective political militant. "Lena's got too much temper," he would tell people. Or, "She likes nice things too much." Both of which, I fear, are true. But in private he did everything he could to reinforce my weakened, mostly dormant sense of racial identity. "You are a Negro—and that is the whole basis of what you are and what you will become," he said. "When you live and learn some more you will be Lena Horne, Negro."

He used to claim that I was like my grandmother—"a very fiery, very strong little woman"—and I think he was right about that, too. Whatever petitions I've signed or benefits I've played I've not done because I had any broad or deep political program I was pushing. I had just learned from my father and from my grandmother not to take any nonsense from anybody. They had instilled enough of the snob in me to make me believe I was as good as anyone else. I was never taught by them that I was not as good as any white person and I figured if this was true for me it was true for all the other Negroes as well. Maybe some of this pride had wavered during the period in the South and most especially during my teens in the lower levels of show business, but it came back now.

Thanks to Paul and Josh White and to the whole atmosphere around Barney's clubs, which was friendly and secure, I began to interest myself in matters like Civil Rights and equal opportunities for everyone. Even Hazel Scott was helpful in teaching me a new sense of pride. Hazel and I have never been terribly close or very comfortable together, but we were friendly in a guarded sort of way. Hazel is a beautiful West Indian and like most people from those islands she has the fiercest sort of racial pride. Down there, apparently, no one ever taught the Negroes that they were inferior. As a result they have a superiority that can be infuriating to an American Negro. I can't totally explain why they should be different from us, but I imagine it is because they are not kept in line by false promises. They are not fed any falsehoods about the nature of democracy or about the possibilities of getting ahead if they'll just be good and quiet and stay in line. Very simply, they are not slanted from birth to think there is a possibility of squirming their way into the higher levels of a basically white society. Without this promise they have no one they feel they have to please but themselves. Marcus Garvey, the first black nationalist, was a West Indian and I realize they have, since his time, been especially interested in movements like his because they have no need of the white man's love or respect and have no trouble turning their backs on him. Even when I was a very tiny child in Miami—where there was a large group of West Indians—they would never stand for being called "nigger" themselves, though they would use that term when they addressed American Negroes. I'm sure Hazel was not a black nationalist or anything like that, but she did have many of the fierce characteristics of her fellow West Indians and she was an influence on me, despite the frequent clashes of our temperaments.

So this was a time of awakening for me. Besides these people I began to meet others from the larger world of the arts—writers and painters and actors. Canade Lee used to come in a lot, and through him I met Orson Welles, with whom he had worked in the Mercury Theater. There were others. I did not become close to them, but their attitudes were good for me—the respect they showed for talent, the interest they had in politics and the social order, the vibrancy of their beliefs and ideas—all this made me feel a part of the life of a much larger world than I had ever known before.

My association with Paul Robeson was used against me

later, when the political witch hunts were on, when I was
actually banned from radio and television for a time. Oh,
yes, I did benefits, and the old left-wing newspaper, *PM*,
was very fond of me as it was of most of the people who
played Barney's clubs, and I was friendly with all kinds of
people who were active in left-wing politics. But I had a
kind of ingrained suspicion about all the promises that were
made, because I had had a lot of promises made to me
when I was a kid, promises of permanence or of some future
good that was going to come to me but never did. So I held
myself back from a really serious involvement in politics. I
was hungry to know something, period. And these people
taught me much, about all kinds of things.

I found that among the artists and intellectuals—and especially with the musicians like Teddy Wilson and Duke
Ellington—I felt comfortable as I did not when there were
outsiders around. Among the musicians especially, I could
even forget my prejudices against white people. They are a
great, gently protective, marvelously tolerant fraternity.

So this was also a very happy time for me. For the first
time in my life I felt free to set my own course. I could accept or reject anyone or anything according to my own standards.

Even my private life seemed serene. I was so happy living
in the old house in Brooklyn and seeing some of my old
schoolgirl friends occasionally. Gail was with me and
Teddy had been allowed by his father to come for an extended stay. I was only making $75 a week, but it was
enough for a good life.

I had late gatherings there with Brooklyn friends, some
of the old gang from school days, then I would sleep late,
but get up in time to spend the afternoon with the kids. I
would watch them play out in the same back yard, under
the same cherry tree, where I had played. Then I would
feed them their dinner and give them their bath and tuck

them in and take the subway over to the Village and go to work. It was a good life, the best, I thought, that I had had up to then.

I renewed my relationship with my Uncle Frank; he was now working in Washington and he used to come up to the city frequently. My Uncle Burke, the youngest of the brothers, was also around and it was good to be with him again. Everyone else in the family has a terrible reserve. But Burke is a very human and warm person and he is the one member of the family with whom I feel great closeness and empathy. He worked out a good destiny for himself, marrying a wonderful woman (she was the daughter of a woman who was poor and widowed and who put her ten children through college by herself). Burke finally became manager of the Apollo Theater. So besides having a decent job that held a certain promise for the future and fine new friends I also had old friends and family around me. Perfection!

It did not last long. After about five months Louis came up from Pittsburgh and took Teddy away from us again. Shortly thereafter, Harold Gumm, who was still technically my agent, showed up. He told me that a man named Felix Young was about to open a club in Hollywood. It was to be called the Trocadero, a name from Hollywood's palmy past, and he wanted me for his first show. Apparently he had heard that "Good for Nothing Joe" record that I had cut with Charlie Barnet, and perhaps my little New York reputation had reached him. The offer was only interesting to me because the show was to feature some of the big Negro stars I most admired—Duke Ellington's band, Ethel Waters, Katherine Dunham's dancers. I was proud to think of being included among them.

There were influential people who asked me to take the job. Through Paul, I had met Walter White, the head of the NAACP and an old friend of my grandmother's, and he thought it would be an excellent opportunity for me. I think he felt that exposure in Hollywood might lead to movie work for a lot of other Negro people, and he was anxious to bend the color line in movies still further; at the time, about the only work available for Negroes was playing servants or low comics or natives in the Tarzan pictures. It was never openly expressed to me, but I think they felt a pretty Negro woman might be an interesting weapon to try on the moguls, though why they picked me out I don't know. There were many pretty women in Hollywood at the time.

I remained dubious. I did not even like to sing uptown in New York. Sometimes I would substitute for Hazel Scott in Barney's uptown club and I never felt comfortable there. The audience was more chic, but in those days I felt that the people who best understood me were downtown. Los Angeles was even farther away from the life I had come to like. Besides that, I did not want to uproot Gail and leave the house in Brooklyn. And, of course, Barney Josephson was very upset. "My God, you can't," he cried, "what do you think they're going to do, put you in the movies?" Everybody in both clubs took sides. In the end to get away from the turmoil I fled, but I said: "Barney, I'm only giving it a certain amount of time in the cabaret show with Duke. If it fails, will you take me back?" He turned his back on me and walked away. It ended our friendship for a long time.

Felix Young sent the carfares and Edwina and Gail and I set out for the Coast.

III

Felix had an apartment listed in his name which he gave to us when we arrived. Appropriately, it was on Horn Avenue, just off the Strip. I believe he neglected to inform any of the neighbors that we were Negro. Edwina was white, white, white; Gail, as a baby was rather Oriental looking; and stupid people often mistook me, as noted, for a Latin type. We caused a good deal of speculation in that neighborhood and the questioning glances we kept receiving did not exactly make us feel welcome. In fact, I felt damned uncomfortable. I spent most of my time inside the apartment waiting for the club to open and thinking that Barney and the other people who had told me not to come out to L.A. had been right and that the contrary advisers had been wrong. The only thing that kept me there was pride, and the determination that finally I must follow something through.

That club never did open. Katherine Dunham and most of her troupe were in worse shape than we were. They were living in a little house down the Strip a few blocks. They had given up other jobs to take this one, and now they were forced to cook their meals, and wash their clothes in communal pots, and sit around waiting for Felix to get together the rest of the money he needed to open.

We were perilously close to being stranded, though as long as we had Felix's apartment and as long as he kept dropping by with a little money for food we were in no immediate danger. But I was angry and I was lonely and it was hard to stick to my determination.

I did not fit very readily into the life of Dunham and her dancers. Both the discipline of their medium on the one hand and its freedom of expression on the other seemed to shut me out of their society. Cabaret life had not taught me the control, the discipline of their profession laid down centuries before. I felt not good enough for them.

What saved my sanity was the fact that Duke Ellington and his band were appearing in L.A. in a show Duke had written, *Jump for Joy*. I had seen Duke, but not been seen

by him, on occasions at the Cotton Club when he
visit backstage. His European success was even then
dary and that he was absolutely beautiful was also quite
evident. I learned his music after I was adult and I am
still learning about it. We saw each other in 1940 in Café
Society. Of course, Barney and everyone adored him and
I was thrilled to come out from our little backstage cubby-
hole and join Teddy Wilson and everyone in the show in
talking to Duke whenever he came in. It was wonderful
because here was one of "our" great artists. The aura of his
importance was heightened for me at Café Society, in a way
that I had not felt before, when we all had to crowd around
him backstage at the Cotton Club. I could see him being
paid homage by the white people in the audience at Café
and his greatness enveloped the performers—we were all in
his orbit. During the time we spent together I was proud to
be with him. He spoke often of Swee Pea. "Who was Swee
Pea?" I asked.

"You will meet him," he said. "You and he need to know
each other." At this time, the decision of my going to Hollywood was already being chewed on, I was pulled back
and forth, and making everyone miserable. Duke threw out
no advice, but offered, instead, a typical Ellingtonism:
"Baby, you must not be selfish, let the whole world benefit
from your incredible radiance." Oh Boy! He is the world's
greatest snow man, and all women love it. But he added,
"You'll get to meet 'Pea' because we're getting ready to
open *Jump for Joy* out there."

When I finally arrived in California, *Jump* was running.
And as soon after I arrived as possible, I was taken by someone, I can't remember who, to see it. Duke had reserved
seats for us, and I proceeded to enjoy. The seat to my right
was empty and at intermission, a pixie, brown color, horn-
rimmed glasses, beautifully cut suit, beautifully modulated
speaking voice, appeared as if by magic and said "I'm Billy

Strayhorn—Swee Pea." We looked at each other, clasped hands. He sat down in the seat and I loved him. We became one another's alter egos. We were both at that time necessary to other people, me as a provider, Billy as Duke's collaborator. But when we were together, we were free of all that. We seemed sometimes almost siblings. We knew what each other was thinking, the same things were funny, the same food was so good. We seemed wrapped in a web of good will that people spun around us. It was Lena and Billy, Billy and Lena. Everything we thought and said to each other made sense—and I began to talk, and it poured out of me. I was talking about me instead of being told about me. I could only tell it to Billy and he to me. I had a friend.

Sometimes we would go and visit Jimmy Blanton, Duke's great bassist, who was miserable because he was ill and being made to rest by Duke. We'd sit and talk to him and we'd listen to music and Jimmy was like a flame, fragile as a whisper, but blazing like that beam that cuts through steel. It would shake me. Other times Billy and I would go to the west side of Los Angeles, in the Negro section where there was a club called the Alabama. All the musicians went there after hours to hear the great singers and musicians who always seemed to be playing there. It was there, for example, that I heard Winonie Harris, one of the legendary blues singers, for the first time. The guys from Duke's band would come in, and some of their wives, whom I also knew from New York. And I ran into some of the girls who had been at the Cotton Club with me and even some of the girls who had been in that little quickie picture I had made, *The Duke Is Tops*. They helped to make me feel a little less lonely and strange. Billy and I would often wind up at a little after-hour joint called Brothers. It would be crowded and hot and funky, and yet muted and wonderful, and I know those were some of my happiest, most feeling moments.

Meantime, Felix still could not complete his financing for the club. So Billy made a couple of arrangements for me so I could audition for Irving Berlin, who was planning something back in New York. But nothing came of that. All I had going for me was Felix Young's insistence that he would find a way for me to perform. "I've got to show you out here; you've got to be seen," he kept saying.

And then the war came. Billy and I were rehearsing at the house of some friends when the news came and I can remember the shock, the feeling that everything was all over, not just for us, but for everyone. We just sat and stared dumbly into that radio, unable to speak.

Among the first, and the most minor, casualties of the war were Felix's dreams of a big club. He was at last close to having the money he needed, but the wartime restrictions on building material meant that he could not do the building and remodeling he needed to do. So with the little money he had he determined to open some other kind of club.

The place he opened was called the "Little Troc," and little it certainly was—not much bigger than a three- or four-room apartment. Katherine Dunham's dancers and I were the first attractions. The place could not have been worse for Katherine. There was no room for her dancers to move and their costumes were always trailing through someone's drink. But that small room was perfect for me. I had some material I had used at Café Society and Billy fixed up two or three things for me—"There'll Be Some Changes Made" and a couple of Harold Arlen things, "When the Sun Comes Out" and "Blues in the Night" which was a very famous song at the time. I was beginning to perfect "Honeysuckle Rose" and that was on the program too.

Word got around very fast. We quickly became that

year's "in" place for the Hollywood crowd. I did not see any of them socially, of course, but I remember John Barrymore coming in several times. And Marlene Dietrich, and Artie Shaw, whom I had known in New York, and Artie's immediate ex, Lana Turner, who was going around with Steve Crane at the time.

Somehow, rumors about me started up. She hates white men, they said, she's just like Billie Holiday—she will leave a job to go with whomever she thinks she loves at the moment. This was the first time I had ever been the victim of that kind of story. It was not to be the last. In fact the rumors amused me. Since I was a breadwinner I had time to see very few men. When I did it was usually on my day off. I was much too egotistical to be a kept woman. In fact, the only dates I specifically remember were with Billy Strayhorn and Billy Daniels the singer. Billy Daniels is a very fair-skinned man and when we went to a restaurant once we were asked to leave because I was too dark. They thought Billy was a white man taking a Negro woman into a place where they were not allowed.

These stories about me were the beginning of a kind of trouble that has existed throughout my career. I guess I confused a lot of people, particularly those who liked to think in terms of images, instead of realistically. I sang popular songs, romantic songs, even some songs that parodied sex, like "Let's Do It," most of which were written by whites. I did not do "race" material, blues, for instance. Nor did I sing things that were automatically associated with what I suppose some people would call the Negro style. Now this was not a conscious choice on my part. I sang what I could sing best, period. But since I was Negro I was amazed to discover that I was assumed to carry on the stereotype sex life. Nor could there be any doubt that part of my appeal was sex. I dressed as beautifully as I could afford and I used to move about a good deal, in what I suppose was a provocative way, when I sang. All this had made me a target for a certain kind of gossip.

I was, though I hate the phrase, the first Negro "sex symbol," or so I have read, working outside the context of the all-Negro show, where, of course, the plots and even the love duets kept sex carefully segregated behind the color line and where the white audience was invited merely to observe, not to entertain the possibility of involving themselves imaginatively in miscegenation. In a cabaret, where your success depends on establishing a certain intimacy with the audience, this barrier had to be swept away. So, less by choice than by accident, I found myself involved in a peculiar kind of pioneering. Beside the usual run-of-the-mill prejudice every Negro must encounter and learn to deal with in some way, I had a special kind of racial problem to deal with—hidden, sometimes ugly, always embarrassing.

Nothing in my earlier career had prepared me for this. A singer with a band leads an isolated kind of life, and my youth had protected me at the Cotton Club where, in any case, I was just one of many pretty young chicks in the chorus. As for Café Society, the crowd that came there had been a sophisticated one—musicians, actors, writers— capable of differentiating between performance and personality. The crowd that came to the Little Troc was simply not like that; social attitudes in Los Angeles in those days were not as "liberal" as you were likely to encounter in New York or, for that matter, elsewhere in the East.

The contrast between my first Hollywood party and the parties at which Charlotte and I entertained in Pittsburgh has always been particularly vivid in my mind. In Pittsburgh I came in with Charlotte and she would play and I would sing and they were charming to me and said "Thank you" and I never saw money change hands. I stayed in a corner, at the piano, and it was fine. In Hollywood my first party was at Cole Porter's house, and it was something of a social *coup* to invite the latest singing sensation to the party. Nothing was said about money, and, ostensibly, I was a guest, but it was perfectly understood that I would sing for my supper. I didn't want to, but Felix Young thought it would be good for the club and good for me. Cole Porter was, as always, perfectly charming, and I was to be a guest in his home many times later. But some of the guests took the opportunity to sit down and play games with me, among them Miriam Hopkins.

It was hard, then, and hard now, to put my finger on just what she did to me, and I'm not certain she was being mean. But she was a white Southerner and I had heard that damned accent before—so gracious, so condescending. It is the same tone they use when they tell the rest of the world that they and they alone "understand" Negroes—such happy, carefree, rhythmic people, like children really. In the context of that party it was both a put-on and a put-down. And I was not equipped to respond like your housebroken house servant. I couldn't respond nicely, or shuffle modestly as she offered false praise. Neither was I then sure enough of myself to deal directly or angrily or satirically with her. I froze and went sullen and stiff. Later, when she was working on *Lifeboat,* I met Tallulah Bankhead and she pulled the same act on me. But I took it better from her. I had the feeling she was a lady and that she was a genuine, dyed-in-the-wool Southerner who really thought she was protective of Negroes—misguided, I thought, but essentially kind. When she talked about how cute the little pickaninnies were and discussed the "non-Negro-ness" of my features she was being honestly herself. And we were talking in private. I might not have been able to respect her attitudes but I could be amused by her, especially when she commanded me, in her imperious way, to "look at yourself" as she tried to illustrate some point she was making.

I went home furious and I told Felix Young that I was

unavailable for parties thereafter. Of course I went when I was invited as a real guest, and sometimes I would sing— if I were asked in the right way, by which I mean informally, casually, and uninsistently.

I never went to the bigger and flashier Hollywood parties. Maybe I was intolerant of strangers. But it doesn't matter. I had to lay down some kind of rule and I made a pattern that I set my whole life on for a long time. They were white and I was a Negro—that's the simplest way to explain it. But I also excluded most people who weren't themselves performers or otherwise involved in the creative end of the "industry." You develop certain opinions and attitudes when you are a performer or a creator and, in my case, I found that these attitudes set me apart as much as color did. The other people in Hollywood didn't feel to me like the people I had got to know around Café Society. Eventually I would wind up with the Gene Kelly group, the Easterners who had been transported out West and who did their best to transpose their old style of life as well. They were the same people who had come to Café Society, and even though I did not greatly care for some of them personally they were decent and interesting. Which was very important to me as I moved, very quickly, from the little stage of the Little Troc to the big sound stages at M-G-M.

CHAPTER SIX

I was discovered for the movies by a man named Roger Edens. The truth of the matter is that he had heard me at Café Society, and one night he came into the Little Troc to hear me sing. At one time he had been Ethel Merman's accompanist. He had come to Hollywood to work on special material and had written stuff for the Andy Hardy pictures and had done "Dear Mr. Gable"—the song Judy Garland sang at an M-G-M party and which served to bring her to the attention of the studio bosses after she had been under contract for months and had received no parts. Now he was working mainly for Arthur Freed's unit at Metro-Goldwyn-Mayer which produced most of the big musicals there. Apparently Roger liked my work at the Little Troc and he got in touch with Harold Gumm who was in Hollywood, following my fortunes at this time. Harold was not licensed to handle movie deals, so he in turn got in touch with the large agency run by Louis Shurr and they agreed to handle any negotiations that might develop.

In a few days Harold and Al Melnick from the Shurr office accompanied me to Culver City to talk about my being in the movies. I suppose I was excited, but I could not seriously believe anything would come of it. I remembered what Barney Josephson had said to me when I talked to him about going to the Coast. So my hopes were not exactly high.

Roger Edens met us and escorted us to Arthur Freed's office. I could tell from his voice that he was a Southerner, but for some reason I didn't feel that instant distrust a Southern accent usually creates in me. I felt that he was a gentleman.

"I heard you sing and liked it so much," he said. "Would you sing for us?"

With that, he ushered us into Freed's office. Roger played and I sang "More Than You Know." There was some artfulness in my choice of a song, because my agents knew Freed was anxious to produce a movie version of Vincent Youmans' *Great Day*, the score of which contained this song. Apparently the stratagem worked, because Freed asked me to stay and sing for Louis B. Mayer, the head of the studio.

While we were waiting to go see him Vincente Minnelli, the director (and Judy Garland's second husband), walked in. I had met him in New York when he had been associated with Vinton Freedley in musical productions. They had briefly toyed with the curious notion of having me play Serena Blandish in a musical. He was terribly cordial to me. "Wouldn't it be wonderful if we could finally do something together," he said. Among all these strangers, sitting in Arthur Freed's big, impressive office, it was good to get such a greeting from Vincente. We seemed to be the "New York group," a little bit at bay, making a sort of informal, unspoken compact of friendship among the Hollywood crowd nervously awaiting to see whether the great man, L. B. Mayer, would deign to see us.

In a little while there came a cryptic-sounding phone call and then we were excitedly informed that Mr. Mayer would see us. Off to his office we went.

He was a short, chubby man and by now everyone is

familiar with the tales of his temperament. But on this occasion—as upon most of the very few others that I dealt
personally with him—he seemed very genial and fatherly to
me. I sang for him and I remember him just sitting there,
beaming at me through his round glasses. After I had done
a couple of songs he disappeared into some inner sanctum
and reappeared with Marion Davies on his arm. She was
just visiting, but I had to sing for her, too. It was kind of
funny. But not funny, too. By this time everyone was all
charged up, excited by some possibility that I could not see.

It turned out that M-G-M had bought *Cabin in the Sky*,
the all-Negro musical, a fact I discovered as the afternoon
wore on. But I also learned that it would be some time
before they could put it into production. There was obviously a part in it for me, but what would they do with
me until they were ready to shoot?

The question did not seem to bother any of my companions. In the car on the way back to my apartment they
were all absolutely certain that I would be signed by the
studio. By the time we got back to Horn Avenue they had
convinced me that the possibility was a real one. I decided
I needed someone I could absolutely trust to talk all this
over with, someone who had no interest in the business
except my interest. It was not that I distrusted Gumm or
the Shurr office but in my dealings with them I carried
with me my habitual distrust of white men.

Now, just before the possibility of this contract had been
presented to me, my father and I had had the most wonderful renewal of our life together. He had come to Los Angeles
to visit with me and we did everything together. After I
finished at the Little Troc in the evening we would go to the
Negro night spots together. We danced, we ate all the foods
we liked, we drank champagne. In the daytime we went
sightseeing. Later, he rented a bungalow at Lake Elsinore,
a Negro spa outside the city and took Teddy and Gail

there to stay with him a few weeks (I visited on weekends).
I loved it when people said things like, "You look like
sweethearts" or "you're such a handsome couple." I hoped
it would be like that always and I was very sorry when he
had to go back to Pittsburgh to attend to his business.
We talked often by phone. Now, when it began to look as
if M-G-M were serious about hiring me I called him and
said, "I'm alone and don't trust any of these people. Come
to me." He quickly agreed.

At the same time Walter White happened to be on the
Coast and I consulted him, too. He had a personal interest
in my welfare, since he had advised me to come to California. But he also saw the dangers and opportunities that
would be presented to me.

At the time there were no Negroes under long-term contract at any of the studios. All the Negro actors in town
were free-lancers, hired for a job here and a job there as
the need arose. Walter's concern, and mine too, was that
in the period while I was waiting for *Cabin in the Sky*
they would force me to play roles as a maid or maybe even
as some jungle type. Now these were the roles, as I have
said, that most Negroes were forced to play in the movies
at that time. It was not that I felt I was too good or too
proud to play them. But Walter felt, and I agreed with
him, that since I had no history in the movies and therefore
had not been typecast as anything so far, it would be es-
sential for me to try to establish a different kind of image
for Negro women.

A few days later I went back to Freed, this time with my
father along, as well as the agents. My father was great at
that meeting. His basic mistrust of white men is so deep he
was able to be very cool with the studio people. Flattery
and empty promises get you absolutely nowhere with my
father. I know those M-G-M executives had had to deal
with the parents of child stars at the start of their careers,

but I'm sure this was the first time a grown Negro woman ever arrived with a handsome, articulate, and unimpressed father who proceeded to show them the many disadvantages, spiritually and emotionally, that his daughter might suffer should she be foolish enough to sign with them. It was marvelous for me to watch them listening to him. Since neither one of us believed in the damn thing, we must have been infuriating.

"I don't want my daughter to work, I want to take care of her myself," my father said. "Now many people are telling her how wonderful it is to be a movie star. But the only colored movie stars I've seen so far have been waiting on some white star in the picture. I can pay for someone to wait on my daughter if she wants that."

Well, they assured him they had given a great deal of thought to all the problems he raised, they appreciated his sense of dignity. To make a long story short, if they had filmed that interview it would have made a great movie scene, but in a sense they were as good as their word. They didn't make me into a maid, but they didn't make me anything else, either. I became a butterfly pinned to a column singing away in Movieland.

The agents took care of the money—which was something like $200 a week to start—but, as I had occasion to discover in later years, agents are interested in very little besides money. For a Negro performer, that is frequently the least serious problem. Generally, every actor should have written into his contract all kinds of special protections. This was especially true in my early days working alone on the road, when I had to have it spelled out in writing that I could have room service, or use the front door of the hotel, or the swimming pool. Actually, I had no trouble of this kind on the M-G-M lot. Arthur Freed and Roger Edens were men of a certain sensitivity, and as long as I worked with them I was treated with great decency and respect.

Even so, my first screen test, which came after the signing of the contract, was a farce. They were planning a picture co-starring Jeanette MacDonald and Robert Young and were thinking of Eddie Anderson (Rochester) and me to play their servants and, I guess, to have a romance in the film too. It was a good role—the maid was to be just as flippant and fresh as anyone. She was a human being, not a stereotype. They asked Rochester and me to do a test together. They wanted me to match Rochester's color so they kept smearing dark make-up on me. And then they had a problem in lighting and photographing me because, they said, my features were too small. Meantime, poor Rochester had to stand around and wait while they fussed over me. It was embarrassing to me, though he was very pleasant about it. In the end, the test was a disaster. I looked as if I were some white person trying to do a part in blackface. I did not do the picture; Ethel Waters got the part.

My friends thought it was all nonsense. Roger Edens said, "It's ridiculous; they should photograph you as you are. That's why they hired you in the first place." My father just laughed, and so did Billy Strayhorn and Vincente Minnelli. It was even funny to me.

But the consequences weren't funny at all. For one thing, they set the make-up department to work on creating a kind of pancake that would make me look as dark as they thought I should without turning me into a grotesque. Eventually the came up with a shade that they called "Light Egyptian" which had an unfortunate side effect. They used it on white actresses they wanted to play Negro or mulatto parts; which meant there was even less work for the Negro actors, with whom I was already in trouble.

They were afraid of what they called "my attitude," by which they meant the terms I had insisted upon in my contract. They feared the studios might think it was the

beginning of a large-scale campaign on the part of Negro
actors to raise their status, or that it might be thought the
beginning of a revolt against roles as menials. They also
suspected that the NAACP was taking an official interest in
me, since the signing of the contract had made me the
NAACP's first available guinea pig. My friendship with
Walter White was suspect.

My chief interest was in protecting my opportunity to
sing. Though Walter White did take an interest in my career, he was also a family friend. And, most important of
all, I was not trying to embarrass anyone or show up my
colleagues. I was only trying to see if I could avoid in my
career some of the traps they had been forced into. It was
no crusade, though of course I hoped that if I could set
my own terms in the movies and also be successful, then
others might be able to follow. But, I must admit, that was
not my main motive.

There was talk about me for many months in Hollywood,
and it finally culminated in a protest meeting. I was called
"an Eastern upstart" and a tool of the NAACP and I was
forced to get up and try to explain that I was not trying to
start a revolt or steal work from anyone and that the
NAACP was not using me for any ulterior purpose. Only
one person among the Negro actors went out of her way
to be understanding about the whole situation. That was
Hattie McDaniel, who was, I suppose, the original sterotype
of the Negro maid in the white public mind. Actually, she
was an extremely gracious, intelligent, and gentle lady. She
called me up and asked me to visit her. I went to her
beautiful home and she explained how difficult it had been
for Negroes in the movies, which helped give me some
perspective on the whole situation. She was extremely realistic and had no misconception of the role she was allowed
to play in the white movie world. She also told me she
sympathized with my position and that she thought it was

the right one if I chose it. I was very confused at the time; the one thing I had not expected was to get into trouble with my own race. Miss McDaniel's act of grace helped tide me over a very awkward and difficult moment and after that the public tension eased somewhat.

But never completely. In a large part of the Hollywood Negro community I was never warmly received.

Here again was a new lesson. I had not been brought up to think that racial solidarity was the way to get a job and to protect it. I had known two kinds of Negroes—those who worked at low level jobs that no one else would take, and those who were educated enough to break out of the pattern, or had a unique talent like athletes or musicians. In a sense, each group was protected; one because no one wanted their jobs, the others because no one else could do them as well. But the Negro actors in Hollywood were not in either category. Plenty of people wanted their jobs, irregular as they were, and the kind of acting they did was not beyond the power of almost anyone. They were mainly extras and it was not difficult to strip down to a loincloth and run around Tarzan's jungle or put on a bandanna and play one of the slaves in *Gone with the Wind*. It seems significant to me that the people who had real talent—like Miss McDaniel or Eddie Anderson or the musicians—did not join in the attacks on me.

The terrible irony, I came to realize, was that the people who did attack me were upholding a continuation of a status quo that was corrupt, and that they were stirred up by the handful who profited most from that status quo. The system for casting Negroes as extras and bit players in those days, before the formation of a strong union, was something like the system of hiring dock workers through the shapeup. There was a small group of leaders in Los Angeles who acted as captains. The studios would call them and ask for a certain number of extras for a certain number of days for a certain picture. They would tell them how many of each physical type they needed and leave it to the actor to provide them with warm bodies, the identities of which they did not care about. In return for this service the leader would be guaranteed the most days' work or the largest part. So if you wanted to work you had to stay in with these gentlemen. You had no personal leverage with the studios. To borrow a phrase from Jimmy Baldwin, nobody knew your name—but nobody. I guess it's not surprising that these so-called leaders were my most vocal adversaries. They stirred things up because they feared I might want to be a potential leader myself or, more likely, that I might establish a precedent that would, in the end, undermine their position. Finally, in the 1950s, more and more talented Negroes came into the movies. They were people with whom the studios had to deal as individuals, and the extras themselves got sick of having to toady to the hiring bosses.

But the full implications of all this became clear to me only after some time had passed.

II

By the time all this agitation had run its course, I had actually made a couple of movies. After my screen test with Rochester, Arthur Freed called to tell me they were giving the part to Ethel Waters. He said I was set for the part Katherine Dunham had played in *Cabin in the Sky* on Broadway, but that it would be a while before they could start that picture. "In the meantime," he said, "we'll have to be very careful about what we have you do."

So I finally made my movie debut—really my second debut if you count that little quickie I had done—in *Panama Hattie*. The picture starred Red Skelton, Ann Sothern, and Marsha Hunt. But I never worked with them. I did a musi-

cal number that was not integrated into the script. The idea
was that it could be cut out of the film, without spoiling it,
by local distributors if they thought their audiences would
object to seeing a Negro. It was ridiculous, but that's how
show business—and especially the movies—docilely bowed
to prejudice twenty years ago. The number I did was a
Latin thing, in which I danced with the Berry Brothers. I
was beautifully gowned, I thought, and the number was directed by Vincente Minnelli. I felt that it came off rather
well. But, of course, it occasioned more criticism. A number
of white people wrote the studio to inquire about their
new Latin-American discovery and some Negroes charged
that I was trying to pass. That, in particular, hurt. At no
point in my career had I ever pretended to be anything but
what I was and so naturally I thought this criticism was
unjustified.

I went from this film into my first big, all-star musical,
As Thousands Cheer. This was the beginning of a long line
of films where I was pasted to a pillar to sing my song. That
was to be my basic screen posture for the next several years.
I no longer remember what songs I sang in that picture,
(which was actually released after the film we shot next,
the long-awaited *Cabin in the Sky*).

By the time winter came around again I was growing
increasingly restless in Hollywood—and increasingly nos-
talgic for New York. I had been more upset than I cared to
admit by the Negro actors' campaign against me, since it
limited the possibilities of making friends among them. I
had, in fact, very few friends at that point on that coast,
regardless of color. Bill Strayhorn and the Ellington band
had left town and about the only new friend I made was
Joe Louis, who was in the Army and stationed out there
for a while. We had kept running into each other through
the years. My father had, as I mentioned, taken me out to
his training camp one time and he had also taken Louis and

me to see the second Schmeling fight in Chicago. I had also seen him a little around New York. Now we met again, and, since he was a good and gentle man, he became my friend.

I was meanwhile preoccupied with my family and the small house we had moved into. So I decided to fly back to New York for a big benefit at Café Society. I didn't know how really badly I wanted to get back to New York until I saw the city again.

It was to be a quick trip—no more than three or four days—and I decided to fly. Little Teddy had arrived in California with his father and was permitted to visit us. So I did not want to be away from him or from Gail for long, even though I felt perfectly comfortable leaving them with Cousin Edwina.

New York was bitter cold that year, but somehow that just made it all the more exciting to me. I felt giddy and high the whole time I was there.

I checked in at the Theresa and quickly discovered a great many old friends were in town and I saw all of them, but the unforgettable night was the last one I was in town. It started at Café Society Downtown. My escorts were Billy Strayhorn and Billy Daniels and so that night when I arrived at the benefit, and saw Barney at the entrance, I felt a flood of emotion. I kissed him and said, "Oh, Barney, I've been so miserable," and started telling him how lonesome I was on the Coast and how much I missed him and the old Café Society crowd.

Barney forgave me. From then on Café Society was my going-home place whenever I had to come in to New York.

After the benefit we went to a place where Count Basie and his band were playing. And Charlie Barnet was there. It was all too much for me. I saw, all of a sudden, too many people who had meant too much to me. Almost everyone who had helped me on my way I ran into that night. I got sentimental, which I almost never do, and drank a lot, which I almost never do. I began to get very weepy.

We stayed at this club until the band quit playing. Then Basie joined us and we went on to other clubs. By this time I was paying for my first "movie star" status symbol, a mink coat which I was wearing, and my most vivid memory is of crossing streets with this fabulous coat thrown open and the New York cold, which I had missed so much, stinging me, seeming to awaken me and make me feel again. At some point Billy Daniels quit our party, disgusted with all my emotion, and the evening ended up with Strayhorn and Count Basie taking me back to the Theresa.

Going in, I told Basie that I wasn't going back to Hollywood. It came pouring out, rather incoherently, I'm sure, in the lobby of the Theresa, after my wonderful New York evening.

"I'm not going back there. I can't go back. I'm lonely; I can't see my own people. I don't want to be a movie star. I want to come home to New York where I belong," I kept saying.

I don't remember when I first met Basie, but in 1940 he worked at Café Society Uptown and when we met there he told me he knew my Dad's little joint on Wylie Avenue in Pittsburgh and that he remembered me from there, too. His personality, which is completely delightful, made it natural that we would become friends. He was both mentor and protector and, in the New York time, I would frequently go uptown with him and Jo Jones, his drummer, and hang out at the Red Rooster or somebody's after-hours joint. He would see that I got home and that no one bothered me. During all the discussions about my going to Hollywood in the first place, he had said nothing. In fact, we had never discussed race, or for that matter, anything serious. I knew he had gone through hell taking his band on the road, getting it established, and had never allowed himself to seem discouraged or angry. I thought surely he was the sort of man to indulge my mood. So I was especially surprised at the seriousness of the advice he gave me when I said I didn't want to go back.

"You've got to go back," he said. "Nobody's ever had this chance before."

"But I don't want it," I sniffled. Part of this was bravado. I had started, in the last couple of years, to try to be serious about a career, thinking about it as something other than a job of work.

Basie wasn't buying. "No, you've got to go back," he said. "They've never had anyone like you."

They. The white people.

"They have never been given the chance to see a Negro woman as a woman. You've got to give them that chance."

He made me believe it would somehow help all of us.

Quite a few people had said the same thing to me at one time or another. People who represented the Negro organizations, the Negro leadership, had said it. White men like Barney, who were my friends, had said it. But the former had not moved me at all, because perhaps they were only interested in creating a new symbol that might be useful to them; I didn't feel they were capable of giving me honest advice. In my mind, my white friends were sort of Great White Father Figures and I felt I didn't dare allow my gratitude toward them to carry me along on something as important as this.

But when Basie said it, I suddenly felt I might dare to believe him. He had some kind of identification with me that the others did not. He was a man. I was a woman. We were both Negroes. Because of this last, shared thing, we could dare to see one another in the former terms. Perhaps he wanted to see if *they* could learn to see me as he saw me— as a woman first, a Negro second. If they could do that, then maybe they could see him as a man and all of us as individuals.

For the moment, there in the Theresa, Basie made me feel more unhappy. This wasn't an organization talking. Or some so-called liberal. This was a Negro man and a Negro woman talking. Its very intensity shook me up. I felt something. It touched me. And I said: "All right. I'll try to understand and I'll go back."

The next day I was on the plane back to Hollywood. On the long flight I sorted some of this out and in so doing, I discovered something else. It was that Basie, whatever his understanding of my possible symbolic value, had also been able to see *me* within the symbol. It was that, most of all, that I needed; a vote of confidence in me. In me, myself and I, who understood only too well what everyone was always telling me: that I was being done a favor, was being given, for no good reason of talent or ability, a special advantage.

A famous Negro bandleader had said to me at this time: "Your people will never accept you. There's millions like you. You just happen to have been given the only chance. Only the white people are stupid enough to think there's something to you." To me, that sounded exactly like those white club owners who wouldn't hire me because I wasn't colored enough.

But there was a little more to it than that. I seemed to be getting, overnight, what people like Ethel Waters, who had served so much time perfecting their craft, had struggled years to achieve. It was quite true that Ella Fitzgerald, the world's greatest singer in my opinion, had not worked in the movies. That's an insult to everyone. When something like that is presented to you, its truth can stop you cold.

I had nothing with which to combat it. I did not want to prove them wrong—I could not. I just needed some way of keeping myself going. All I had, until I talked to Basie, was a bleak kind of pride. I had never been able to accept a gift easily. That goes for friendship or love. I just had this ingrown thing of wanting to be independent, to make it on my own, to not be placed in the position of having to accept favors or seek them out.

I knew I was not a great talent—but I had a brain and I had used it in performance to keep me from being too amateurish, because I had no one but me to depend on. I wanted to preserve my independence, to be beholden to no one for the work that insured that independence.

That had been enough when I was bumping along at the lower levels. But now, thrust toward greater importance, I needed something more. I did not have a total involvement with the medium, the kind of professionalism that would have helped me. Nor did I have pure personal ambition. What Count Basie gave me at Christmas time, 1942, was exactly the thing I needed to survive at this new level. He was the first person who I thought had some objectivity about me, to imply that I was worthy of this favor that was being done me after all. What I took away from my encounter with him was the knowledge that this was the kind of a favor you prove yourself worthy of only after it is given. That is, the way you use it is the important thing, not the question of whether you really deserved it in the first place. Beyond this explanation, he also implied that he had confidence in my ability to be worthy of it in the end.

So I got what I wanted—what I had secretly wanted from New York after all. I returned with the sense that I belonged somewhere, that somewhere there were people who cared about me and believed in me.

Some years later, when The Count was tendered a beautiful testimonial banquet, I sat on the dais with many famous names who made beautiful speeches about him. Al Collins, the brilliant disc jockey, cracked the whole place up when he introduced me as "the President of the United States, Miss Lena Horne." After we had all simmered down I looked over at that beautiful kisser of Basie's and forgot what I'd written down and began to talk about that wild night and his words to me—his hopes and aspirations for me. The tears came into my eyes—and into his—and suddenly that banquet was all family.

III

I was to return to New York sooner than I expected. When I got back to Hollywood I discovered that shooting on *Cabin in the Sky* was still being delayed. I would be facing another couple of months of idleness and I was very depressed by that fact. But then word came to me that the Savoy-Plaza in New York wanted to book me for an engagement of a month or so. It was a huge break for me, so the agents wangled permission from M-G-M to let me accept it.

The offer came about through the intercession of Ivan Black, who had handled publicity for Café Society. He suggested me to the young guy who was booking the room for the hotel. His name was Dick Dorso, and he has since gone on to be a very prominent packager of television shows. I don't know what he went through, trying to make that hotel take a chance on me. They had never had a Negro work there and they had never had a single act work the room. They were afraid somebody would object on the first count and that audiences would stay away on the second. Even after Dick persuaded them to give me a try, anyway, there were still more troubles.

First of all, there was not enough money to pay for my accompanist, Phil Moore. He had played for me at the Little Troc, where I discovered that he was the husband of Jeanne

Le Gon who had been with me in *The Duke Is Tops*. We renewed our friendship when I was working on *Panama Hattie*. I had found the white rehearsal pianist was an awful square. With the help of Roger Edens we got Phil hired at M-G-M to work with me. I began to spend a lot of time with Phil and Strayhorn, working on my material. I had already begun to realize, even then, that one should always have the best musicians to work with. No matter what the sacrifice I wanted him with me at the Savoy-Plaza. I had, in fact, promised him the job. So there was a scrap with my agent about raising the money to bring him East.

More important was the business of a room for me. The hotel would not let me stay there, and that was ironic, considering how far away from the Noble Sissle days it was. They gave me a suite where I could change and rest between shows, but I could not sleep there. It seemed a very fine point to me. If the patrons did not object to a Negro using the elevators or taking a shower or entertaining visitors in a suite, how could they object to her staying overnight? The contortions of logic which segregation forces on people would alone make it worthwhile to abandon. I accepted this compromise, however, on the grounds that getting a Negro performer into the cabaret was more important as a victory than this was as a defeat. Besides, I enjoyed staying uptown at the Theresa anyway.

We finally opened and it was a perfect little room. I didn't have to use a microphone and the intimacy of the setting suited me perfectly. The newspaper write-ups were great and *Time* and *Life* did pieces about the young Negro girl who had broken into the chic cabaret circuit. That's when this business of my being the *café-au-lait* Hedy Lamarr started up. I did not like that much, but I did enjoy the success, and the first burst of truly national publicity.

The hotel's strange policy of semi- or demi-segregation damn near killed me, though, before the engagement was finished. I was ill almost the whole time I was at the Savoy-Plaza. One night I collapsed on the floor right in front of the audience—too ill to even stand up. They carried me up-stairs to "my" suite and sent for a doctor. When the doctor told them I was seriously ill, they begged me to stay. But I refused and made Phil Moore hire a private limousine and take me back to the Theresa. By this time I was hemor-rhaging and he didn't want to move me. I just yelled at him: "I don't care if I'm dying. Don't leave me where I'm not wanted."

So we piled into the car and drove to Harlem where Phil called the great Dr. Shag Morgan. "My God, you idiot," was all he said.

He shot me full of some kind of medicine and I went back the next night to work.

By this time the hotel was frantic. They had lots of reser-vations. Now they couldn't show enough concern for me and, of course, urged me quite desperately to live at the hotel. But what a great delight it gave me to sweep out of the place every night and strike out for Harlem and the Theresa.

At that time I met a girl who was to become one of my best friends. Her name then was Zulme O'Neill. She turned up at the Theresa one afternoon at a party for some soldiers I knew who were about to go overseas. We clashed im-mediately. She was very light-skinned and I am very thin-skinned and I thought she was some white hanger-on. I had all the proper prejudices too. You see a white girl hanging around with a Negro man, you immediately think she's a tramp. That's the nub of all prejudice, I suppose, and the irony is that it is always the woman for whom you feel contempt, not the man.

We picked each other out immediately and started duel-ing the way women will. I had to give her credit—she was terribly bright and I was always attracted to brainy people. I admitted that even before I found out she was Negro.

I had to go away to work and when I came back she was still with the group. I drew one of the men aside and said, "What the hell is that white bitch doing here?"

The guy was amazed. He said, "Don't be silly, Nuffie ain't white" and proceeded to reel off her list of credits—she was a graduate of Howard University and had worked as a researcher with Gunnar Myrdahl on *American Dilemma*.

I went up to her and admitted my mistake, and apologized. I was especially ashamed and I had to admit—as both of us cracked up—that I thought it was only white folks that couldn't tell what we were. I guess that established a bond between us, because Zulme and I have been friends ever since, growing especially close after she turned up in Hollywood, married to Cab Calloway. One day the two of them—I didn't even know they knew each other—just appeared together at my house to tell me they were married.

IV

I started to work on *Cabin in the Sky* the minute I returned to Hollywood when the Savoy-Plaza engagement ended. This was not only the first picture in which I was to play a real part, it was also to be the first completely directed by Vincente Minnelli, who up to that time had been employed by M-G-M only as a director of musical sequences.

I was very glad about that, because Vincente and I had drawn close in the months since I ran into him in Arthur Freed's office. It was a completely undemanding relationship, with no pressure of any kind on either side. We did not go out at all. He had a beautifully run house with a won-

derful library and fine paintings on the wall and we spent
most of our time together there. Occasionally he would
come over to my place and Edwina and I would cook dinner for him. He was living like a displaced New Yorker, just
as I was, and we shared a dislike at that time for Hollywood
life. It gave me a great deal of confidence that he was going
to direct this picture; I knew I could trust him and lean
upon him.

I knew I was going to need all the support I could get,
because Ethel Waters was to be one of the stars of the
picture. Long before we met I began hearing rumors
around the lot that she was—to put it mildly—a rather difficult person to work with. We only had a couple of scenes
together, and they were not scheduled to be shot until we
were well along in production. The kids who were working
in her scenes told me she was violently prejudiced against
me. Miss Waters was not notably gentle toward women and
she was particularly tough on other singers. Billie Holiday
had told me she cost her a job once, when she desperately
needed it, by refusing to go on with the show if Billie was
hired. I suppose she had all the normal feminine reactions
toward another woman who might be a potential rival.

Besides that, she was very unhappy with the studio.
Ethel Waters had spent many hard years playing small
and unpleasant clubs before she achieved stardom, and had
been terribly exploited.

In my own career, I had been aware of this kind of exploitation but I had not been too hurt by it. When I did encounter it, I was well enough established to be able to fight
it or ignore it. Miss Waters had not been so lucky and
she was, therefore, chronically suspicious of her employers
and somehow she had got the idea that I was in league
with them in some way. So as the day approached when we
were to work together I knew I would encounter a good
deal of antipathy from her, taking place against a back-

ground of extreme distrust of the studio which had, I heard, already led to many minor incidents in the course of shooting.

Up to then, *Cabin* had been heaven. The story, of a good woman (Miss Waters) contending with a bad one (me) for the soul of a man (Rochester) was warm and funny, despite its underlying seriousness. There were wonderful songs, some from the original Broadway version by Vernon Duke, John Latouche, and Ted Fetter, some written especially for the movie version by Harold Arlen and Yip Harburg, among them "Happiness Is a Thing Called Joe," Miss Waters' song, destined to become a standard, and a big show-stopper for Rochester and me, "Life's Full of Consequences."

Unlike Miss Waters, I was enjoying myself hugely on this picture. For the first time I had a real role to play and for the first time I felt myself to be an important part of the whole enterprise, not just a stranger who came in for a few days to do a song or two. By this time I had made quite a few friends around the studio. The make-up men and cameramen were basically friendly people and more inclined to be democratic with me than with some of the big stars. Also, I think they respected me because I always showed up on time and knew my songs and my lines and therefore was a "pro" in their eyes. And they were interested by the challenge I presented. The cameramen finally decided they liked the way I photographed and the make-up people finally invented a shade for me that didn't make me look like Al Jolson doing "Mammy" and Sidney Guilaroff, the head of the hairdressing department, did great things with my hairdos. Mostly I did not have characters to play, so there were no restrictions on what he could do —I was only supposed to look beautiful leaning against my pillar. He would invent Victorian hairdos or coronet braids or whatever his fancy dictated and there was no one to say, "No, that's not right for her character."

For quite a while all these people kept reporting to me about how difficult Miss Waters was in general and that, in particular, she resented my appearing in the picture. She thought others deserved the part more and that I was part of the plot against her that she was sure the studio bosses had concocted. Maybe they were unhappy with her, but it seemed to me that it would be out of character for them to hire her and spend the money to do the picture and then turn around and make trouble for her on the set. And I just couldn't believe that she would dislike me without knowing me at all.

Miss Waters did have one legitimate complaint against me. She was supposed to do a parody of me doing the "Honey in the Honeycomb" number. In it, she drops her righteousness, her good-woman attitude, and sings a steamy hot version of the song in an attempt to show up the hollowness of our values. Of course, I had recorded the song before we started production, as we always did, so it could be played back on the set when it came time to stage the number. Miss Waters went up to the sound department and heard my version of the song. She claimed that I had imitated her and that it would be impossible for her now to parody the song.

If I had imitated her, it was completely unconscious. She was a great singer, someone to be admired, and of course some of her style had come into that number. I'd worked hard to get it there so her parody would come off. Still, sometimes it's hard to see things that way. I'm always being told that some young singer is doing me nowadays and I'm not complimented, though my husband tells me I should be.

With all this tension building up, I was prepared to be very, very careful when we finally started working together.

While the picture was shooting, I did not see much of Vincente. Like most directors at work on a picture he used the nights to prepare for the next day's shooting. But we did talk occasionally about how I should play my scenes with Miss Waters. Up until then I had done nothing but fun comedy stuff with Rochester and Louis Armstrong. Now Vincente suggested that the only way to compete against Miss Waters' intensity was to be terribly helpless, almost babyish, when I confronted her. He thought it would make a good contrast with the hoydenish way I had played the comedy and musical scenes and that since she had the basically sympathetic part—the good woman trying to protect her marriage—this would be the best way to give my part a bit of complexity.

It might have worked—except for an accident. The day before our scene was scheduled I was rehearsing a big, dancing entrance into a night club with Rochester. We were to arrive in a Cadillac and make our way through a big crowd and then do this production number involving a huge number of people. Just as we started to do a full rehearsal with the music, I twisted my ankle and I heard a snapping sound. Rochester made a joke about it later; he said Ethel had put a hex on me. Hex or not, they carried me down to the studio infirmary and the doctors there sent me downtown to a bone man. He discovered that I had chipped a bone in my instep and he put me into a cast. It was painful and cumbersome and, of course, it meant extra trouble for everyone, restaging musical numbers, setting up difficult camera angles so my plaster cast wouldn't show and so on. For example, "Honey in the Honeycomb" now had to be done with me perched on a bar instead of moving through the set.

This caused a certain amount of the attention to be focused on me, which was just exactly what I did not want to happen when I was working with Miss Waters. The at-

mosphere was very tense and it exploded when a prop
man brought a pillow for me to put under my sore ankle.
Miss Waters started to blow like a hurricane. It was an all-
encompassing outburst, touching everyone and everything
that got in its way. Though I (or my ankle) may have
been the immediate cause of it, it was actually directed at
everything that had made her life miserable, the whole
system that had held her back and exploited her.

We had to shut down the set for the rest of the day.
During the evening, apparently, some of the people at the
studio were able to talk to her and calm her down, because
the next day we were able to go on with the picture. We
finished it without speaking. The silence was not sullen. It
was just that there was nothing to say after that, nothing that could make things right between us.

When the picture was released in the spring of that year
I went to New York to appear with Duke Ellington's band
at the premiere showing at the Capitol Theater. That was
a wonderful time. It was a Negro picture—a Negro movie—
and the people were lined up all around the block waiting
to get in and see it. Even Duke, who had been feted by the
crowned heads of Europe and who's normally so cool—he
has the artist's need to wrap a protective wall around himself so he can do his work without distractions—even Duke
was impressed. I had an arrangement of songs from *Cabin*
that Phil Moore made and it was just a fantastic engagement.

I went back to Hollywood to find a couple of pictures
waiting for me to do. The first was a little segment in a Red
Skelton picture, *I Dood It,* at M-G-M, the second was a loan-
out to Fox to do *Stormy Weather,* another all-Negro picture.
I Dood It was a silly little thing about the romance of a
pants-presser and a movie star. It was of no importance
to anyone and I doubt if I would even remember being in it
if it were not for the fact that while we were shooting the
picture my life began to take a new course.

V

In many ways, of course, my life had already changed quite radically. I found it a very different experience to be in demand as a performer and to make from my work a little bit more than subsistence wages. For another, I found myself naturally gravitating to the Eastern group in Hollywood and this led me, in turn, to adopt many of their concerns as my own. I was active in war work, helping out at the Hollywood Canteen, touring the Army camps with USO shows and so on. Once I had the honor to christen a Liberty ship that was named for George Washington Carver and that was to have a Negro captain. The group I was with was liberal and took this kind of war work seriously—for them it was not just a way of getting publicity, which is the way the studios sometimes used it.

I had begun to work very actively with the then Assemblyman Gus Hawkins, to promote a Fair Employment Practices Commission in California and there was also a committee, called HICCASP (Hollywood Independent Citizens Committee of the Arts, Sciences, and Professions), that took an extremely active interest in all manner of liberal causes, membership in which caused a lot of people, me included, considerable trouble during the red-baiting days in the late forties and early fifties. In short, I was beginning to commit myself on public issues for the first time in my career.

Anyone who is a performer, not a politician or a spiritual leader or some sort of expert, must surely wonder about using his position and influence to sound off on issues; he does have a power that is more than that of a private citizen, after all. One always runs a chance of being exploited. But there was one issue—that of civil rights—that was a real gut issue with me. People who agreed with me on that one found it easy to recruit me for other causes where the rights and wrongs were not quite so clearcut.

Still, I was in a rare position for a Negro. I could do something—even if it was only a little bit—about discrimination. I would have had to have been super-human to turn that chance aside, especially since my slightly improved economic status by no means made me exempt from discrimination.

The first serious incident occurred when we moved a couple of blocks up Horn Avenue, to a place on the eastern side of Sunset Boulevard. Down where we had lived there were a lot of cracker accents—Okies and Arkies who had come out to find work in the war plants. With Gail growing up, and able to venture out more and more in the neighborhood, I was afraid of exposing her to some kind of racial incident. With Teddy being allowed to visit us, the original two-room apartment was no longer big enough for us. So the management found this house across Sunset. It was a double house and in the other side lived a woman who was, I believed, the niece of Aldous Huxley. Her husband was the brother of Lady Mendl's secretary, and she became, in time, one of our family's good friends. Anyway, it was a perfect house for us, with congenial people renting the other half.

But we had hardly settled in when trouble began. A petition was passed around the neighborhood seeking to have us removed. Now there was a house across the way, Spanish style, with a red tile roof, high walls. After we lived there awhile we realized it was occupied by Humphrey Bogart. We knew it by the sounds not of wild parties, but of wild scraps. This was the period when he was married to Mayo Methot and they were known far and wide as the Battling Bogarts, which they certainly were. We did not meet them until this petition started going around. Even then, we did not see a lot of Bogart. We just heard that he threatened to punch anybody in the mouth who bothered me. Some of our other neighbors also rallied around. If Bogart was just plain abusive to the petition peddlers, Peter Lorre was suave and abusive and Vera Caspary, the writer, was indignant. Pretty soon the petitions stopped being circulated.

Strayhorn was often in California and we were very, very close. Roger Edens frequently dropped over in the evenings, usually with a couple of people from the M-G-M music department. Marie Bryant, who is still one of my dear, dear girl friends was there too. Of course, whenever I did one of my rare movie scenes she and the other girls were always included. And sure enough, Zulme O'Neill showed up one night with Cab. Their first baby was on the way and when Cab had to go back on the road she stayed with us and we drove her to the hospital when her time came. Christopher was my first godchild.

It was during this period that I started noticing Lennie Hayton who was, of course, to become my husband. I can hardly claim that ours was love at first sight. Quite the opposite, in fact. I had met Lennie around the studio, since he was a staff composer and arranger at M-G-M, following a career in which he had been a pianist and arranger at nineteen with Paul Whiteman, and after that a famous bandleader on the "Hit Parade" and on his own.

Now Lennie is a very quiet man and though I spent a lot of time around the studio music department, since musicians were just about the only people on the lot whom I was comfortable with, Lennie and I did not exchange more than distant nods for several months. The first time we ever exchanged words was one time when I went up to the music department to hear some recordings I had made for a sound track. Somebody asked him what he thought of them.

"They'll raid the joint," he said. I thought it was a very nothing remark—I couldn't figure out if that meant he liked the recordings or not. That's a problem you're always running into with Lennie.

I then ran into him at a party at Ella Logan's house. She was married to Fred Finkelhoffe, the writer and producer, who was, it turned out, an old friend of Lennie's. I admired Ella's singing and had met her in New York, so Vincente Minnelli and I broke our rule against parties and went over.

Lennie was there, sort of noodling around at the piano and Rags Ragland, the comic, was also at the party. Ragland told a couple of bad-taste jokes about Negroes and I got mad and insisted we leave. I remember taking the anger out on Vincente on the way home. "Goddamit, you decide to go out for a change, you let your guard down for a minute, just because you're tired, and then it happens again. So why bother . . ."

Now Lennie had been in another room when Ragland told those jokes. He had had nothing to do with them. But he was associated in my mind with that rotten evening and I knew he was a friend of Ragland. I remember asking Vincente, "How come that Lennie Hayton, who seems like a nice enough guy, can go around hanging on bars with a guy like Ragland." I held it against him for some time. It was not until later, when we were friends, that Lennie explained that Rags didn't know any better. He had come from burlesque, which was full of stereotyped jokes about all kinds of minorities, and as far as Rags was concerned the jokes had come loose from their original meanings—they were almost stylizations. I don't think I bought that line completely, but at least, by the time I heard it, I was able to see Lennie as an individual, not as part of a terrible evening.

I didn't think about Lennie again until I started to work on *I Dood It*. At the time Kay Thompson, who later wrote the *Eloise* books, was a vocal coach at M-G-M, and we were working together a great deal. She was a famous singer and

an arranger and later she helped organize the Williams
Brothers, of which Andy Williams was a member and with
which she appeared in a great act. The most important
thing she taught me was breath control. She had a very easy
way of showing you how to use your breath, which is really
the whole trick about most popular singing. I hadn't realized some of the power I had until she worked with me and
showed me how to utilize it. I had a ball with her. We
were working on her arrangement of "Jericho" and it really
extended me and I was hitting the notes I didn't know I
could.

The number was to be a big and complicated one, featuring Hazel Scott as well as me and a choral group and
full orchestra. Hazel was also going to do one of her boggie-
woogie piano solos in the middle of it all, besides singing,
so it required a great deal of preparation. The recording
session was a long one. It was scheduled to start in the afternoon, but it soon developed into an all-night thing.

It started off pretty funny. Hazel was always known for
her fabulous clothes and jewels and furs and back in New
York people were always telling me to get some clothes like
hers. That wasn't so easy on my salary—but this day I
was determined to outshine her and I came to work in my
best dress and wearing my mink and my few little pieces
of jewelry. Of course, that was the day Hazel decided to
go California. She came to work in slacks and a blouse. It
was a laugh all around, with Kay Thompson leading the
chorus. I have said that Hazel and I were always edgy with
each other, because we were both stubborn and strong-
minded, but we were always professional and we found we
could work together on this job. It was fun.

But during the course of a long, weary evening, conducted by a gentleman that I never did enjoy working with
—too Prussian in attitude, with everybody—Kay and I began
to gripe.

"God, what a drag," Kay said. "If Lennie were doing this we'd have been finished eight hours ago."

"Lennie? You know him? What's with him?"

Well, it seemed Lennie could do this, and Lennie could do that. There wasn't anything that Lennie couldn't do. She had known him since they had done the old Lucky Strike radio show together back in New York. He had a reputation for working well with singers, and very quickly.

"Every time I've run into him, I can't stand him," I said. "He's very sarcastic."

"I don't think it's that," Kay said. "It's that he has a strange sense of humor. Very dry."

Which is true. He has almost no small talk and he's inclined to be extremely quiet, so when he does say something you pay more attention to him. The dryness comes out more barbed than he really intends it to be.

Kay pointed out that he was basically a loner and tried to sum up by saying he's a man's man. I've never known what that means, exactly, and I still don't know. I would say Lennie is more a musician's musician. He likes best to stand at the bar and drink and talk with the other musicians at a party. He's as typical of the type as anyone can be. They're a hard group to sum up. They do tend to be quiet and a little impractical, as if they're listening to sounds only they can hear. They do their drinking quietly and those of them who are chasers, tend to chase quietly, if determinedly.

Toward the end of the evening Kay said, very firmly, as if making up her mind about everything: "He's very much the kind of man I think you'd like."

"How do you know," I shot back, "when I don't know what kind of man I like myself?"

"I just know. In the first place, he's a musician. In the second place he's . . . you know . . . very sensitive."

You know how your girl friend can plant something in

your mind. I admitted I'd never really had a chance to know what Lennie was really like and Kay had managed to pique my interest. "Why don't you ask him to show up some time," I said very casually.

"Okay, I will," she said.

I didn't think any more about it. And it was to be several months before Lennie and I were really to discover each other.

CHAPTER SEVEN

In 1942, Metro lent me to 20th Century-Fox to make *Stormy Weather*. I knew the studio made a nice profit on the loan-out, charging Fox more for my services than they —M-G-M—was actually paying me. But I was happy to know they were going to make an all-Negro picture. The picture was made quickly. It reunited me with a lot of my friends. Katherine Dunham and her dancers were in it and so was Cab Calloway and his band and the Nicholas Brothers. In addition, dear Fats Waller and Bill Robinson played star roles, while the supporting cast included Ada Brown, who had been featured at the Cotton Club in the old days, and Flournoy Miller, the comic who helped make it possible for me to work with Noble Sissle. The plot was one of those backstage things in which Bill Robinson and I were partners in an act and kept splitting up and reuniting. Some of the critics said that the whole thing was patronizing toward Negroes. *Time,* for example, said that Hollywood, on the evidence of this movie, apparently regarded Negro performers "less as artists (despite their very high potential of artistry) than as picturesque, Sambo-style entertainers." I did not think *Stormy Weather* was anywhere near as good as *Cabin in the Sky,* but every five minutes there was a great big musical number and it gave Fox a chance to use a lot of fine songs they had acquired through the years, as well as some new ones Jimmy McHugh wrote for the picture. There were some wonderful moments for individuals in the picture; Katherine and her group had a great dance number and the Nicholas Brothers did a fantastic acrobatic dance on a flight of stairs that a number of critics singled out for special mention. For me, of course, it was the beginning of my association with the title song, which I suppose I've sung more than any other song in the years since.

It was Cab Calloway who helped me to display some sort of creditable emotion when I sang "Stormy Weather." Andrew Stone, the director, seemed to me to represent the rock-bound coast of Maine. He simply couldn't pull any emotion out of me and I could not respond to him. Now, I supposedly sing this song when I'm grieving over having decided to leave Bill and go it alone on my career even though I'm still secretly breaking my heart over him. So Cab took me off in a corner of the sound stage and told me to forget all about what Mr. Stone had been telling me and to think, instead, about my own marital problems. For good measure, Cab called me a few good dirty names, just to upset me, and it worked. I was able to give a passable performance.

The only other memorable occurrences during the shooting of *Stormy Weather* were my lunches with Joseph Schenck, who was, as they say, "one of the pioneers of this industry," and at that time was one of the heads of 20th Century-Fox. He was a rather elderly gentleman and for some reason he took to inviting me to take lunch with him in his office. It must have been a pretty funny scene—me bewigged, bedaubed with make-up, and refusing to be beholden, sitting at a small table with a tray in front of me; he behind his desk, benignly staring at me while I ate and chattering away. The invitations kept coming and I kept reporting to that office for a week, until I had just about run out of light chatter. Then the invitations stopped, leaving my reputation intact, which is to say I was still, as far as gossip was concerned, that dumb broad who dug musicians instead of people who could do something for her.

Stormy Weather may not have been an all-time great, but I'm still grateful to it for the reputation the song gave me —particularly in the European countries I eventually visited. Not that everyone liked it. Another review—this one from one of the major New York papers—stuck in my mind. The critic liked everyone in the picture but me. I seemed tepid and treacly to him, with none of the rich earthiness of Ada Brown or Bill Robinson. I was looking for the little ol' earthy me, also, but I must say every time some white person said something like that I jumped salty.

The course of my search in the year following the completion of *Stormy* took many different directions.

II

After finishing *Stormy* at Fox, I returned to M-G-M to shoot the scenes for which I had recorded my songs during that almost all-night recording session when Kay Thompson and I had talked about Lennie Hayton in such girl-friend fashion. After we had completed our first morning's shooting, I was having lunch in the commissary, as usual, with Vincente and some of the New York writers when Lennie came in. He just said, "Hello," and I said "Hello" and we just looked at each other for a slightly longer time than the brilliant dialogue required. I guess it would be fair to say that we really saw each other for the first time there in that big, noisy barn of a place. It was like the recognition scene in the movies, when the boy and girl, in a blinding flash, realize that they like each other after all. It seemed terribly romantic at the time.

That afternoon he turned up on the set. I looked up to see him standing there with Kay, watching me work. He left in a few minutes. When we were done I said to Kay: "I see your friend Lennie showed up."

"Yes."

"What did he say?"

"Oh, I don't know. Something silly."

That night a group of us, Hazel Scott included, went over to the Alabama to hear Winonie Harris sing. I loved to hear him and T-Bone Walker, who both played that joint regularly. We spent the night having a ball and I had to drag myself to work the next day, but Hazel and I finished our scene anyway. Vincente suggested that to celebrate we all go over to the Francis Edwards, which was a bar and lunch room across the street from the studio where the M-G-M people liked to hang out. Hazel and Vincente and some of the kids who had worked in the scene came along. But it was not a large group. We hadn't been there long when Lennie turned up again. Vincente saw him and asked him to join us.

There was a piano, so he sat down and started playing. I started to sing and Hazel sang and everybody sang and everybody was drinking more and more. Lennie, too—but he wasn't saying anything, just playing.

He knew everything I could think of—all the songs I'd ever heard, it seems. It got later and later. Vincente left, and then Hazel, and finally everyone was gone except Lennie and me. And I found I liked him, liked just being with him.

A few weeks later, when we began to see each other constantly, I asked Lennie how come he seemed to dislike me so much at first, for it was this sensed dislike which had made me bristle back at him. He said:

"I got sick of hearing people tell me how great you were.

I just didn't believe anybody could be that good. And besides, I hate singers anyway."

That's a kind of half-true teasing that goes on between band leaders and singers. They all think singers spoil their arrangements and they would rather hear the sections play, really.

I asked him why he didn't come to the Little Troc and listen for himself. He just said: "I never go to hear anybody who's touted that much." Typical Lennie!

And it was typical, too, that it was music and not personality that was the basis of his judgment. That is an important thing to understand about him, and about our relationship.

At first it was not an easy one. I couldn't see him much at home, because of the children. We couldn't go out much either, because we were both public figures, at least around Hollywood, and naturally our racial difference made us a curiosity. The two people themselves, no matter how enlightened they think they are, just have to feel a certain amount of discomfort.

As it happened, my meeting with Lennie came at a moment when all sorts of crises, involving my children, my divorce, and my public life reached their climaxes. I do not believe I could have solved any of them without his help. I began our relationship in the most awful mental state, but going ahead with it made me grow up a great deal in a relatively short time.

III

The first in the series of difficulties that assaulted me in this period was caused by the fondness developing between Lennie and me. Edwina, my father's cousin and my longtime companion and nursemaid for the children, decided she disliked Lennie intensely and declared that she could not remain as long as I was seeing him.

It was a case of simple prejudice on her part. She was quite vehement about the old saying that "they'll screw you but they won't marry you." In fact, she often sounded to me like my mother as she said again and again, "You'll ruin your career if you marry this white man." To which I replied, as I had replied to my mother when she had warned me about marrying Louis Jones, "What career?" My movie career, at this stage, seemed only a little more promising than my career as a band singer had seemed in the middle of the thirties.

Finally, though, Edwina laid down an ultimatum. It was her or Lennie. I had to choose Lennie. I chose him mainly, of course, because I was beginning to fall in love with him. But I also knew that I was essentially a married-type woman, with no real drive or the tough guts to be a loner in show biz. Finally, in the back of my mind there were all those admonitions from my childhood—don't be a tramp, don't be promiscuous like they say we are. I already knew that two or three of the town's most eligible pimps, white and Negro, had their eyes on me. So I returned from the road where I was either playing theaters or playing USO shows and I turned more and more to Lennie.

A most wonderful miracle occurred when Edwina left. I desperately needed someone to take care of the children and I was just beginning my search when I met Mrs. Ida Starks. She is a wonderful woman whose husband was then in the Army and who, although she too had a child, was as lonely as I was at the time. So we joined forces and she was a source of great, quiet strength to me in the next years.

It was only a little while after she and her daughter had moved into our house that we confronted together that thing every Negro parent must someday confront—the day when your children come home from school crying and asking you what it means when someone calls you "Nigger." Up until Little Rock, when I suppose untold millions of small Negro children were confronted all at once with the word, on television, shouted by the charming fat white ladies in hair curlers as they tried to enter Central High School, it was the Negro parent's duty to face up all alone to the day when your baby wants to know what that word means and why it hurts so much.

My day arrived when Gail and Teddy and Mrs. Starks' little girl came home crying from the public school where they attended kindergarten and first grade and asked us what the word meant.

I discovered they had been called it quite a bit before they told me. I had always been dubious about living in California with the children. From the beginning I held the fixed idea that New York was the only possible place where a Negro had at least a fighting chance to escape some of the worst aspects of prejudice, and now I decided to look into the possibility of moving back there and commuting to Los Angeles to do my movie work which, in any case, usually only took a few weeks at a time to complete.

I told the children that they did not have to go back to school, that they could take a little vacation until I worked something out. Then I went to the school myself and found Gail's teacher and complained. She replied that our three were the only Negro children in the school and that, just naturally, a great deal of prejudice was focused on them.

"What can I do?" she asked. For all I know, she was prejudiced, but she didn't seem like a bad dame. She was just one of those helpless people, too timid to fight the system, incapable even of imagining how to begin.

"All kinds of people from out of state have come here to work in the aircraft factories," she said. "They're really just Okies and Arkies, and their kids come to school and they're full of prejudice and I don't know how to cope with them."

I didn't know what to tell her. I knew she could not protect our children on the way to school or out on the playground. I've always had a great respect for teachers, but she didn't seem to compare favorably with Mr. Young at P.S. 35 in Brooklyn or Mrs. Walden, down in Georgia. I wanted to somehow get across to her that at least she might try to combat, in her classroom, the stuff the white kids learned at home. Her attitude was so negative that I grew more and more angry—called her a cowardly bitch (which didn't help matters) and said, "Don't worry, our kids aren't coming back. But you're passing up a great opportunity."

So I decided to go to New York and look for a place to live. Finally, through Cab Calloway, I found a place in St. Albans, in Queens, formerly a white neighborhood, into which a lot of middle-income Negroes were beginning to move. Eventually, that's where I settled Mrs. Starks and the kids and that was to be our home for a while.

Unfortunately, Mrs. Starks and the children did not get away from California before there was an unpleasant incident with my mother. She and Mike, as I've said, went back to Cuba shortly after my marriage to Louis and though we had kept in touch, there was no great warmth—or even regularity—about our correspondence. Now, suddenly, she turned up in Los Angeles. Somehow she had got into a downtown hotel that was usually restricted to Negroes. I couldn't enter the lobby (that would have given my light-skinned mother away) so I sent Lennie to bring her out to the car where we could talk.

We managed to have a rather strained visit. During the course of it she asked me if I would mind calling a few producers on her behalf. She had still not given up her dream of being an actress. I found it difficult to explain to her that I was not on very close terms with any important people in the industry. From the distance of Cuba she just automatically assumed that I was a big star, traveling in the very highest circles. I tried to make her see that for all the publicity I was receiving I was still just a very minor figure in Hollywood. She seemed to accept this and we parted for a bit. I had to go out on the road to play some theater dates in Loew's theaters.

But while I was away I received a call from Mrs. Starks, very agitated. My mother had come over to the house determined to get my personal book of phone numbers, thinking to find producers' names in it. Mrs. Starks refused to let her have it and there was a fight.

My mother didn't get the phone book, but I got the message. It dawned on me that if I was not careful I could have, at this late date, a classic Hollywood mother on my hands. I did not want that and I did not believe that my mother would like it very well once she experienced all the indignities that role can bring to you.

By this time, however, my mother was terribly upset. She felt, with some justification I guess, that now that I was a success she wanted something more than the allowance I was paying her for her sacrifices at the beginning of my career. She talked vaguely of going to the newspapers with a story of an ungrateful daughter who had turned upon her in the daughter's hour of success. Since I seemed to be unable to explain to my mother the true situation of my career in Hollywood or a career of her own, I worked out a solution with a lawyer. She returned to Cuba and stayed there several more years. In the end, she and Mike returned to New York where, this time, Mike was able to get a good job as an electrician, at which he worked until he died several years ago.

That problem solved, and with the children safely settled in St. Albans, I returned to the road. But, during these war years I discovered that my position as a celebrity imposed a new kind of responsibility on me. You can walk away from prejudice when it is directed at you, personally. You can choose not to fight and withdraw to a better atmosphere. But it is impossible to withdraw from the fight when you are a public figure and you are publicly confronted with evidence of official or semi-official racism. Now, because of the movies I found that I was a public figure in a way I had never been when I was working with a band or singing exclusively in clubs.

This fame began, I'm sure, in the Army camps. Negro soldiers for the first time had a Negro star and I've been told that my picture was pinned up in their barracks the same way pictures of white movie stars were pinned up by the white soldiers. If the officers were white it was hardly safe for a Negro soldier to put up any of the fifty or so white lovelies, ranging from Grable to Lamarr. They did not have fifty or so Negro lovelies to choose from. They only had little ol' me. I therefore chose not to accept my status as a pinup queen as a compliment. It was, rather, an afterthought, as if someone had suddenly turned to the Negro GIs and said: "Oh, yes, here fellows, here's a pinup girl for you, too."

But setting aside the question of pinup publicity, there's no question that *Cabin in the Sky* and *Stormy Weather,* which were evidently shown time and time again in the Army camps, established my name with young Negroes of my own generation in a way it could not have been established if I had not got into the movies. The pictures also established me with Southern Negroes in a way that many other Negro stars had not had the chance to be established. Our little segregated sections were always cut out, as I've said, from the basically white musicals in which we appeared. But the all-Negro pictures were shown in the South because there was no mixing of the races to which the whites could object. And the Negroes responded enthusiastically to *Cabin* and *Stormy*.

Anyway, these movies created a demand for me on the

Army camp circuit—especially at the Negro camps. I was glad to go, but on these USO tours I received a most unpleasant education in the niceties of segregation, Army style. The basic, terrible irony was plain to see. Here were Negro men drafted to fight for their country—for freedom, if you will—and forced to accept the discipline and customs of a Jim Crow Army.

Several times I performed for the all-Negro 99th Air Force, both at its first base at Tuskegee, Alabama, and later at Camp Huachuca, and I was also crowned the Queen of the 99th.

It was officered by white men, and the whole disgraceful history of what those soldiers suffered until they were allowed to fly in combat is well known. Naturally, I loved entertaining these men, but I never felt completely right about the fact that I rarely was allowed to entertain any enlisted men socially, either in the Negro camps or on the bases where there were both whites and Negroes. Usually the GIs had to return directly to their quarters after we did a show and we would end up having drinks with the officers. That did not go down well with me, nor did the knowledge I acquired of how rough the Army was on Negro soldiers—all the little niceties of training Northern men in the South and the great doses of segregation that prepared these men to be in a good healthy spirit to fight for their country. My tours for the USO were continually filled with the sights and sounds of this. I was always expected to entertain the white soldiers first, then the Negroes—and often under the most degrading conditions for both the soldiers and me.

I was getting full—up to here—with the whole situation, but I wasn't about to quit USO work, for I was genuinely lovingly received by the men of both races and I wanted to be with them. At least when we appeared we gave the guys a little recreation, a little respite from the Army and, for the Negro soldiers, a respite from the special hell to which they were assigned.

I guess I should have known that I could not go on forever in this way. The stuff hit the fan at Fort Riley, Kansas. I was traveling with Horace Henderson, Fletcher's brother, who was my accompanist on a lot of these trips. We arrived late in the afternoon and got billeted and almost immediately set out for the huge auditorium where we were to perform. I looked out from backstage and, as usual, saw all the officers sitting down front in the best seats. It was always irritating to me, but I grudgingly accepted the notion that Rank Has Its Privileges. But behind them, where the enlisted man were, I did not see any Negroes. Now I knew there had to be Negroes on the base, because Joe Louis had been stationed at Riley for a while. So I turned to Horace and said, "Where are the Negroes? There must be some Negroes here, you know."

"Yes, I heard that we entertain them in their mess, tomorrow."

"Well, why should we have to stay over and do that when they could all have been here tonight?" It was toward the end of our tour and we were both anxious to wind it up and get home.

"They're just not allowed in here," Horace said with a shrug.

"Well, that's damned inconvenient," I said. The inconvenience of Jim Crow always seemed to hit me first. I suppose it's the way I made personal, inner logic out of something that's so sick and stupid.

"I won't do it. I won't do it," I shouted at Horace. Well, he got me calmed down long enough to do some kind of show for the white guys. The whole situation was not their fault, after all. They didn't issue the orders and there was still a war on. Then Horace and I beat it out of there and found the Negro USO lounge in town. A few of the guys gathered around and started telling us the whole story of their particular Jim Crow. By this time I had agreed to stay overnight to do the show for the Negro troops, of course. But I remember saying to the guys at this lounge, "I gotta do something, I gotta say something about this."

Next morning we hustled over to the Negro mess hall—much smaller than the auditorium we had worked the night before. They had improvised a little platform for us to work on and I looked out and saw the Negroes were all there all right. Except the front rows were occupied by white men.

"Now who the hell are they?" I asked somebody who was standing around there with me.

"They're the German prisoners of war," he said. Now I don't know if this was an insult calculated by some cracker colonel who had heard me blowing off steam the night before or it was just the usual Army stupidity showing itself. I don't think I have ever been more furious in my life.

I marched down off that platform and turned my back on the POWs and sang a few songs to the Negro guys in the back of the hall. But by the third or fourth song I was too choked with anger and humiliation to go on. I went backstage.

Some of the guys came back to see what was the matter and to ask me to go on. All I could say was: "I have to go. I just can't."

A young Negro soldier had been assigned to us as an escort and driver and I turned on him and demanded to know why he hadn't warned us about the POWs. Well, the poor guy, he had been afraid to say anything. Now I think he was afraid that if we left he would get blamed for it. He said he didn't know how to get us out of there ahead of schedule. The Army—indignation upset its plans.

"Don't worry," I said, "I'll make my own arrangements. You just call a cab."

Big mouth. We had been flying around in an Army plane

and staying at Army bases and eating Army chow. We didn't have enough money on us to make it back to Hollywood. I would have to wire for money.

Anyway a cab—a little jitney—came for us. The driver was Negro and I said, "Take me to the local NAACP office, wherever that is."

So I got there. It was some very unfancy place upstairs over a store somewhere. There was a beautiful woman sitting there at the desk when I came charging in.

"I want to talk to somebody in charge," I said. "My name is Lena Horne."

And she said, "My name is Daisy Bates. What's on your mind?"

Who could know then what Daisy Bates' story would turn out to be? She was, of course, the leader of the Little Rock NAACP at the time they tried to integrate Central High School and Eisenhower had to call out General Walker and his troops to keep the peace. Daisy is one of the great Negro women. Her home has been bombed, she has been persecuted and labeled (libeled is a better word) with a hundred epithets, her husband's business has been ruined, all because she has fought for civil rights and human rights in Little Rock.

When we met, she was just at the beginning of her long struggle. But she already knew, better than I, how to channel her anger, so she could fight effectively.

I was still hot when we started to talk. "Goddamit, how long has this been going on?" I demanded. "The whole situation is bad enough, but this on top—the enemy getting the front-row seats."

She said they knew all about the problems out at the camp and they had been fighting them in their own way—probably better than I could just by opening my big mouth. But she added, "Honey, there hasn't been anybody come right out and say anything about it."

"If I said something," I asked, "do you think anything bad would happen to the soldiers who were there?"

"How could it?" she replied. "Besides, what have you got to lose?—not a damn thing. So yell it out."

Which I did. I wired the Hollywood USO branch that I was quitting the tour. And I told them why I was quitting. When I got back to Hollywood I was reprimanded by two of the organizations which helped sponsor the tour. A couple of movie stars happened to come from around there and they insisted that nothing like this could happen in the old home state. I begged to differ, publicly. The word was very quietly passed down to keep that big-mouth woman out of the Southern camps. So I finished out the war traveling to those camps on my own money, paying my own fares and my accompanist's, and having the good fortune to renew my friendship with my Uncle Burke who was stationed at Huachuca. My friendship with him has lasted all these years and now it's begun with his son—my little cousin—the newest Horne.

At about the same time I involved myself in a local housing fight—some Japanese-Americans who had fought in the war and been wounded and now wanted to move their families into neighborhoods that had previously been restricted for them. These were the kinds of fights I seemed to look for. I was frequently involved, in my own work, in similar fights—hotels that would not let me use the front elevators even though they might be bragging that I was the first Negro artist to play their room, or who might let me live in the hotel, but not let my musicians stay there, too. This made me identify, quite naturally, with any cause where people or institutions denied rights and conveniences to individuals on the basis of color. I suppose I would have got into these fights even if I had not acquired a certain celebrity. But when you get a name you are made aware that you can make a bigger noise about a problem than if you are just an ordinary citizen.

Fame has its disadvantages, too. I began to find that out as Louis and I began to move toward our divorce proceedings. By this time he was living in California, and up to then he had let Teddy stay with me. Louis and I had remained politely friendly, but it was clear to us that there was no further hope of reconciliation. I was warned by my lawyers to try to make the proceedings go smoothly and without acrimony and they did—so far as the public was concerned. But for me, they were certainly not pleasant. In fact, the settlement we arrived at was the beginning of a very painful part of my life. I had to share custody of Teddy, getting to see him only during school holidays and vacations. Louis would not settle on any other terms. There had been some talk between us about Louis' managing me, but I knew this couldn't hold together a bad marriage. So that was the end of any hope for a friendly reconciliation.

The idea of his managing me was a foolish idea on our part, anyway. The few managerial partnerships I had seen between husbands and wives in my business (and especially in my race) had not given me a very good picture of the relationship. In any case, at that time a Negro manager could not get jobs for his clients, because the agencies who had the Negro talent under contract were not about to let a Negro personal manager in. And how the hell could a Negro book clients in to more than a few places when they couldn't even come in to the majority of them as customers? So even though many of us would have liked to have had Negroes as managers the system prevented us from doing so. You have to work with whoever gets you the most jobs.

All this was very realistic thinking on my part, but perhaps it seemed cruelly unfair to Louis. Anyway, I was fated to pay for this realism by having to give up my son.

I regret most bitterly that I did not press my fight for

him harder, yet at the time I could see the point my lawyers and agents raised. There would have been a great deal
of unpleasant newspaper coverage, with all the sympathy
going to Louis as the husband seemingly dropped by the
ambitious wife with no concern but her own career. More
important to me, however, was the fact that I had myself
been the child of divorce. When I remembered the bitterness I had been exposed to by my mother after her divorce,
and thought how much worse it would be for our children
if Louis and I began slinging mud in a courtroom and the
papers, it sickened me.

And so my son grew up as a partial stranger to me. I
only saw him a few months out of the year, and I kept up
with his progress in school through lawyers and accoun-
tants. I am certain our love would have been stronger if
we had been together more. We have never really been able
to communicate very well, and perhaps he blames me alone
for the divorce. I wish we could have been in a position
where it would have been easier to understand each other
better.

But there is no point in dwelling on might-have-beens. As
with any showbiz parent, my work kept me away from Gail
(custody of whom I did keep), more than was good for
her—or for me. In the years 1943–45 it grew increasingly
clear to me that I would never be able to settle down for
any length of time in a single place. M-G-M simply could
not give me enough work to occupy me more than a few
weeks out of the year. Nor did it provide enough money
to pay my mounting expenses. I needed to travel to find
work—in clubs and theaters.

IV

M-G-M was glad to let me play the Loew's theater chain,
and my agents were allowed to let me work in night clubs

wherever they could get bookings, so long as they did not interfere with the theater bookings or with the occasional scenes I did in pictures. But, as I quickly discovered, there is a big difference between getting a job and being happy in it.

I was worse than naïve. I actively resisted involvement in the detailed workings of my contracts. And from the start, I was constantly being embarrassed by nagging over money details. The first incident I recall occurred just before *Panama Hattie*. M-G-M arranged a booking for me at the Orpheum in Los Angeles. The arrangements were made through my manager, Harold Gumm, and the Louis Shurr office. The headliners on the show were Jimmie Lunceford and his band, whom I had known and loved in the Cotton Club days. Jimmie and I were happy to be working together, and I knew most of the guys in the band. I showed up for a midnight rehearsal the night before the opening as happy as I could be.

And then some of the guys in the band told me that I was taking the place of a great, talented Negro singer, June Richmond. When M-G-M had made me available, the theater just dumped June out of the show and put me in because, at the moment, because of the picture, I was hotter.

I was crushed. This was to have been a big moment for me, too—my first big theater date in Los Angeles. I did not want to carry a load of guilt out on the stage with me. I was hurt for June's sake, too. I don't think she ever believed, through all the years afterward, that I had not connived to take her booking away from her. The morning I opened she was there, in the first row, watching me silently. I'm sure the same thing has happened to white singers. But you feel it more—the resentment on the part of one, the guilt on the part of the other—if you are a Negro and the opportunities so few.

I should have realized right then and there that I, more than most performers, needed a personal manager who did more than write contracts and balance the books. I needed someone there to fight my battles side by side with me, someone who could talk the language of the owners and managers and be tough in a way that I could not be.

It would be quite some time before I got the kind of management I needed. Meantime, the incidents piled up. Not long after the unhappy experience in Los Angeles I was booked into the Howard Theater in Washington. I was excited about it. It was a famous Negro theater. I had played there with the Charlie Barnet band and we had packed the place.

But the first afternoon we played there, the house was almost empty. After the second show, I was worried. There had been plenty of advance publicity, including a press conference, and still no one came. The only way I could explain it was by believing what people had been telling me—that the Negroes would not accept me, that they resented me getting ahead of them. As that orchestra leader had told me, there were plenty of pretty girls who could do the same thing if they had got a few breaks.

Now my good friend Tiny Kyle was traveling with me as companion and hairdresser. Sidney Guilaroff had employed her as my hairdresser at M-G-M when the white hairdressers showed a certain reluctance to do my hair. I'm not certain Tiny was ever accepted into the union. We just had this quiet arrangement. In the course of the long hours on the set she had become a good friend.

Now I sent her out front to find out what the management's explanation was. She came back and said:

"Lena, do you know what's going on? The prices out front are higher than they charge for anybody—even Ella Fitzgerald."

You see how vague I was. I knew what my salary at other

theaters usually called for. It was a good, stiff price. But I had not thought to ask if I were getting that amount at the Howard or ever to relate that figure to box office prices, or to inquire whether a theater like the Howard could meet my salary without raising its prices.

My agents didn't care. They simply asked the Howard for the same salary I got in the white theaters. I got mad. How dare my stupid agents ask the same salary of a Negro theater as they did at a white theater? The people didn't make the kind of money the white people did. They couldn't spend what the whites did at a theater. To make matters worse, this was Washington, where there was only one theater at that time the Negroes could go to; they weren't welcome elsewhere. Besides which, who was I to ask more money than Ella Fitzgerald?

I asked the manager of the theater, Shep Allen, a nice man, to come and talk the whole situation over with me. He confirmed that he was paying my regular price for me. "That's what they're asking, Lena. And I have to ask this amount if I'm going to pay."

Of course, it was too late to change the signs out front. So I said, "Call the press."

He got in touch with the Negro newspapers while I got in touch with my agents back in California. I said, "I'll cancel myself if you don't lower the prices," and they had to agree. When I talked to the newspapermen I explained my ignorance and apologized. I was able to promise that the prices would be lowered for the rest of the engagement. By that evening the word was around the community and then the papers confirmed it, and from the second day on it was a tremendous engagement.

That was one kind of problem. There were others, sometimes with members of my own race. Shortly after the Washington performances I was booked on a tour of Loew's the-

My children, Gail
and Teddy—Lake Elsinore,
California.

The boat departures were
glamorous with a vengeance.

Irene Lane, my friend and companion—
and Lila, the "Peke."

9

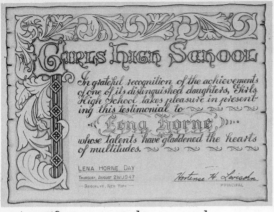

A certificate presented to me one day in Brooklyn.

I think my name looks ver nice in Hebrew.

My father has acquired glasses by now, and Lennie a beard.

The very opposite of a boycott and one way to thank the sponsor for presenting a Negro TV Special.

One of many simpatico moments with Perry.

10

Avedon looks at me and Lennie.

aters and I took a new, and very good, Negro band out with me. I was paid a flat fee, out of which I paid whatever musicians accompanied me. The band I decided to take had been organized by a man who had played with a famous orchestra leader and musician and had recently cut out from that orchestra to form his own.

Right from the beginning there was trouble. He did not respect me and he did not respect himself for taking the job with me. He needed the work all right, but he thought he and his men were better than me. In a way, we were acting out, in a different context, the old Negro drama in which, typically, the woman finds it easier to get work than the man, and he must resent the fact that he is dependent on her.

His defense was to declare repeatedly and loudly that I couldn't sing. He was, by nature, a temperamental guy anyway. So he allowed the sidemen to fool around and talk and even read the paper behind me when I was singing. In short, they were unprofessional, even in rehearsal.

I tried to make do for a while, but by the second week of the tour I could barely sing. That's the way with me. Any sort of emotional reaction hits me in the throat. I don't mean that I fake it. I mean I really get so I can't work. The origins of my throat trouble may be psychosomatic for all I know, but the symptoms are real. This guy had got to me.

It was not hard to do in those days. I knew I had not sung long enough in places like Café Society, where there was a good, perceptive audience to test you and tough, smart professionals to help you learn your craft. As a singer, I needed to make a tremendous effort, and the reviews would have told me so, even if characters like this had not told me—even if I had not told myself.

But the reviews told me—and I knew myself—that something else was operating for me. The reviews nearly always said that I was not the greatest singer going, but that I had a way with a song that covered up my vocal inadequacies. I think this is what Lew Leslie had seen in me when I worked in *Blackbirds*—a sense of theater, a sense of drama. I may not have been the singer this band and a lot of other people thought I should be, but I was beginning to be a good entertainer. I was beginning to have a sense of my own presence on a stage—and I was beginning to sense that audiences could respond to that. Now, I can't claim a lot of credit for this. This is a thing that people either have or don't have. But you have to have it if you are going to be a star—I don't give a damn what a great amount of great singing you do, you can't go far without it. At the time I could not express all this as clearly as I can now, so what kept me going was the feeling that I might as well do my damnedest anyway, because I didn't know how to do anything else at all to make a living. I just had to fight his mental blackmail as best I could.

So after about the thousandth time he said to me, "You're just getting by on your looks," I fired him. I replaced him with a guy I had known when I worked for Charlie Barnet. His name was Georgie Auld and he had a fine band. He was completely professional. Naturally he was not plagued by the same stresses as a Negro leader. He finished the tour with me. Once I got a little respite from the emotional pressure, my throat cleared up and I was able to work hard. But situations like this, if not always as serious, were to occur off and on and they made me anxious to get off the vaudeville circuits.

I must say going out on tour was not always this bad. There were some good times, too. And one of the best came early in my association with M-G-M.

After the first day that I had sung for Louis B. Mayer, I

rarely saw him. I'm glad now that I had not read anything about him or heard anything about him before I went to M-G-M, or I would have been much more scared than I was. And I had reason to get to know all about the tyrannical side of his nature a little later. But all I knew about him for several years was what I had seen of him at the first audition—a jolly, stout fellow with twinkly eyes, benign, not even very Olympian except in retrospect when everybody kept saying, "How fantastic—you mean you and your agents really stayed and visited with him for three hours?" When I did see him on the lot, it was usually when they gathered a bunch of us together for some publicity picture or when they were starting up some big production. On those occasions he would smile and pat me on the back and say something like, "Good girl." That was all. Once the word got passed down that he would like me to do a recording for him of "I'll Get By." It was one of those songs that made him get all sentimental. He was a famous crier. I cut the record for him at the end of a recording session for some sound track or other—me and a hundred-piece orchestra cutting a record of an old standard for the head of a studio! That's why I say the whole M-G-M period was kind of unreal to me.

One day I was walking toward the commissary when he approached me. He always seemed to have a couple of personal assistants with him—Benny Thau or Eddie Mannix usually. He hailed me and asked me if I'd do him a big favor. He had a dear friend who had a cabaret in Chicago and he would consider it a tremendous personal favor if I would go and sing for him. Well, what do you say to the head of the studio? Of course I went.

The cabaret turned out to be the Chez Paree. And it turned out to be, in the early years I worked there, a beautifully run club—the first very large night club in which I worked, after the Mocambo in L.A. and before the Copa in New York.

One of the good things that happened there was on a Sunday afternoon before the night show. I went out to the Great Lakes Naval Training Station to entertain the guys. I was escorted by an old friend Reginald Goodwin—and I remember how impressed I was by his beautiful white dress uniform. There were thousands of Negro sailors there and I was wearing a hibiscus in my hair and a crazy dress I used to have and I'll never forget the scream that went up when they saw me. It was one of the few times in my life that I ever felt like a movie star.

When I was about to close at the Chez that first time I was made to feel like a star again. I did not receive a very high salary, probably because of Mayer's friendship with the owner, but we had done tremendous business. One of the owners had started a conversation with me one night about jewelry and I had said that I liked rings and that I liked star sapphires. On closing night he came in with five star sapphire rings held out to me in the palm of his hand and told me to pick out one I liked. They were all very glamorous. I made some polite protests, I guess, but in the end I took a ring. After all we had broken attendance records and I deserved it. It was the first present I ever got from someone I worked for. Lennie used to kid me about it. He said, "How'd you know there was no blood on it?"

Nevertheless, it was clear that I needed better management, by which I mean an agency that had the time and the staff to personally handle the details of the special problems my career caused and details that could not be handled by phone or telegram from Hollywood.

I did nothing about it for a long time. I really didn't know where to turn. It was not until a rather serious crisis developed in my relationship with M-G-M that I finally was desperate enough to make the change.

V

This crisis occurred in 1945 when Arthur Freed, who produced most of the musicals in which I appeared at M-G-M, asked me if I would like to star on Broadway in a musical he was backing with Samuel Katz. The name of the show was *St. Louis Woman*. It was based on a novel by a well-known Negro writer, Arna Bontemps, who had joined with Countee Cullen to write the book. A producer named Edward Gross had got Harold Arlen and Johnny Mercer to write the score. It was a fantastic one, including among others, the great song "Come Rain or Come Shine." I loved the music and they began to have me sing it there at the studio for different people—I think Mayer even heard it. I was very enthusiastic and so was Freed. He thought it would be a great opportunity for me. After all, they didn't have much work for me and it would be much better for me than touring around the theaters and clubs.

But it was not until I had fallen in love with the music that I received the script to read. The role I was to play was a flashy whore who was in love with a jockey. There were all sorts of the usual cliché characters in it and I thought it very melodramatic and old-fashioned. I knew the book had been written by Negroes, but I still resented its pidgin English and the stereotypes they had written. In fact the play seemed just another of those tired rehashes with *Porgy and Bess* overtones.

I was pretty bored with the cliché presentations of Negro life. The only Negro shows of modern times, so far as I remembered, were those folksy things—*Mamba's Daughters* —about a dedicated Negro mother trying to save her daughter from a yaller pimp; *Green Pastures* with God and all those darling angels; *Porgy and Bess*, which, for all the greatness of the music, showed the usual slum attitudes. It just seemed to me, at that time, that it was a drag to do another show about Negroes that created the same old atmosphere.

I didn't deny that a lot of Negroes had to live in such an atmosphere. I had lived in it myself not so long ago. But I saw nothing romantic about it, the way audiences apparently did. I knew there were other sides of Negro life you could write a play about, and I said so to Freed and the other M-G-M people who were putting a lot of pressure on me to take the part. Even then, I had an eye toward playing a part that might have been played by a woman of any color or nationality.

I don't know about the others, but I believe Arthur Freed's motives were good. I think he was just glad to finally get a good piece of material for me. I know he also thought that if the show was a success—and if I was a success in it—he would have an easier time getting permission to make another all-Negro picture with me. Maybe he was even hoping to convert *St. Louis Woman* into a movie if it turned out to be a hit. I don't know. In fact, since the show was, as I understood it, a personal project of Freed's, I don't know why the rest of the studio hierarchy took such an interest in it. But they did.

They kept telling me that it had been a long time since Negroes had had a chance to work on Broadway—which was certainly true—and that if I didn't do the show I would be robbing deserving people of a chance to work. Guilt again!

On the other hand, people representing the Negro organizations were telling me that I must not do the part. They were concentrating very hard just then on trying to end cliché presentations of Negro life.

So I was caught between two very important forces in my life—the opinion of the Negro community and the opin-

ion of people who had been important in my career. The
discussion of this decision stretched on for days and weeks
and the people at M-G-M kept asking me if I were really
speaking for myself, acting on my own personal wishes, or
whether I was being used by the organizations. Freed insisted that I tell him my own feelings. He was not insensi-
tive about the situation. I found out from him that a Negro
woman whom I respected very much, and who had con-
demned the script to me, had secretly sent her sister to
Freed to try out for the part that she was, simultaneously,
advising me not to take. There are always lots of ambi-
guities in a situation like this.

I hoped, as the talks went on, that something might be
done with the book so that I might, in honesty to myself,
and at the same time to the people from the organizations,
do the show after all. But it was hopeless, and I finally had
to make a clean-cut decision. I said no—finally and flatly.

After some delay the show got on anyway. They found
a fine young singer named Ruby Hill to do the role. Harold
Nicholas played the Jockey and Pearl Bailey—anything she
does is super—sang a couple of great songs, and June
Hawkins was also featured. The show was plagued with
troubles. Countee Cullen died before rehearsals could begin
and Chuck Walters, the choreographer, was called in to replace the original dance director, and Rouben Mamoulian
had to be called in to take over-all direction while the
show was out of town. It did come into New York in March
1946, and it did run about three months, but it was hardly
a hit. Over the years the memory of the bad book has faded
and the Arlen-Mercer score has come to be regarded as one
of the best they did—together or separately.

The people in the show didn't have any more trouble by
doing it than I did by not doing it. From the moment I
definitely turned it down M-G-M ceased giving me permission to work in cabarets. They also forbade me to work on

Broadway in a revival of *Show Boat,* even though Jerome
Kern personally requested me for the part of Julie. I was
still booked on the Loew's theater circuit, but by this time
my expenses were heavy—there was the home in St. Albans,
and I had bought a small house in Los Angeles in Nichols
Canyon. Besides which, traveling expenses with three musicians were now heavier than they had been. Beyond that,
there was a growing sense of frustration brought on by the
long period of enforced idleness and increased by my
absolute inability to talk to anyone at the studio or to get a
straight answer about why my requests to do outside work
were being rejected. I was being punished and it hurt.

It was Joan Crawford who helped get me out of the jam.
I met her at a party—and I'm not at all certain but what our
accidental encounter may have been arranged by friends
who knew of my predicament, and knew that she had once
solved a similar one for herself.

We fell into conversation, and I discovered that she knew
in a general way what my situation was. Then I filled her
in on the details. When I finished she said, "But you'll never
win unless you do certain things."

"But there is no legal way," I replied. After all, the contract existed and it was drawn up perfectly properly. The
only hope was that the agents could persuade M-G-M to
let me work again, but they weren't having any luck.

"It depends on who the agent is," she said. "Maybe
there's another agency that can help."

But I couldn't go to another agent because my original
New York agent had tied me up good and tight with the
Shurr agency.

She just replied that there was usually a way out with an
agency and that she was sure a bigger firm, with more
leverage at the studios and with better personal contacts
there, could help.

But then she added: "Of course, none of this will do you

any good unless you go to *him*." She meant L. B. Mayer.

Well, I had been to *him*. And he had not had much to say. He was terribly surprised and hurt at my attitude and I was an ungrateful girl after all they had done for me. I was in no mood for all that and I told Miss Crawford so.

"You've got to do it," she said.

"Well, I can't."

"But I did," she said very quietly. Many people had. She was very honest about it. She knew I would detest begging from him, just as she had. But he was running a dictatorship there and he demanded this of his subjects. It was the only way out. I believe he thought that I—or anyone who thwarted M-G-M's will—just had a goddam nerve. I was somebody under that roof. And anybody under that roof was his property. He was the father of us all, the Grand Seigneur.

I thanked Miss Crawford for her advice and not long afterward I went to MCA and explained my trouble and asked if they could help. They got me out of my contracts with my previous agents. Very simply, MCA bought out their interests—and I paid for the buy-out on the installment plan while I was under contract to them. It still came to less money than I had been paying to the first two. Then MCA went to work softening up people around Mayer—convincing them to convince him to see me.

I finally got my appointment, and his secretary, a very powerful woman around the studio, and one of the loudest and longest of the lecturers who addressed themselves to the subject of my ungratefulness, my lack of thoughtfulness toward "my people" and the lack of respect for "a great man" (L. B. Mayer) ushered me in.

I remember very little about the interview that followed, except that he cried. He was always emotional. I think the tears probably started when, to salve my own pride, I told him that I disliked being a burden to the studio, taking money when I wasn't working and therefore didn't deserve it.

I don't believe he promised me anything directly at that interview, but apparently he decided that the months of punishment had gone on long enough. I was allowed to work after that. The crisis had passed—though things were never very friendly thereafter at M-G-M, especially as it became clear to them that Lennie and I were serious.

Throughout this period, despite my long absences to make my various road trips, we were growing closer and closer together—almost against our wills. I continued to be hard on him. I believed he would never marry me, because I had it drummed into me for so long that white guys will never marry you. Clichés! Lennie had always said he would marry me whenever I was ready. But in the back of my mind I would not believe it. I could not believe it. So I kept challenging him on the subject. In some perverse way I guess I was trying to get him to confirm my worst fears. He never did.

Instead, I began to learn how to love him. I depended on him already, because I had nobody, really, and he was a friend. He was there. But real love posed a new problem. We knew that if we made the marriage we were sincerely coming to want we would have to work harder at it then most marriages must be worked at. We knew, for instance, that for a long time we would have to work together as a unit, professionally. We knew that he would eventually have to leave M-G-M. Lennie simply felt that, the way you sometimes can feel those things. That meant that we would have to spend more time together—living together *and* working together *and* traveling together—than most couples do. That meant neither of us could afford to be a drag on the other— and I don't mean just emotionally. I mean as companions and as professionals. We were going into something a lot deeper—or so it seemed to us—than simply a marriage. This was going to be a partnership in every way.

Obviously, we did not rush into anything. We had known each other a good three years before we actually married.

In recent years I have been asked, usually by Negro journalists, how I feel when I see pictures of white men turning fire hoses or police dogs on Negro children in Birmingham and then look over at my white husband. Do I see in his face the same thing I see in the twisted, hating white faces of the news pictures from the South? The simple answer is, No, of course not. The idea is absurd. Lennie is a gentle, loving man, a much gentler and more loving individual than I am. Like most people, of whatever color, he could not possibly do such things.

But the question is a loaded one. What they're really asking is how could I be so disloyal as to marry a white man. What they are demanding, by implication, is racial solidarity in all things. They are trying to require conformity, the sacrifice of every inch of yourself to the large goals, the great shining end they envisage.

It is hard for me to answer these people. They cannot know that I wrestled with all these questions for years before Lennie and I finally married. On the very first page of this book I said, in effect, that my lifelong search was for an identity. I came from a class of Negroes that had very little racial identity to begin with. I led a life in which I was equally exploited and equally aided by individuals of both races. When I met and fell in love with Lennie I desperately wanted to find some kind of personal security. I wanted to make a private life in which I could, to some degree, let this question of identity alone. The thing I noticed first about Lennie was not the color of his skin, but the fact that he was a musician. They were the ones, white and Negro, with whom, all my adult life, I had been able to be easy and relaxed. Music was, and perhaps still is, the area of my life where the question of color comes second and the question of whether you play good or not is the one you have to answer as a test of admission into society.

But I was not unconscious. The more I saw of Lennie, the more I realized that it was unrealistic to think we could simply exclude the question of color because we were in love. It did not bother him, but it bugged me hard. Falling in love with Lennie represented, I now realize, a culmination of the battle within me between two forces—the need for racial pride and identity and the need simply to be myself, to assert my rights as a private, even selfish, person.

In the early days of our affair I swung wildly from one extreme to another. There were always people around reminding me that I was a symbol of certain Negro aspirations. When those reminders were made too often I would try to assert myself and say, in effect: "All right, I'm a symbol. But I'm a person, too. You can't push me so hard. I've got a right to my own happiness too." Then, at other moments, when I was angry about some raw deal visited on my race, I would turn on Lennie, and he would be nothing but a convenient white whipping boy. "You bastards think we're inferior? O.K., I'll show you." And then I would make his life a hell for him. I gave him all the psychological punishment I could not give the rest of the white men. I took advantage of him. I demanded more of him than I would normally ask in any relationship.

I used to tax him with the things all Negro women are taught to believe, which is that they will lay us, but they will never, never marry us. "You won't, you know. You're not going to. You don't mean what you're saying," I would cry out at him.

In those early days, I now know, I wanted him to pay for everything the whites had done to all of us. It was the most unfair thing I have ever done in my life, because I honestly believe Lennie is one of those rare people who never had even one secret moment of prejudice ever. He was a musician. That's what he thought about—and very little else. When it came to dealing with people he is one of those instinctively nice guys who wouldn't think of hurting anyone, even if he was hurt first.

Falling in love with me did not represent, therefore, any big upheaval which he had to turn over and over in his soul the way I did. I never heard him make any excuse for this lack of anguish. He just quietly began to learn to think as a Negro. He had to become aware of everything I was aware of. I think, perhaps, he was surprised at the dues everyone expected us to pay, and which we did pay and even now, after eighteen years of marriage, continue to pay, because a lot of people still find our marriage some kind of curiosity.

As the years have gone on, I have begun to realize that for Lennie there was a secret price in all this. When Lennie took on the job of learning to think as I did it meant that he had to efface a certain amount of himself. The way I saw the world became the way we both saw the world. It had to be so, because my problems were the hard ones to solve. The lucky thing is that we share a great many tastes and opinions in the smaller, everyday matters. We both like to avoid crowds, we tend to like the same books and plays and what-have-you. And, in our professional lives, we really do function as one.

But building that kind of common understanding which is the thing that glues most marriages together, whatever their problems, took a long, long time. I believe it would never have happened if Lennie had not been the kind of man he was.

The most important thing I learned about him was that he had grown up in a closely-knit and very loving Jewish family which was free of all the ordinary prejudices. His mother, for instance, was very open and loving with me when we met. Just as important, when I met him, Lennie had *grown up*. He had already achieved professional success as a composer and arranger. As I got to know him, I realized that he no longer felt driven to prove himself (if he ever had), that he had already achieved a great deal of what he wanted and needed to achieve, and that he therefore had room in his mind to understand my drives and ambitions, and to help me deal with my inadequacies. He helped me professionally, of course, but more important, he helped me emotionally. He was not subject to the terrible pressures a Negro man must deal with, but he was also not under the kinds of pressure that drive most men in our society to prove themselves. In short, he had no ax to grind with the world. I've learned, through the years, a great many lessons in simple decency from him.

Meantime, I worked at my profession and I began to improve vocally. Working in the big theaters and at the Army camps I had grown dependent on a microphone. Before that, I did not need them in small clubs. Now, with Lennie helping me, I started to develop and strengthen my voice. He was also making arrangements for me, the first really exciting ones I ever had, using my best capabilities and making them interesting musically to the ear. They gave me a new confidence. As a performer, at least, I felt some of the pressure was off me. And I found that I was beginning to be written about seriously as a good singer.

I recently came across an old clipping—an article written by Elsa Maxwell—in which she said I lacked "the ability to project herself beyond herself." She called it the fault of the "cultured introvert" and added that I lacked "the great, warm, human quality which takes in all feeling—the quality which makes a great artist like Ethel Waters." I knew she was right about my seeming to be an introvert. I had developed an isolation from the audience, that was probably only a cover for hostility; most of them were so

bemused by their own preconception of what a Negro
woman should be like on a stage, and my difference from
the preconception, that they did not see the hostility. The
image I gave them was exactly the one Miss Maxwell saw,
that of a woman they could not reach. I rarely spoke on
stage. I was too proud to let them think they could have
any personal contact with me. They got the singer, but
not the woman.

Some of this had to do with race. Many of the cabarets
I played in those first years had never had a Negro performer working them, so none of us knew what to expect
from the audience. I felt unconsciously that if I created
an atmosphere of reserve, a wall between me and the audience, I would not be hurt or angered by anything that
might happen. But this introverted quality in my work was
also a response to something much simpler than race—the
atmosphere of a cabaret. In a play, the story and the character you play and the costumes, scenery, and lights all
create a framework for the performer. But cabaret work
gives you no framework at all. You must create your own,
without any outside help.

My distance, my aloofness gave my performance the psychological framework it needed. In a funny way, the audience and I reversed roles. Usually performers seek the audience's approval, but in my appearances they, in a sense,
had to seek mine. In effect, I challenge them to break
through the wall I create, challenge them to interrupt what
seems to be my self-absorption. I believe, anyway, that is
where the tension, and therefore the excitement, is in my
work.

I can't claim that all this was arrived at through conscious
artistry. It developed pretty naturally out of my personality,
my prideful refusal to ask anybody's favor. Nor does it
mean that I did not work hard to try to perfect the voice,
the range of which has grown wider over the years, the

strength of which has grown as I have used it more and more. Does that sound conceited? I don't mean it that way, even though, like most artists, I think we have a right to our conceits. Singers talk rather objectively about their voices, I find. It is an instrument, really, even though it is, physically, a part of you.

I was, then, at least becoming a solidly professional singer in the late war years and the early post-war years. After I met Lennie I gradually stopped being a girl who happened to sing for her living and began to be a woman who derived part of her identity from her profession. And part of her pride. Now I began to insist on having only the very finest musicians working with me, and I began to insist on certain standards of professionalism in the way I was presented, the way I was costumed, and the way I was treated by managements. Even then, when I could not afford it, I spent two-thirds of my salary for music and clothes.

In all of this MCA was a mixed blessing. It is true, that like some of the other larger agencies, they controlled the bookings in certain important rooms. That meant that I could get into places I otherwise might not. And, because I was a Negro, this opened the doors for a lot of talented Negro performers to follow. There was nothing altruistic about MCA's doing this for me. I was their client and they wanted me to do well only because that was the way they could make money out of handling me. But I won't deny that I received a lot of satisfaction out of the barriers we broke down in the process.

On the other hand, there were a lot of things MCA never thought of. The joke always was that the good-luck telegram from the agency never arrived on the opening night of an engagement. It always came the second night. Then on the third or fourth night the local MCA man, whoever he was, would turn up to see if everything was OK. I

don't think this was a conscious put-down on their part.
Let's just say that for the white talent the telegrams usually
arrived on time.

But all of that was minor compared to the problems they
simply never dealt with. They never quite managed to spell
out in the contracts all the things that had to be spelled
out in those days if you were a Negro working in show
business. We might arrive somewhere to find that the Negro
musicians in my group would not be allowed to stay in the
hotel, even though I, as the featured attraction, might be.
Or we would find that we could not use the front entrance
or eat in the main dining room or use the public elevators
or drink at the bar. And somehow you could never find
anyone from MCA to help you straighten it out. We fought
a lot of fights alone in those days. Nat Debbin was then
my personal manager and I would get on the phone to
New York and he would put the pressure on the hotel or
cabaret to solve the problem—never MCA. Nat remains one
of my good friends, but he had other clients and he could
not travel with us. I was beginning to realize that I needed
someone who could be with me on the road all the time.

Several incidents reinforced my awareness of this need.
The first was in Philadelphia, where I had a bad cold when
I reported for work. I could hardly open my mouth to
sing. I told the management I couldn't go on, that it would
be ridiculous for me even to try until I felt better. They
told one of my musicians that I'd have to prove it. Why,
I don't know. All they had to do was listen. I told them
to call the doctor I had already gone to. He told them I
could not and should not work. They still didn't believe.
They made me go to their own doctor, who of course, said
that I was a little hoarse, but that I could work without
hurting myself permanently. I couldn't find the local
MCA man and I had to wire the main office, and I had to
get Nat to talk to them and to assure them I wasn't trying

to use the cold as an excuse to run out on the whole engagement—that I would work as soon as I was better.

That was just a personal matter, though. The next important incident occurred in 1945 when I went into the Copacabana in New York, and that involved out-and-out racial discrimination. I have to say that I don't believe the business in Philadelphia would have happened to a white performer, but I could never prove that. The thing at the Copa was something else again.

I was booked in by MCA and it was an important engagement for me—I had not been back in New York for a club date since the 1942 engagement at the Savoy-Plaza. The Copa had never had a Negro play the main room downstairs, although a couple of us had played upstairs in the lounge. I was a success, business was great, and, at first, I did not pay any attention to the composition of the audience. But then my friends started calling me, saying they could not get in to see me. There were the usual excuses—no reservations or, "Sorry, I have no record of that reservation."

Now this was a problem I had not encountered much, oddly enough. In the theaters I had been working it never came up. They were mostly big, downtown theaters in large Northern cities and there was no question that Negroes could come if they wanted to. In clubs like Café Society there had been no problems either. Nor in that terrible place in Philadelphia had there been any question about Negroes coming if they wanted to. Now, suddenly, here it was—and in liberal New York.

There were protests, and even picket lines. My first reaction was simple and selfish: "Oh God, why me?" You just can't help that first resentment. The management was very bland. They said there was nothing in my contract giving me the right to force them to change their admission policies. Besides, they said, Negroes have never wanted to come in here before.

I could understand that. It was a lot more expensive to go to the Copa than to some theater. I remember thinking, why should they make a fight over this when they couldn't get an apartment in most good New York neighborhoods?

The more I thought about it, though, the madder I got. It was just damn wrong. I thought it was a waste of any-one's hard-earned money to go to a nightclub, but since I was making my living in them, who was I to say how you should spend it if you've got it?

And if the people wanted to come, well then they should be able to get in. And probably more and more of them would want to, since other Negroes were also getting a chance to work the more expensive clubs. Why should we work so hard to play in these clubs, to break down the bar-riers for performers, if our own people couldn't come and watch us? I put it to myself in the most selfish possible terms. If the people were quietly discriminated against, or even if they stayed away just because they *thought* they might not be allowed in, I was in for years and years of thinking that maybe if I had been someone else they would have come. I would never know for certain if my own peo-ple would accept me if they did not have absolute free choice to come or not as they pleased.

A lot of people continued to think as I did at first that getting into the Copa was worth fighting over. I remember Billie Holiday came backstage one night and we talked it all out. Naturally, she had had no trouble getting a table, but she made it clear she was not interested in any test case.

"Hell, baby, the only reason I'm here is because I wanted to see you. If I was working here I don't know what I'd do about it. You're not supposed to do everything. You can't fight it all."

But by this time I had to do something. There was a very decent man named George Evans handling publicity for the

club then and he and Nat Debbin helped me work out a
statement. I said that I could not break my contract over
this. I had no right to do so. But I said that in future I
would not work anywhere without a clause in the contract
guaranteeing everyone the right to come in, without discrimination. The club promised that in the future there
would be no discrimination. For all I know, they lived up
to their word. The next time I played the Copa, everyone
who wanted a table got one. What I could never be sure of,
however, was that Negroes could get in to see white performers. They never tested the club then. I returned there
in '46 and there were certainly Negroes in the audience, but
I was never absolutely certain that this was more than tokenism. Right after that a guy named Bill Miller opened a
club called the Riviera over in Jersey and he was very anxious to have me play it. He not only guaranteed a no-
discrimination policy but offered to let us test his good faith
in any way we could devise. We did and it was clear that
he was as good as his word. So I played the Riviera for the
next few years.

By the early 1950s, of course, there were laws on the
books in New York that were pretty effective in preventing
the more obvious kinds of discrimination in public places.

Not all the incidents of these years were as serious, objectively or emotionally, as the one at the Copa. For instance, right after the war I made what amounted to a pioneering trek to Las Vegas—pioneering in the sense that I
was the first Negro to star in a big club there and pioneering, also, in the sense that I went there right at the beginning of the expansion and glamorization of the big clubs on
the strip.

I was playing the Flamingo, sharing the bill with a very
famous Latin band. The leader was a real jerk—very snide
when he introduced me, and not rehearsing and not disci-
plining the band at all. I took it for a couple of days and

then called Lennie in California to ask him what to do. I was furious and ready to walk out on the whole thing.

He calmed me down a little and said he would call the manager of the club who was, of course, just the front man for the gents-up-top who really owned it. He made the call all right and told the guy what was happening. They discussed it back and forth for a while and the manager was sort of noncommittal. What did he care?—we were both under contract and business was good. Why should he stir around in the situation?

But then another voice came on the phone and said: "Don't think any more about it, Mr. Hayton. I didn't know that she was having any trouble, but she will not have any further trouble."

Lennie didn't recognize the voice, so he said, "Who's this?"

"This is Mr. Siegel."

Lennie thanked him and then called me back. "Darling, I just want to tell you not to worry. Mr. Siegel says he'll take care of everything."

"And who the hell is Mr. Siegel?" I said.

"You know, Bugsy Siegel."

Well, apparently Mr. Siegel sent a couple of his boys around to see the bandleader and give him a little lecture. At the next show he did not introduce me. One of the men in the band did, and it was a beautiful announcement. After that, the leader made very proper announcements. And I noticed that he and his band, who had been hanging around the club between and after the shows to gamble, were suddenly in a big hurry to pack up and get outside when they finished work. I thought it was pretty funny, watching them scurrying around, being nicer than nice. And I thought there was a kind of rude justice in it, too.

Which does not mean I was ever in favor of life in Las Vegas. I continued to go back there—usually to the Sands—

for the next decade or so, but I never liked the atmosphere and I have finally quit going there at all. That may be foolish on my part—they pay the best prices of any cabarets in America and one engagement a year there would bring me enough so that I would never have to work in any other clubs.

One time a representative of a rival club in Las Vegas visited my manager, Ralph Harris, at some hotel where he was staying. He was carrying a big bulging paper bag. He asked Ralph if there was any way to get me to come to his place. Ralph said he doubted it. Whereupon the guy overturned the bag and what Ralph guesses must have been about $50,000 in small bills came spilling out.

"That's for you," the guy said. "Just for talking to me."

Ralph was scrambling all over the room grabbing the money and stuffing it back in the bag and telling the guy "No, no chance, sorry." I'd love to have witnessed that scene. In the business we were always considered crazy because we were frequently passing up little opportunities like this.

Ralph, as much as anybody, is the man who has made it possible for me to go on in this business. He was the answer to all the problems I had been encountering. But he does not enter my story for another year or so.

By 1946 I decided that I would marry Lennie at last. He had taken a leave of absense from M-G-M and had come to New York to conduct my engagements at the Copa, and it had been great to actually work with him on the stage with me. We were both anxious to breathe a little freely. It was possible to go to Europe for the first time and we decided to give it a try. We were not well known over there, and we felt that perhaps it would be possible to get married there without the publicity, and the questions, that would be inevitable if we married in the United States. In the back of our minds, too, was the hope that we could start to build a following there, second careers, in case our marriage was simply not accepted at home.

Accepted! I hate even to think in those terms. Yet we faced it. Of course, I received a lot of crank mail from white racists once the marriage was announced—some of it so sick and filthy that Lennie and Ralph Harris did not allow me to see it. Ralph had two to three of the worst offenders traced by the post-office inspectors and frightened into stopping. That sort of thing makes me angry. But it was the letters and comments from Negroes that hurt. They said, "you are one of *our* women—how could you marry one of *them?*"

It hurt and I wondered why I should be regarded as such an important symbol. Why should people think I'm so important that what I do or don't do is going to hurt the feelings of people I don't even know?

I'm afraid those questions are rhetorical. I know the answers. When a Negro woman marries a white man it is yet another put-down of the Negro man. It wounds his already deeply wounded vanity and masculinity. For a hundred years the system has decreed that he take the worst jobs, the worst education, that he not be able to give his family as good a home and neighborhood as a white man of the same status. Then he sees a Negro woman marrying a man of the race that has oppressed him, and it's impossible for him to believe that it was a purely personal decision. In fact, he is unwilling to concede her the right to make such a decision.

Once I was talking to a very famous Negro athlete and he suddenly started a tirade about what the Negro men would do when they were free. He told me how they would take back their possessions and their women whom the white men have stolen and they would not let them go with white men again.

I said to him: "What you mean is that even when black people are free, their women will still not be free."

I told him that at heart I was a feminist before I was a Negro, because if you are really getting down to basics you probably respond to a situation on the basis of your sex even before you do on the basis of color. Or maybe that was just my suffragette grandmother speaking through me. Anyway, he turned me off by saying something like, "Oh you and your college friends"—though he had been to college and I had not. What he meant was that it was educated Negro women, mostly, who had mixed feminism into the struggle for civil rights. Anyway, it was a hopeless argument, involving something that runs so deep that there is no way of keeping the discussion cool. We let it drop.

But it was to spare us a hundred encounters like this— and much angrier ones, at that—that we decided in 1946, that if we were ever going to get married we had better do it outside the United States, and then keep it quiet for a while, letting people get used to the idea of our being together before we made a public announcement.

In October 1947, Lennie and I sailed for England.

CHAPTER EIGHT

I

With Lennie and me when we went to Europe was my friend Tiny Kyle and Luther Henderson, who was already becoming a famous pianist, conductor, and arranger, and who was along to play piano for me and lead the small group we expected to recruit in London and Paris where we had engagements.

London was our first stop and I have two vivid impressions of it—the gray coldness of the weather and, in contrast, the tremendous warmth of the people toward Americans. Practically no one had come over from the states to entertain in these early days of post-war austerity. So even though I was not well known, I was given an amazingly warm reception.

No newspapermen welcomed us at the pier, except for two young men who worked on the jazz paper there, which was called *The Melody Maker*. They had to search for us, but when they finally caught up with us they said that they knew me from a record I had cut with Charlie Barnet and a couple of bad ones I had made with Artie Shaw. I was flattered to discover that anyone at all knew who I was, and especially to think that they had gone to all that trouble just on the basis of a handful of indifferent recordings.

I had done very little recording up to that time. I had yet to develop what I call a record voice. Some people don't have to—they just naturally sound good on records. But I didn't, I suppose because the way I learned to project was essentially theatrical. When you're seeing someone, you use your ears differently than when you can't see her, and my style was essentially developed for an audience that could see as well as hear. I know two or three important singers who think they do not record well—and I list myself among them. It's only lately that I have come to like recording at all.

I mention that just to explain how little I was known, which made the reception I got such a wonderful contrast. I was booked by Lou and Leslie Gray, who were then relatively small agents, but who have now become multimillionaires, owning one of the two independent television networks. Their brother had a lease on a little theater in Soho, the London Casino, and that's where we played. Soho was not the famous entertainment district (in the widest sense of the term) that it now is. It was just an old section that had been heavily bombed during the war. We had the good fortune to be on the bill with Ted Heath and his orchestra and Ted lent us his drummer, Jack Parnell, to play in our small group. Jack was to go on and form his own band, appearing with me on the TV special I filmed in London in 1964, and which first appeared on the Grays' network. Lennie and Luther went out hunting for other musicians in the little jazz clubs that were just starting up then. It was not easy for musicians in London in those days. One of the men who worked with us worked in a bicycle factory all day, then came and played with us all night. I don't know how he did it.

Some wonderful things happened to us during that first stay. For example, Hilda Sims was there, playing in *Anna Lucasta,* and we spent a lot of time at the digs members of the company had rented. We had brought over canned hams and other sorts of food that were almost impossible to get in England at that time, so we were able to contribute materially to the good parties they had.

At one of them I met Dylan Thomas. I understand our encounter is mentioned in one of the books about him. He was a strange-looking, fey creature—a red, freckled drunk with an odd accent, who kept staring at me and never said anything memorable—just maudlin, I'm sure. I didn't know a thing about him or his fame at the time.

To me the parties were memorable because they gave me my first chance to meet English writers and actors and painters. They were also memorable because it gave us a chance to discuss something I had heard a little about before—the racial question in England.

When we checked in at the Piccadilly Hotel, I found that although I was acceptable, Tiny and Luther were not. There were the usual excuses and I made my usual fuss. At home I could make a fuss—I had that much importance. I certainly wasn't going to stop fussing over there. They got their rooms, all right, but the very first night we were there some West Indian friends of ours were refused rooms in the same hotel. About their case I made a public fuss. The big papers didn't do much about it, but the music papers did carry some interviews with me about the problem. At the Chelsea parties, I learned more about the growing numbers of West Indians coming into the large English cities, and the growing prejudice toward them. In the years since, I have watched the prejudice spread inland from the port cities to the industrial cities. But this was my introduction to it.

I was also introduced, in this first visit, to the arrogance of the African Negro. I was invited to speak at a tea for a group of students. I was asked to tell them a little about life in the United States. I could tell from the questions they asked, and from some of the statements with which they peppered me afterward, that they had nothing but contempt for what they regarded as the servility of the American Negro, pity for what they regarded as his attempts to ingratiate himself with white society. They were, they said, going to have freedom in their countries some day soon, and they didn't want to hear about the difference between the conditions in theirs and in the United States. They only wanted to criticize. So naturally we fought violently.

So, I was discovering that travel could be broadening.

But mostly it was fun. It made me feel free—freer than I had felt in a long time at home. And most of the people we met went to such pains to make us feel welcome.

I especially remember James Mason's family. I had met James at the Copacabana. He had just made *The Seventh Veil* and those dark, broody good looks set a whole passel of feminine hearts a-flutter—mine among them. He had given out, in an interview, a list of the women he most wanted to meet when he came to America and I was on it. One night he came to the club and sent word back that he would like to come and meet me. I hadn't felt so schoolgirlish since I saw George Raft at the Cotton Club when I was sixteen.

When I met him I found that he was a marvelously intelligent, witty, and very independent man. We spent a lot of time with James and his wife Pamela—and it became a friendship that carried through the years. When they heard we were going to England they insisted on writing their relatives to tell them to look us up. His mother had a little farm not far from London and she visited us several times—usually bringing some eggs for Lennie. He's no good in the morning unless he has his egg and you couldn't get them in London at the time. They gave us our first insight into a different sort of England—a kind that most American performers don't easily get to know.

Warm as the English people were to us and as exciting as our engagement had been, it was toward France I was really drawn. Partly, this had to do with my mother's fam-

ily. I have said that her grandmother had been Senegalese,
but the family had also spent sometime in Martinique. So
it and France, the country that colonized it, had always
been places of romance to me.

Besides that, I felt that Lennie and I could at last really
lose ourselves there. We had heard that the French just
didn't give a damn about anyone's private life and more
than anything else at that time, that's what we wanted. The
English press had been perfectly polite, but we had detected a questioning attitude, a slight air of askance, when
we were seen together. Then, too, London was rather like
a small town. When I was a success at the Casino people started recognizing us on the street. We even found, as
we moved about, that quite a number of the English armed
forces had seen me in *Stormy Weather*. I was just a little too
well known then to feel the anonymity I craved. All this,
of course, has changed in the years since. I feel complete
acceptance in England now and love to work there—more
than I do almost anywhere else. The French grant you your
right to be yourself automatically. The English have to learn
to respect you a little bit before they grant you that right.

II

So just getting on the boat was exciting. The Channel was
rough, as it always is that time of year, and Tiny spent most
of the trip being sick and none of us could relax because we
were so excited. We had hardly any money between us.
England had extremely tight currency restrictions then
and I don't believe we were allowed to take more than a
pound apiece out of the country. We splurged on shots of
cognac on the boat.

We hit the pier at Calais late in the afternoon. It was
cold and blustery, and the French were having one of their

typical wildcat strikes. The boat train was going to leave
the dock on time, but they had announced on board ship
and again after we landed that it would probably be stopped
about halfway to Paris by the strike. We couldn't decide
whether to chance it or not, so we called our management
in Paris and they said they would send a car for us if we
would just wait on the pier.

On the boat we had run into Johnny Galliher, and old
acquaintance, who said he was going to try the train. He
volunteered to look after our heavy luggage and we accepted the offer. And then we settled down to wait for the
car.

We waited and waited. Nothing happened—except the
need to go to the bathroom grew and grew. I decided to be
a pioneer—we had all heard about the primitiveness of the
French facilities and we were all a little nervous. I had
learned to say "toilet" in French because I could never
bring myself to call it the WC. It made me think of W. C.
Handy, which seemed impolite in a way. So I asked one of
the porters in blue denim around the pier to direct me and
he sent me hiking down this long jetty while the rest of the
group waved me on my way.

I found the place and opened the door and discovered a
gentleman there standing at the urinal. He nodded pleas-
antly and I nodded back, as I headed for the little booth,
feeling very sophisticated and cosmopolitan, and delighted
that I had the proper reaction, which was no reaction at all.

I was wearing a fabulous long coat, sort of a monk's coat
with a tie. It was a copy of a Schiaperelli and I loved it. But
I had a terrible struggle to keep it up off the floor of this
little booth. Besides that, I had a huge traveler's pocket-
book to manage and I was cussing away to myself in there.

When I came out, another gentleman had replaced the
first one and I gathered that he had been somewhat amused
by the cussing he had overheard. But I said "Bonjour" very

gaily and sailed right on past him. Somehow, having managed the French toilet so successfully I was convinced that I could handle anything that happened in France. I was also convinced that any country that could manage co-educational bathrooms with such aplomb would probably grant us the kind of indifference we needed.

Indifference of this kind, of course, breeds indifference of another and less convenient sort. The car from Paris simply did not arrive and we kept getting hungier and hungier. We were sharing the waiting room with a group of Italian immigrants who were on their way to Canada. They all carried big straw baskets of food with bottles of wine sticking out. They kept nipping and nibbling at the stuff and it was driving us crazy. So we decided to pool our resources to see what we could buy to eat. We got a hard-boiled egg apiece. They cost something like seventy cents each.

But still our chauffeur did not show up. We decided we would have to make our own arrangements. Luther suggested we hire a car to drive us to Paris. He and Lennie hunted one up and with Luther's little bit of French and mine we managed to communicate what we wanted. The man was agreeable. He had never been to Paris and a paid trip appealed to him. Naturally we didn't tell him we had no money.

We piled ourselves and our hand luggage into his ancient cab, which had been through both World Wars, I'm sure, and set off. We jounced along down the road a while, which was still rutted from tank traffic of the war. And then we stopped. The driver said his girl friend lived in this house and did we mind if she rode along with us? She had never been to Paris either. We said sure. He popped inside and returned with this chick a moment later. She was carrying a nice big bottle of wine and a mysterious package.

By this time it was completely dark and colder than ever. The driver and his girl chattered away to each other up front, while Lennie and Luther bounced along on the jump seats. Tiny and I shared the rear seat but it was not much more comfortable than the jump seats. No springs. We were cold and hungry and tired, but we didn't care. Every once in a while I saw a little scrap of scenery and once there was a great cathedral looming suddenly up out of the darkness. It may even have been Abbeville, though I'm not sure. It was very moving.

After a long while, the cab stopped again, this time at a dark, shuttered house on a corner in one of those little, narrow villages that are strung out for a couple of hundred yards along the road. Suddenly there was lamplight and someone let us into a large, drafty room. There was a big coal stove in the center of the room, but it was not giving off much heat. The floor was hard-packed and very cold dirt. The place had a little bar and it was clear that the family who owned it lived upstairs. Now our driver's girl friend opened the parcel she had been carrying and out of it came long loaves of French bread and meat and sausage and cheese. Oh boy, how we wished they would offer to share. But they didn't and we could hardly ask. Nor could we offer to buy food from them. We put what was left of our money together and it was only enough to buy one glass of wine to be shared between us. The host went down into the cellar and came back with a huge jug of Beaujolais. It was heaven—cold from the earth of the cellar and rough to the taste.

We had more experience of French facilities—Tiny and I waded around back, squatted, me still in that damned long coat, and then we climbed back into the cab.

Paris appeared to us first as a glow in the sky. We were not sure it was Paris, but we knew it had to be a big city. All excited, we asked the driver if it was Paris. But he didn't know. He had never been there. Soon it was clear that it had to be Paris. But we did not plunge directly into it. We kept stopping to ask directions, which the driver refused to believe. He thought they were all playing tricks on the hick from the country. Besides, he had managed to convince himself that he knew the way from what his friends had told him. So we wandered around the suburbs for an hour and a half until suddenly, totally by accident, we found ourselves in Montmartre. We seemed to suddenly turn a corner and there before us was life—bars and nightspots and people playing pinball machines. On Pigalle we stopped to ask directions one last time and this time all four of us screamed at him to listen and then to do what the man said. Within a few minutes we were at our hotel.

It was the Raphaël—then the best hotel in Paris. The German High Command had taken it over during the war, and they had taken over nothing but the best. Our French agent was waiting for us there and, of course, there were profuse apologies from him about the inconvenience and then, of course, there was a fight between the cab driver and the agent. The driver, when he saw where we were staying, decided he had asked too little for the trip. Lennie kept trying to mediate and I was, by this time, hysterical with exhaustion and I kept laughing and saying, "Pay the man the two dollars."

I guess someone finally did, because the next thing I remember we were being escorted up a huge, curving staircase, then heavy wooden doors being thrown open on what was to be our sitting room. A crystal chandelier dominated the room. Under it, there was a table with a cold buffet spread on it. I remember the paper-thin slices of salmon, the little curls of butter nestled in their beds of cracked ice, the necks of the wine bottles peeking out of the ice buckets. It was a movie director's vision of a welcome to Paris. But hungry as we were, we could not touch it. Exhaustion had overcome us all.

"Take it away. Show me the bedroom," was all I could

say. Lennie and I, who had always been so discreet, simply
fell into bed together. I had no idea where everyone else
went.

I have no idea of how long we slept. I woke up in complete darkness. But it seemed unnatural darkness, so I
reached out my hand and touched taffeta. I shook Lennie
awake and said, "Lennie, there's silk all around." Sure
enough, there were red taffeta curtains drawn tight around
the bed. I felt around and found a switch and a light under
a little silk lampshade on the night table and it came on.

"I've got to see everything," I said and I pulled the curtains aside and jumped out of bed. I came out of the bed
alcove into the main sitting room, where there were chaise
longues all around and silk walls and rococo decorations
everywhere.

Lennie had rolled over and was trying to get back to
sleep, but I shook him more. "Wake up, wake up. You just
can't imagine this room we're in."

There was a bell pull next to the bed and I pulled it
and the maid appeared. She asked what I wanted and I
understood her and I said, "I want a cold bottle of champagne."

Lennie was awake enough to say, "Sweetheart, she isn't
even surprised."

She was back in a moment or two with a valet who was
carrying the ice bucket with the bottle in it and two beautiful glasses.

And everything was fine. They left and we sat on the
bed and had our wine and I said, "I don't care, even when
she called me 'Madame' I didn't feel like a whore." They
don't care if you're married or not, they just think that
being an adult entitles you to a title.

Afterward, I decided to explore the bathroom—two big
sinks, a bidet, a shower with a head you pick up like a
telephone. I splashed around in there for hours, it seemed.

Of course, we had fallen for the jazz about not drinking the water over there, so when Lennie pulled the bell rope and ordered cognac, he brought a glass in to me so I could wash my teeth with it.

Finally we managed to pull ourselves together and get dressed. Then I opened the draperies and threw open the windows and leaned out and there was the Arc de Triomphe and that was too much, it was so beautiful. I started running through the suite. It seemed there were rooms and rooms. We found Tiny in one and Luther farther down the hall. And it was hurry, hurry, let's get out on the street.

Lennie was hungry so we stopped for breakfast and he managed to get a couple of eggs. I didn't have anything but croissants and coffee. And then we started to walk and cry and laugh and it was so damned beautiful. Even the doorknobs seemed beautiful.

We walked and walked. Down the Champs to the Tuileries and then finally we crossed over to the Left Bank. Whenever I got hungry I would just stop in somewhere and get a piece of that great bread. Finally we called a friend, Auren Kahn, who was an official of the Joint Distribution Committee, and he agreed to meet us for dinner.

It was just magical, that first day in Paris. And we were lucky. They were in the midst of what amounted to a series of general strikes. One day the lights would go out and another day there would be no heat. And the next there was no postal service. The club in which we were to play kept postponing the opening until the unrest was over. So we spent days and days exploring Paris, mostly on foot. One day we went to the Louvre and were politely turned away by a guard. "Please come back tomorrow," he said. "Today we have decided to be on strike." The French it seemed were always doing things like that. As the wonderful mood of Paris that fall wrapped itself around us we finally said, All right, let's try to get married here.

We had been through so much at home, trying to keep our love a secret, that just to be able to walk down the street and go where we wanted to and sleep where we wanted to, was good. You could probably be very lonely in Paris unless you have an absolute need for the lack of interest the average Frenchman shows in everyone else's emotional, sexual, or even professional life.

It helped, also, that we had this sort of naked adoration for their country. They are such chauvinists that this was bound to intrigue them in a way that attempting to invade our privacy never could. A couple of restaurants took to us because we so obviously loved the food and what we were drinking. As a result, we ate and drank even better.

I guess the simplest way to say it is that France lived up to our expectations. It's possible to read about the expatriates and the biographies of the artists and then have France not meet your expectations. But for us it did. That's why it was such heaven. And that's why we knew that if we could not get married here we would never get married anywhere.

Auren and Lennie and Luther attended to most of the arrangements, which are complicated and require the services of an advocate, while I worked at the club. Our chief concern was not to let the press know. Which was not easy because we had taken to eating and drinking in places near the club which were frequented by newspapermen, among them our friend, Art Buchwald, just beginning his career in Paris, and Robert Capa, the photographer. The favorite place was called Calvados, and there was a very elegant whorehouse nearby and the ladies from it often dropped in, particularly one we called the Duchess, who was terribly chic. If she seemed to approve of my apparel, it made the evening for me.

All this made my work in the Club Champs Elysées— nouveau-black-market-type chic club—in the basement under a theater—seem extremely unimportant. The reviews were puzzled but pleased. They took the line that since I didn't wear bananas I was obviously not an exotic and, therefore, they could not say just what it was that was interesting about me.

They had had very little experience of American performers then, and the only Negroes of any nationality that they had seen had concentrated on giving them a very exotic style. They did, however, think that I was chic. It was not a matter of clothes, but rather an aura of womanliness I seemed to project (perhaps because I had never felt more womanly myself) and we were fortunate to be working with Bernard Hilde's orchestra, whose blonde vocalist was named Jane Morgan.

As my two weeks in the club came to an end, most of the arrangements for the wedding were completed. I had a few days' work to do at a spa in Belgium, and we set a wedding date for the day after I finished there. We would pass back through Paris, get married, and then catch the boat train that was to be the first leg of our journey home.

Before we started out we had to have blood tests made. Lennie and I went to the doctor together and I discovered in the waiting room that he was deathly afraid of needles. I gave him all the usual good advice—don't look at the needle, think about something else. But by the time he rolled up his sleeve he was a lovely shade of green, and when the needle went in he looked up rather sadly and said simply, "I'm going." Then he swooned in my arms.

The doctor was terrified, and so was I. But we brought him around and repaired to the Ritz Bar where we met Auren and drank a concoction we enjoyed, cherry herring mixed with vodka. We were on a kick of trying all kinds of exotic drinks in those days. Under the disapproving eyes of the Ritz bartender we celebrated the last big step on our way to marriage.

A couple of days later we left for Belgium by car. It was an all-day trip, and we sampled the beautiful beer all the way into Brussels. All I remember of that first night was a table of fabulous food displayed at the entrance to a restaurant. Of course, we had eaten well in Paris, but not since leaving home had I seen anything like the fruit on that table —mangoes and peaches and plums and grapes in wild profusion. I said, "My God, where did all this come from?" and Lennie answered, "Remember a little place called the Belgian Congo."

Up till then I had *never* seen anything like the spa we were booked into in Belgium, Chaudfontaine, near Liége. This was old-world elegance—mahogany and gilt and chandeliers—the like of which an American gambler will not see frequently in Las Vegas. They would bring a glass of mineral water to the table and set it discreetly next to you as you gambled. Your finances might be stricken at Chaudfontaine, but you could rationalize your losses by thinking about your improved physical health.

We played just two days there and then headed back to Paris by car. We were terribly conscious of the need for perfect timing. We left very early in the morning, planning to arrive in early afternoon, get married, and catch the boat train the next morning.

Of course, everything went wrong. We were at the border at dawn and the guards were sleepy and slow. The top of the filtre coffeepot broke in my hands because I banged it impatiently, afraid that the delay would spoil our plans to get married later in the day. In the confusion the guards forgot to stamp a re-entry visa into Lennie's passport. And then our driver got lost and we wandered around the back roads near Paris again for an hour and a half. As we rattled around I got hysterical and started screaming at Lennie. "It's all on purpose. You're never going to marry me."

They laughed and made me calm down and we made

it to Paris in time for me to change into my wedding dress, a very elegant black daytime dress by Balenciaga.

There was just one remaining problem—a wedding ring. I wanted one, and Lennie had not thought to get it. So Lennie and Auren set out to buy one while I changed. What we had not counted on was the gold shortage. At that time in Paris in order to buy gold jewelry you had to give an equal amount of old gold, and we had none. Lennie and Auren ran in and out of the jewelry shops in the Place Vendôme. In desperation they went into one of the most elegant of the shops and told their story. Apparently it touched the romanticism of the salesman and he let them buy a very plain band—red gold and yellow gold mixed.

But that took a lot of time, and I had just about convinced myself that I was about to be left at the altar. I had finished packing for the trip home by the time they got back. Besides the ring they had bought a bunch of violets from a street vendor—my wedding bouquet.

They grabbed me and we rushed off to get married. Auren had arranged for the ceremony to be performed in one of the nearby *arrondissements*. We arrived at the official building and found another party ahead of us. We sat on straight wooden benches, waiting, Lennie and me and Auren, who was to be the best man, and Luther and Tiny who were to be witnesses.

Then the other wedding party came out. The girl looked cold, all dressed in white on this freezing day, but she also looked happy and they both had their families with them. It was then that I had the typical bride's reaction of, "Oh, God, let's don't do it."

But we were ushered in immediately, and the Mayor turned out to be a lady. After she started the ceremony she made a little speech:

"How wonderful that you chose my country in which to marry. America, what we feel for her and the friendship that exists between us—it could not be better exemplified than by this, that you choose to marry in France."

I started to cry and cried intermittently through the ceremony. The tears continued as we drank champagne at the Café Rond Pont on the Champs. Afterward we got in a cab and said, "Drive very slowly up the Champs." It was not lighted and it was not yet dark out, just that deep gray of late twilight. The tone fitted my mood. Our dream Paris was fading with the light and, often as I have gone back since, and much as I still love the city, I have never recaptured, for any length of time, the mood of those few weeks in the fall of 1947.

The next morning we got on the boat train, heading for Cherbourg and the S.S. *America*. The minute we boarded the boat train I slipped off my new wedding ring because of our decision to keep the marriage a secret. Almost everyone on the train was an American and when we heard those accents we self-consciously drew apart. For two months we had been able to walk down the street with our arms around each other, but now we sensed the disapproving stares and all the problems we had set aside for weeks returned with a new force.

The customs and immigration officials came aboard the train and proceeded with their routine inspection of baggage and passports. When they came to our compartment all the baggage was OK'd and all the passports, too—except Lennie's. They took a very long time with it and after many suspicious glances at him they informed us that they would have to keep it and that he would have to report to the passport office on the dock. I told them very sweetly that since I had learned to love France I hoped they could find a good reason not to let us leave.

At Cherbourg we found out what the trouble was. It was the failure of the officials at the Belgian border to stamp the entry visa into the passport. I'm sure if we had acted guilty they would have kept us in France, but instead we explained what had happened, they accepted our word, and they stamped both an entry and an exit visa in the passport. We thanked them. But in a way we didn't mean it. We both would have been glad for an excuse to postpone our leaving.

I especially would have liked to avoid that passage on the *America*. The Negro crewmen had been trying to get into the union and had been refused. They were hardly mutinous, but they were in bad shape with the captain, who apparently regarded them as troublemakers. They sneaked one of the women in to tell me about it, so I joined their protest the only way I could, refusing to entertain the first-class passengers at their gala, the benefits of which were to go to the crew's welfare fund. There was considerable unpleasantness about it.

A day or so before we were due to land we called little Gail in St. Albans on the ship-to-shore telephone and I said: "Darling, we'll be home in time for your birthday. And this is a secret—Lennie and I are married, and we need your help to keep it a secret. Just tell Mrs. Starks and no one else." It was quite a burden to place on a sensitive and perceptive little girl, but she never told anyone.

CHAPTER NINE

I

Our trip home on the *America* had been a rough awakening from the dream in which we seemed to move in Europe, and the world refused to allow us to slip back into that euphoric state again. We arrived in New York on December 22, were allowed to spend Christmas quietly together in St. Albans, then plunged into a hectic series of recording sessions on the 26th. The musicians' union and the record companies were involved in a dispute that was to end in a strike beginning on January 1, 1948. The companies were frantically trying to record everything they could before that deadline. We had to try to put our entire repertory on records before it. We began on the 26th, in the midst of a snowstorm that was to stop traffic and even trains for several days. We worked night and day, our schedule and the weather preventing us from going home to St. Albans until the 30th. We spent New Year's Eve recuperating instead of toasting the beginning of our first full year of married life. That was the way it was for us for several years—the constant harassments and interruptions of show business.

We kept our marriage a secret until 1950. Of course, Lennie's family knew about our marriage and so did mine. Most of my family stopped speaking to me and my father and I were estranged for quite a while. Our best friends suspected that we were married, but we did not publicly confirm or deny the rumors that circulated about us.

There were several reasons for this. One had to do with the Negro press specifically and the Negro community in general. They were already dubious about me, I believed, because of my build-up by Hollywood as a glamour girl. By the time those technicians get through with you, if you're not very strong in the head, even you begin to wonder what became of the real you. Nobody, black or white, looks that good in real life. So the Negro press was hardly to be blamed if it was suspicious of me. If it wondered if I was becoming a white Negro, sometimes I wondered myself. But it did seem that if I announced my marriage just then I would only confirm their worst suspicions. I was not strong enough to face that. It took a long time to accept their distrust and dislike on an impersonal basis, as the kind of thing that would be directed at any Negro who had been thrust into my position. Isn't it ironic? For three years I preferred to let the world think I was a woman living in sin rather than admit that I had married a white man.

Circumstances also conspired to make it simpler for us to dodge the questions about whether or not we were married than to face up to them. Lennie was still under contract to M-G-M and he remained under that contract until 1953. That meant that he had to stay in Hollywood most of the time, while I continued to go on the road. We had a little house in Nichols Canyon and I would go there between jobs. But the only other time we could be together was when Lennie could sneak away from the studio for a long weekend and make a flying trip to wherever I was working. Since we were not constantly together—and since we had a great deal of privacy in the Nichols Canyon house—it was easier than it might have been to avoid public statements about the marriage.

It was not a good life. I hated being separated for so long

from Lennie and I hated the fact that Gail was now established in the house in St. Albans, which forced me, when I had some free time, to choose between seeing her and seeing my husband. I didn't feel that I should uproot her again and ask her to move to the West Coast, especially since I would be unable to spend significantly more time with her there than I could on the East Coast.

Unfortunately, I could neither slow down my work schedule nor find a job that allowed me to stay put in one location for any length of time.

I made only one more short movie sequence in this period, and the Broadway parts I was offered were not good. I had no choice but to keep going on the cabaret circuit, especially since my expenses were heavy—my gowns, the house in St. Albans, three musicians always under contract to me, whether I was working or not, the need to pay off the money MCA advanced me to buy out my contract with my previous agents, insurance for Gail's and Teddy's education. It was a treadmill—plushed-carpeted, to be sure—but still a treadmill.

Two things made it possible to go on—Lennie's love, and my association with my old friend, Ralph Harris, who became my manager shortly after we returned from Europe. I had met Ralph for the first time in 1945. At the time, Ralph was a song-plugger. The job was to bring your company's music to the attention of bandleaders and singers, and try to get them to record it or play it on the air or at least include it in the repertoire. The competition between the song-pluggers was fierce, and any tactic that could ingratiate you with a bandleader was considered fair. You lined up broads for them or, alternatively, distracted the wife's attention so the leader could make time with his current chick. You did them favors, you made sure restaurant headwaiters got them good tables, you played tennis with the athletic ones, and drank with the non-athletic ones.

Naturally, I'm only describing the more esoteric aspects of this work, but all in all it was not a very pleasant business, especially for a guy like Ralph.

He was from Syracuse originally, and had gone to work when he was a little kid, helping out his mom after his father died. His family was large and he had been brought up in a mixed neighborhood—German, Italian, Jewish, Negro, and oddly enough, he was without prejudice of any kind. By the time I met him he had worked at all kinds of jobs. He had been an ice man, a gravedigger, he had learned to be a tool maker and he had worked on WPA road gangs. He had also been in show business as a performer. He and another Syracuse boy, Jimmy Van Heusen, had toured in tank vaudeville with a singing act and later Ralph had joined a couple of Negro guys from Philadelphia to form a singing group, the Three Clefs. He had met Lennie as early as 1935, when Lennie was conducting the "Hit Parade" orchestra. Van Heusen, who was then a songplugger himself, had introduced them and when Ralph became a plugger he kept up the contact.

During the war, Ralph left show business to work for a firm that developed parts of the Norden bombsight. With the end of the war, he had gone back to song-plugging, but he was a very non-conforming, very disenchanted songplugger when he and Lennie picked up their friendship again, mostly around a bar at a hangout called Lucey's which was owned by a good guy named Nate Sherry. It was one of the very few Hollywood restaurants I would go to. Of the chic ones, Romanoff's was the only one I went to, because Mike Romanoff made a point of inviting Negro GIs to eat there during the war and he also made a point of asking any white customer who objected to this policy to leave. The other places I would go to were the Key Club, the 331 Club, and Brother's, but Nate Sherry's place was rather special. The only customers he really liked were actors and people from the music business, so I was made to feel comfortable there. If some cracker insulted me Nate was always pleased to let Scotty, the bartender, aided by Ralph or Lennie, escort him none too gently to the door. I think Lennie and Ralph were the first white men I allowed myself to believe in and to accept their love.

It is hardly possible that I was always pleasant company for Lennie when I was able to be with him. Or, on a different level, for Ralph or any other friend. As for their loving me, the realization came in painful stages, since it took years for me to understand that love is renewed constantly through the reception of it, and that I took everything in those days and gave nothing back. But what I could see in Lennie, and then in Ralph, was their attitude of going along with me, right or wrong. A few fights in a bar, our mutual dislike of musical phonies, companionship—that was important to me. Lennie and Ralph used to put me on by telling me I'd never sing as good as Ella Fitzgerald and we would have mock fights about that (they had to be mock, because I agreed with them). More important, Strayhorn liked Ralph, and so did my friend, Marie Bryant. They saw what I saw—that Ralph was the kind of man who would be completely for you in a scrap, that despite the hard-nosed knowledgeability he had picked up in his years of knocking around show business, he remained a sensitive and sympathetic person.

It was Lennie who finally asked Ralph if he would like to stop being a song-plugger and start being my manager. He just couldn't stand the idea of my going out alone any more, trying to solve by myself all the problems that came up, or having to depend on the musicians who went with me to take care of them, when they had their own troubles (and were not, in any case, being paid to look after me).

From the start, Ralph was the perfect manager. While I was buying myself off from MCA he took nothing but living expenses. When he couldn't get rooms in the hotel we were playing he would make sure that we all had a place to live. He worked the lights when there was no one else to do it; woke up the musicians and carried their bags so we could catch last-minute trains; found songs for us and food for us and good doctors for me when my bronchitis acted up in strange towns. He worked out ways to most effectively co-operate with Negro organizations so they could get the best possible use of me, and took the threats from some bosses who were going to "finish that bitch in the cabaret business," when I would refuse to do something or other that they wanted done.

He was, in short, great at handling the nitty-gritty of the business. But more important, he and Lennie together made a great team, giving my career a sympathetic direction it had not had before. Lennie helped make me a better singer, helped me to develop and broaden my musical tastes. Ralph, meantime, protected me from the most unpleasant aspects of life on the road. He understood completely when I preferred to work for less money in a club that offered more congenial surroundings than usual. Gradually he began to get written into my contracts protection against discrimination, making sure, in writing, that Negroes could get in to hear me if they wanted to or, on the personal level, spelling out, again in writing, that my family or my musicians could use the front door or the front elevators of the place I was working. While he was doing all this he never made me feel that he was just humoring me, keeping the performing seal healthy and happy so she would work harder and make more money. He respected me and my wishes, even when I would get contrary and just refuse to work at all for a time, or insist on taking off for some place where the money was poor but the surroundings or the audience or the management were good.

There were always incidents for him to cope with. In

In the long run it's a lonely business.

Royal Command Rehearsal Palladium Theatre, London, 1964.

PHOTOS BY MICHAEL COOPER

My granddaughter, Amy Lumet.

1948, for example, we went into St. Louis to play a room in one of the big hotels there—another first. They refused to let my musicians eat or drink in any of the hotel's restaurants. Since I didn't feel welcome to partake Ralph had a ball shaming them. He would march into the bar and order a trayful of drinks, then march out of it, through the lobby, into the front elevator and bring the drinks to our room. A man who seemed to be a paying guest unable to get a waiter to carry his drinks for him—it didn't look good to the other guests, and it drove the management crazy. Even after we were a smash and had been invited by the management to make ourselves at home, we continued our usual procedure.

I don't know how soon thereafter they changed their policies, but at least we had made our protest.

We also devised a way of making sure we had no recurrence of the incident at the Copa. Wherever we suspected a management of not allowing Negroes in to hear me, we had Negro friends make reservations by phone. Armed with a list of their names, Ralph would stand next to the *maitre de*, making sure he did not pull the "sorry, sir, we have no record of that reservation" bit.

He also learned how to protect me from myself. My father had always believed in generous tipping. Whenever he and I would get on a train every porter would have cash pressed on him. One time I asked him why and he said, "Because we're Negroes—and besides you get the best service when you tip." It was the first part of his formula that was important to him, I believe, and it was to me, too. If you're a Negro, your relationship with people whose jobs call upon them to serve you is bound to be difficult. Other Negroes are bound to resent it—and so are prejudiced white people. So I was an overtipper, and also an easy mark for handouts; because I could remember my father standing on the sidewalk in front of his hotel on Wiley Avenue in

Pittsburgh, giving money to everyone who came along. Ralph helped me to control my tendency to do too much of this.

One time late in the forties, when I was playing at the Capitol Theater in New York, a huge crowd was at the stage door, many of them being hangers-on looking for handouts. The crowd was so large that some of my friends and relatives could not get through to see me. Ralph asked me if I really thought it was a good thing to give away so much to these strangers. I agreed that I probably shouldn't. So what we did was work out an arrangement with a restaurant across the street. If anybody approached us with a hard luck story he was given carte-blanche to all the food he could eat in the restaurant. The really hungry ones— they were very, very few in number—took the privilege. Those who were just looking for a fast, easy buck soon stopped hanging around. This and many other incidents had their effect.

Perhaps that is why Ralph and Lennie gained the reputation of erecting a wall to separate me from the hard realities of Negro life. Maybe it was true—but at the time, I was a quivering mass of hang-ups. Without the protection they afforded me, I could not have preserved myself, let alone been any good to my family or my friends.

As for the Negro cause, I did what I could for it by lending my name to various activities, by appearing at fundraising rallies and benefits and so on. But I refused to be drawn out as a spokeswoman every time there was an incident. I always thought, Who the hell can possibly care what I think? I had always insisted that any reactions I made against segregation be a personal one, a response to a situation in which I was myself involved. If my reaction could be used to advantage by the rest of the people, well and good, but it always made me feel strangely guilty when it was. I never thought I had the right to speak for anyone

but me, myself and I. Whenever I made a general statement of belief or commented on some injustice that did not
directly involve me, I felt as if I were reacting like one of
Pavlov's pups, responding not because I chose to, but because I had been conditioned to do so, whatever my true
feelings.

Occasionally, I let those feelings show through. One time
Josephine Baker was refused admittance to the Stork Club
and there was a fuss made about it. I was playing in To-
ronto and the NAACP wired me, asking for a statement. I
wired back that I was sorry to hear about it, but I didn't
understand why she wanted to go to a joint like that in the
first place.

Well, that was the wrong thing to say. I should have fired
off a statement of solidarity and let it go at that. Nobody
cared if I thought getting into the Stork Club was an unimportant aspect of the battle for civil rights.

The simplest way of summarizing all this is to say that
they wanted to use my name all the time, while I wanted
to use the name only in situations I thought were important.
This is why I schooled myself not to be available for com-
ment on every possible issue that did not involve me personally. This decision was my own, not Ralph's or Lennie's.
What they did was draw the fire, accept the blame when it
seemed that I was being unreasonably uncooperative. In
fact, in a lot of instances, I know they would have had me
do things differently from the way I did. But they never
insisted.

Yet for all the protection I received from my husband and
from Ralph, there is no question that I grew, in these busy
years, both cold and suspicious. I was naturally suspicious
of the bosses of the clubs where I found most of my employment, and of some organizations that wanted to use my
name to advance their interests, and even of ordinary peo-

ple whom I met and who might have been good friends if I had let them.

I had never been a terribly open or loving person. I had not learned much about the nature of love from my family or my first marriage or from most of the people I had worked with, or from in the early years of my professional life. I don't offer any excuses. A different person would have overridden these difficulties, not allowed herself to withdraw from people as deeply as I did. In time, I would pay for this, as a kind of deadness came over me, a lack of joy in life and living. But at first I did not notice. I preserved my tight little world—Lennie, Ralph, some of the musicians who traveled with us, a small group of good friends. I just kept going—just kept trying to meet all my obligations. I could not stop my professional life long enough to establish a true home base, a wide circle of friends, real interests outside my work.

Las Vegas came to be a symbol of a great deal I hated in this business. It was and is where the big money is for a cabaret entertainer. I played the Sands for a decade. It was a beautifully run room, very classy. If you have to play Vegas that is the room to play. But to me there was no gratification to performing there. You never know when you're working in Vegas quite what's happening to you. The audience is a captive one, but the thing that has captured them is the gambling. They really only come to see you in order to take a rest from the crap tables. And since they're still thinking about the crap tables, they aren't thinking about you particularly. There's no challenge in them, so you have no sense of discovery about your performance to gain through their reactions.

Besides that, there is usually, along the strip, no sense of competing with your peers. You're competing with what a headline of the moment has created, what a cliché of the moment has created, what a nakedness of the moment has created.

I might be working next to a place that has an attraction at the moment who is the world's best fire-eater. Well, that's fine; that's all show business, really and truly. But then, on the other hand, I think the world's best fire-eater is more show business than, for instance, the most divorced woman in the world, who is working at the place opposite us both, and who can't eat fire and who can't sing. It made me feel like a freak, that's all. The lure is only money and I'm not being a snob about it, but I have not always found that when you have money you have everything. And besides, it's still a prejudiced town.

Now, a lot of the good performers may think all this, and they still go back. One of them said to me, just recently, "What the hell—take your money and run." But the thing that galled me was that Vegas was the *only* big-money channel open to Negroes. TV was closed to us, movies were closed to us, Broadway was mostly closed to us. The only place we could get the big loot was Vegas!

That was hardly Las Vegas' fault, I know. But I had to resent it. And the resentment grew and grew until I stopped going there. In the end, it was just a personal thing. I welcomed the opportunity to go and work in physically bad, acoustically poor rooms, for less money, rather than go there. Maybe it was stupid. But in those rooms, if I made it, I could find me again. At least sometimes I could.

The trouble was that throughout this decade I found it harder and harder to take pride and pleasure in my work. I could not go forward to new kinds of expression in new media. Neither could I justify what I was doing as something that was, in my off hours, enabling me to purchase a stable, restful or luxurious home life. Quite the opposite. The harder I worked, the less chance I had to be with my husband, my children, my friends. Gradually, without my being aware of it, a kind of despair began to creep over me. It would not manifest itself in a really terrible way until the late 1950s. But I know now that its beginnings were in the first years of extensive cabaret touring.

II

Three things made it possible to go on—the house and the life Lennie and I were able to share in Los Angeles, my visits with Teddy and Gail, and the trips to Europe.

When we moved into the tiny house in Nichols Canyon, we faced a good deal of trouble. Once again, the neighbors circulated petitions, trying to drive us out. This time they were accompanied by implied threats of violence. Lennie bought a shotgun, and the first remodeling we did consisted of constructing a large wall around the property. We discovered, as usual, that it was just one family that was stirring up the trouble. Oddly enough, they were the parents of a white movie star with whom we had friends in common. One of these friends mentioned the problems her parents were causing me to her and, since she was supporting them, she gave them a brisk talking to and our troubles ceased.

We gave a housewarming party and arranged, through a friend, to have four dozen live lobsters shipped to us by plane from Maine. The day before our party we received a telegram telling us the lobsters were en route, due to reach Los Angeles at 4 A.M. We decided to stay up and go to the airport to greet the little darlings personally. We did not know, however, what airline the lobsters were coming on and we had to make the rounds of the many companies only to be informed that the lobsters had been bumped in Kansas City and would not arrive until ten in the morning. We did notice another shipment of lobsters—also four dozen

strong—waiting at the shipping office. They were addressed
to La Rue's, one of the better restaurants. We tried to talk
the man into letting us take La Rue's shipment and giving
them ours, but it was no deal. All we learned from this exchange was that of all the restaurants in L.A. advertising sea
food shipped fresh daily from the East, this was the only
one living up to its promise. All the others were getting
shipments once or twice a week and holding them over. This
at least gave us some hope for our bumped lobsters as we
headed home, and later in the day, they arrived safe and
sound.

We had a great party. I had invited some of our good
friends from Katherine Dunham's troupe and some people
from the New York City Ballet, among them George Bal-
anchine and Tanaquil LeClercq, who were appearing in
Los Angeles at the time. Full of lobster, full of good food
and good booze, the two groups intermingled dance styles
—and the bacchanal went on to the next day.

Our entertaining was always informal. People just
dropped in rather casually—musicians who had traveled
with me like Jerry Wiggins and Chico Hamilton, old friends
like Marie Bryant, and often, Ava Gardener, who lived up
the road and whom I had found to be a wonderfully down-
to-earth girl when we were both under contract to Metro
and whom I had casually kept up with for some years.

Lennie and I established the custom of an experimental
cocktail hour on Saturdays and Sundays. We had bought
The Gentleman's Drinking Companion, and we had con-
verted a closet into a bar, complete with sink and stocked
with every imaginable kind of liquor and mix we'd read
about in this book. We vowed to go through that book page
by page, trying every recipe in it at least once. So on the
weekends when I was home, people would drop in and see
what in the world we were mixing up. Those cocktail hours
always led to the kind of evening that I liked—a lot of good

friends sitting around, talking, getting loaded, listening to everybody's good music.

Our life there was most times very quiet. For the first time in my life I really listened to music. I also did a lot of reading and a lot of relaxing, storing up energy for my next venture out on the road. Very often my son Teddy would be allowed to come and stay with us for several days at a time. (He lived with his father in downtown Los Angeles.)

It was here, in Nichols Canyon, that I was able to indulge myself in the luxury of having pets. I had always wanted to have them, but I had never been allowed to when I was young. But now someone gave us a cat—we named her Hey-You. She contracted rather a hasty marriage with a great white cat, down the road, and produced a litter behind our bed. Of course, we did all the wrong things with that litter, allowing our friends to touch and play with the kittens until Hey-You simply took them away. We went into a panic, searching all over for her and her babies. But she kept them hidden until she judged that we had learned our lesson, then brought them back. Out of that litter we kept a beautiful white, blue-eyed cat we named Shy-Guy.

Not long thereafter, Hey-You got pregnant again. Just about the time she delivered that litter, we took Shy-Guy in to be inoculated. He carried cat fever back from the vet's, infected the new litter, and all but one of them died. The one who survived was a wonderful little toughy we named Runty. How I loved that cat. He was desperately ill with this infection, but he was a fighter. He snarled and arched his back, sick as he was, when we took him to the doctor. He just never gave up the fight. And he won, though ever after he walked with a lurch, the result of a needle that was injected, by accident, in a leg muscle.

Shy-Guy became Lennie's cat. He would sit on the piano when Lennie was writing. Runty chose me. He always brought me presents. When he caught a lizard, which was

often, he would bring it to the side of the bed and proudly
deposit it. He was a real character, the only cat I've ever
heard of who made friends with a frog. There was a huge
bullfrog who lived under our patio, and we would come
home late at night to find them sitting side by side talking
—the frog croaking at Runty, and Runty mewing back at
him. I also have a vivid memory of a flood we had in the
canyon. It had rained for days and it was still raining, and
the men all pitched in to dig run-off ditches to protect the
houses. Even so, we had a mud slide that piled up against
the glass doors that lead to the patio. In the midst of all this
I had to leave on a tour, and my last sight as I went through
the door was of the cats, perched quietly on the furniture,
watching that mud piling up against our house. To me it
was as if they had some primeval knowledge of natural di-
sasters and had an ability to accept them that man does not
have. It was this mysterious quality cats can communicate
to some people that drew me to them in general, I guess.

But my relationship with Runty went beyond that. The
best thing about it, for me, were his welcomes when I came
back from a trip. He always disappeared the night I left,
but Lennie always claimed he knew when I was about to
return, because Runty would always mysteriously reappear
the night before I came back. Usually I would be completely exhausted and all I would want to do would be to
sleep for twelve or eighteen or twenty-four hours. I would
hit the sack and Runty would appear at the side of the bed,
look at me questioningly and talk to me in much the same
tone he talked with that frog. Finally, I'd say, "OK Runty,
let's take a rest," and he would jump up on the bed and
sleep there with me as long as I slept.

Later on, James and Pamela Mason gave us one of their
beautiful Siamese cats which decided, as Siamese will sometimes do, that the house must be run for her benefit. She
made life miserable for the other cats, and we finally par-

celed all of them out to friends, except Runty. He stayed with us until we gave up the house. Then Marie Bryant gave him a home and he was quite old when he was finally struck down by a car while he was out adventuring.

I would have kept cats always, but they are such poor travelers. Our life in the fifties involved a great deal of moving about, so it would not have been fair to try to keep one. In that period, however, I discovered pugs. To me, they are the most cat-like dogs, despite their unfair reputation as playthings of society ladies. When I announced my intention of getting one, Gail was afraid I was going to turn into a dowager-type. But I persisted, and my pug, Nellie, went with us everywhere we traveled.

We gave up both the St. Albans house and the Nichols Canyon house in the early fifties. We sold the latter when Lennie finally finished out his contract with M-G-M and there was no need for a West Coast home. I gave up the former when Mrs. Starks decided she and her family needed to make a home of their own. I was not unhappy to have Gail leave St. Albans, because she had fallen in with a group of youngsters who were, I thought, rather snobbish in their attitudes. I thought she might be doomed to repeat the "first family" syndrome that I had been exposed to at her age and I did not want that to happen to her. For a while she lived with my friend Aida Bearden, who is married to Lawrence Winters, the singer, and attended a good progressive school in New York. But all children do not necessarily fit into progressive education. Since we were now full-scale traveling show folk we knew that Gail's education had to be given serious thought. Through the kindness of friends of ours we discovered Oakwood in Poughkeepsie, and she spent her prep-school years at this fine Quaker School. She went from there to Radcliffe.

As for Lennie and me, we then went through a long period of living without a home. We lived in a hotel suite in

New York. There was certainly nothing wrong with the Park Sheraton, but it is a little expensive compared to an apartment—even a New York apartment.

There were plenty of apartments around that we could have afforded to rent, but we weren't allowed to have them. Ralph Harris, Lennie, and I trudged the streets of New York for years, finding places which became mysteriously unavailable when we appeared eager to rent them. We were caught in three different kinds of prejudice—against Negroes, against Jews, and against mixed marriages. I don't know which of these its management was responding to, but the Eldorado, on Central Park West, refused us an apartment. At the time it was owned by a Negro, Bishop C. M. ("Daddy") Grace.

Ironically, we had to leave New York in order to solve our New York housing problem. We solved it, almost accidently, in the course of a trip to Europe. But that was not until 1956.

Europe continued to draw us back. It was natural, I suppose, given the wonderful experience of our first trip there, and given the relaxation of pressures we always felt there. We returned for the first time in 1950. Lennie had got another leave of absence from the studio—this time for six months—and we made a long tour. It was the first time I worked at the Palladium in London. It's such a beautiful theater, with an atmosphere so different in those days from anything we had here. The stage manager, for instance, wears evening clothes, and instead of tacking a card with your name scrawled on it on your dressing room door, they have it engraved in bronze, and when your engagement is over they give you the nameplate. There was a style to it that I hadn't found here in a vaudeville theater.

In 1950 we also played the provinces of Great Britain for the first time. I also remember Glasgow and Manchester. They were the first cities over there where I found a kind of mass enthusiasm that was comparable only to the first times that Duke Ellington and I played the big New York theaters. In Glasgow I was greeted with a kind of enthusiasm that surprised me no end—stomping, cheering audiences that simply screamed their liking for me. When we emerged from the theater after our night's work was done we would find hundreds of people waiting for us, packed into the alley leading backstage, and overflowing into the street beyond. They had to call out mounted policemen to keep order. Not that there was anything vicious about the crowds. The authorities were afraid someone would get hurt in the crush. I would stand there for hours, signing autographs. When we moved to Manchester we encountered similar scenes. And then, a little later in the same tour, we encountered a curious contrast to this in Stockholm.

The audience at the lovely little "China" theater offered a kind of hushed respect that I had never received before. In the British provinces the welcome was more in the American style. It usually sounded like a cheer at a ball game. But in Stockholm they greeted me almost as if I were a concert performer, with sustained, intense, sober applause. Then when I had finished my opening night, they threw flowers. By the time I took my last bow, the stage was littered with flowers. It had never happened to me before, it has since only happened in one other place, Rio. Then when we came out of the theater there was a huge crowd waiting for us. But there were no cops, there was no pushing and shoving and very little sound. One by one they filed up to the stage door and quietly handed me their programs and autograph books to sign. When I finished, we made our way easily to the street, where a car was waiting for us, the crowd falling back to make way for us. Then, as Lennie opened the door for me, they burst into applause. It was completely unexpected and, therefore, both totally electrifying and completely moving.

I don't think we ever made a trip abroad that did not contain some incident as memorable as this, though perhaps in a different way. One of the most exciting trips we ever made was to Israel. That was in 1952 and while we were aboard ship, en route, they celebrated the fourth year of their independence.

We sailed through the Mediterranean on an Israeli ship called the *Artsa*. It was a very small ship, and so I was able to make friends with my fellow passengers. We carried with us ninety-six refugee children who had been in a Youth Alijah Camp and I found that very inspiring. In America I had done some benefits for Hadassah and other Jewish organizations and this had brought me into contact with some Israeli people who had taught me, phonetically, a couple of their songs which I was able to do at the Independence Day party on the ship and later in Israel.

But the important thing to me was the feeling I got in Israel of being in touch with history, not only the ancient history of Biblical times, but of history-in-the-making in a brand-new country. I also liked the treatment I received there. They were too busy to give me the tourist treatment, or to waste time on a lot of fancy arrangements. Because of my association with Auren Kahn and the Joint Distribution Committee, I was treated as a friend and not as a tourist. I remember visiting a Kibbutz where Lennie got very upset because they were canning sauerkraut and throwing the juice away. He began to think of all the ulcer sufferers in America.

The most fascinating thing to me was a visit to a school for Yemenite children. They are dark and beautiful and they reminded me of my own children—and their people had been traditionally discriminated against before the formation of Israel. There I saw for the first time in my life terribly oppressed people of color, people just emerging from the kind of bondage Negroes have been struggling so long to emerge from.

One of the counselors was an American boy from Chicago, who was upset because the children came to the school very pure, untouched by modern civilization, but by the fifth day, he said, they were chewing gum and the little girls were begging for lipstick. I thought it was funny, the speed with which children can adapt to new conditions and he had to admit that, in general, the sort of progress they made was inspiring. "After a time," he said, "the only thing left is color."

In Israel I had first-hand evidence of how hard it can be to change attitudes once they are deeply ingrained. I got a little teed off at a couple of the Negroes who were traveling with us, because they did something it was quite easy to do. They found some white people they could kick around easier than they could at home—Jewish people who waited on them at the motel. They were not that way with the French and the English, but here they could not resist the temptation. These were people who lived in uptown New York, where the pattern of anti-Semitism is long established. They had learned to resent the Jewish merchants who run many of the shops in Harlem, and they hated the slave-market tactics of the Bronx housewives when they hired domestic help and now, with the situations reversed, it was almost as if they could not help themselves. What an endless chain of unhappiness prejudice forges.

But Israel was not all a learning process for us. I was not well known there, and I was amazed and delighted by the warmth of the reception we received. And then there were the birds who nested on the roof of the theater at Ramat-Gan. We did four concerts there. During the first one they accompanied me through the entire performance. But after that they settled down and it was only at the close of the show, when I sang "Stormy" they all chirped in, as if cued.

Almost as memorable to me as the trip to Israel was the trip to England and the Continent in 1956. I took Gail and Teddy, and Ralph Harris brought his wife along, my pianist brought his wife and their two-month-old baby. Altogether, our party amounted to twelve people (plus my two dogs).

There were so many of us that when we got on a train to take us from Copenhagen to the ferry for Sweden they had to put on an extra car. That was delightful because we had it all to ourselves. But when we got to the ferry we discovered our car made the train too long to fit on the boat. So they shunted us on a siding to wait for a shorter train. The men got off to buy food, whereupon they started switching our car all around the yards. The women were on the train without passports or money and the men couldn't find the car. Panic all around, compounded by language difficulties. The men kept dashing up and down stairs, up and down different tracks. Finally the next train for Stockholm, via the ferry, pulled in and they climbed on. But by this time the railroad officials had forgotten our special car entirely, and it took hurried consultations with the yardmaster to join our car to the train and set us on our way again. Lennie remembers that as just about the wildest hour in all our travels.

But it was a grand trip. Gail was the perfect little girl, finding girl friends her own age all over and taking tea with them. In England she even visited one of them on a houseboat. Teddy, two years younger, was having none of that. He wanted to see the "real" world. Already he was a proud, sensitive, tremendously brilliant boy. On this trip he would wander off alone, looking for unfortunates (bums, really) whom he called "world travelers." He would ask them if they would like to meet another world traveler and they would agree and then he would bring those old, bleary-eyed, red-nosed drunks around to the stage door to meet his mother. I think they were far more shocked at these meetings than I was. I can still see their puzzled faces peering up at me.

There were certain constants in our travels. One was at a gala at Monte Carlo that we played every other summer for a decade. The salaries were not equal to what we usually received elsewhere, but it was a chance to rest up in perfect surroundings, to eat and drink well and soak up the sun.

Sometimes we followed this with an another engagement in Juan-les-Pins, the famous resort between Cannes and Nice. During a rehearsal for one of these appearances Sidney Bechet came to visit us. He was to appear that same night in the club next to us. He was very popular in Europe, especially France, where he made his home. He was famous for the shrill, penetrating tone he could produce on his clarinet. We had a very pleasant meeting, but imagine our surprise when, a few minutes before I was scheduled to appear, the sound of Sidney's clarinet, amplified by many loudspeakers, reached into my dressing room. Both of these clubs were open air places, with only a high hedge separating them. We quickly sent one of our management around to see if we couldn't stagger our appearances, because it was clear that my singing would also interfere with his playing. We would have been perfectly willing to postpone our appearance until he was through, but he very graciously insisted that we go first. He was a wonderful gentleman.

These engagements in the South of France were welcome vacations for all of us, but they were especially useful to Ralph Harris. We usually took off for Europe with only a couple of dates lined up and we tried to separate each engagement by a week or more in which we could be free to act like ordinary tourists. But we had to pay our musicians every week whether we worked or not, and we always had our own heavy living expenses which meant we usually arrived in Monte Carlo nearly broke. Ralph would heave a

sigh of relief over having made it that far (especially if we
had played Italy, which had serious restrictions about the
amount of currency we could take out of the country with
us). Knowing that we were safely settled in a hotel for a few
days, all expenses paid, he would get on the phone and line
up some more bookings for us, enough to pay everybody's
salaries and the cost of the trip home at least.

Good things occasionally resulted from those phone calls.
One time we got booked into the Olympia Theatre in Paris
at the last minute. I had never done variety in France and
was leery about it. I wasn't at all certain I could hold a
popular audience, especially with the language barrier. But
it was a success, and Ralph told me later, a historic first
for us—the first time I had ever got a guaranteed salary in
France, paid out at the end of the week by check. Usually
we took a cut of the gross and watched while the French, in
their inimitable way, scurried around to collect the cash
owed us at the end of the engagement.

Ah, the French: They can bug you if you let them, with
their don't-give-a-damn attitude, and they are mysterious
about money, but there's no denying their charm. I had a
special wardrobe trunk designed to hold my working overalls (my gowns) and the French customs men always took
a special delight in checking it over, letting me know their
opinions of my choices and more than that, letting me know
that they were up-to-date on *haute couture*. They would
admire with extravagant gestures and sounds or, if they
did not approve, they would purse their lips in that inimitable way of theirs.

I enjoyed all this—the new theaters and audiences and
places every year, as well as the fun of returning to old
favorites like the Palladium or Monte Carlo. But I think
best of all, I loved the food. Poppy Cannon, Walter White's
beautiful widow, used to say "you could always find Lena
in Les Halles in Paris, looking for gumbo filé and then bor-

rowing somebody's apartment to cook in." The reason for my interest in food, and for the particular kinds I adore, can be traced to my childhood, I'm sure.

For example, one of my vivid memories of Florida is buying crayfish, bought from some guy who had a roadside stand, or who peddled it from door to door, then eating it after the herbs, garlic, onions, and maybe a little shrimp were added. It was, therefore, natural for me to welcome bouillabaisse years later in Villefranche like an old friend. Similarly, as a child in the South, guavas off the trees, all pale pink and green, sapodillas, mangoes, figs (purple and green), prepared me for the fabulous fruit that Italy offered. And chitlin's—I always adored them—put in a pot with all the right things and cooked all day, making the house funky, prepared me for calamare in San Francisco and squid in Italy and snails everywhere. In my mind, at least, the only thing you can compare those things to is chitlin's.

Negro dishes are directly comparable to the famous delicacies of Europe. Rabbit, fricasseed, for instance, was standard Sunday fare at my Uncle Frank's home in Fort Valley and it did not taste appreciably different at Lapin Agile where I had it in Paris. By the same token, grits tastes to me almost exactly like farina in Rio or polenta in Italy, and a great French cassoulet calls to mind the taste of turkey neckbones and fatback and dumplings all cooked together, in Macon, Georgia.

It sometimes amuses and amazes me that poverty is a better preparation for *haute cuisine* than is a good solid, middle-class upbringing.

It was, then, when we traveled abroad that I found the good life this profession can offer. This is not to say we did not occasionally have good times in the United States. I remember, in the early years, working at a joint up at Lake Tahoe, the State Line, where Harrah's is now. It was a terrible joint. The entertainers worked in a big long room in front of a green baize curtain and you'd be doing some soft thing like "Bewitched" and right in the middle of it you'd hear somebody in the gambling room yell, "Crapped out" at the top of his lungs. We had to laugh.

I worked there with Chico Hamilton, and we lived in log cabins scattered around the area, because the motels would not take in Negroes. But even so, the show people had a kind of community there. When we finished work we would load a burlap sack with cans of beer and take a pile of sandwiches to the lake. At 4 A.M. the water was icy cold, and we would submerge the beer in the lake and sit there eating and talking until mid-morning when the sun would be high and burning the chill out of us.

It must have been about the same time that I went on stage for the first and last time soaking wet. This was in Vancouver, Canada. It was a big, dreary joint called the Cave and decorated with papier-mâché stalagmites. Because of government liquor regulations, the customers had to bring their own bottles, and the joint made its money selling set-ups and tickets at the door. You got a plate of spaghetti and meatballs—no choice—for the price of admission. Well, no one had told me what a vociferously enthusiastic audience Canadians can be, and by nine o'clock they were all roaring drunk and yelling for me to appear. Chico and the group went out and played and then it was time for me to go on. To get to the stage I had to pass through the kitchen. I was wearing a long white dress trimmed with paillettes, with a huge fishtail of tulle at the bottom. As I came through some woman from the audience was coming from the other direction, looking for the ladies' room. She said, "Hurry up, Lena—we're waiting for you." And with that, threw up the spaghetti and meat balls all down the tulle. Chico was waiting to bring me on and he just threw up his hands and screamed with laughter. The

band was already hitting into the introductory drum roll
and I didn't know what to do. But all the water pitchers
were standing there and Tiny Kyle just grabbed a couple
of them and sloshed me down, and out I went. The audience was marvelous—so family. I think it was probably one
of the best receptions I ever had.

But mostly working on this continent was no fun at all.
It seemed to me just one big night club, a weary succession
of similar cities, one nasty little fight after another over
some aspect of segregation, a series of questioning glances
directed at me and my husband, a gradual deadening of
my responses as an artist, leading me to replace inspiration
with a kind of dogged professionalism.

It was then, in the late forties and early fifties, that
Europe came to seem a real temptation to me, for it was
there I felt alive and free. Lennie and I wondered sometimes if it would not be wise to become full-time expatriates,
putting behind us for good all the problems, personal and
professional, that constantly confronted us in our own land.

Sometimes these problems showed themselves in a particularly ugly way. In the early fifties, while Lennie was
still at M-G-M, I played the Clover Club in Miami. The
first time was great. The place was owned by Jack Goldman
and he had a lovely house, where he invited me to stay as
his guest when I worked in the club. The next time Jack
asked me and Lennie to come back we said, "Sure, but
would you mind if we rented a little place of our own?"
Jack was very understanding and asked one of his waiters
if he would rent us his house. It was a nice enough little
bungalow, and we didn't think he'd rent it to us if there
was a restrictive clause in the lease. The only Negro hotel
was miles away, built around an open court. The visiting
ball teams and orchestra members had a ball all night,
and sleep was impossible.

The waiter was charging us a damned good price, and

saw no reason to spoil the deal by pointing out that there was a restrictive clause. I guess he thought the neighbors would let him get away with it.

It was the winter season, and the audiences were good and the sun was warm and Ralph and Chico and his group were along, and everyone was having a good time. I had even put out of my mind the memories of my childhood in Miami.

But, one night toward the end of the engagement, Ralph was standing in the bar of the club, having a drink and waiting for me to do the last show, when a guy he knew to be a detective approached him. The cop was a habitué of the bar in his off-duty hours and he and Ralph had struck up a casual friendship. The detective engaged Ralph in conversation, and in the course of it rather casually remarked:

"I wouldn't let the girl go home tonight. They've got the house staked out."

Ralph hurried around backstage, found Lennie, told him what was going on, and they devised a plan. They refused to tell me, until later, what was happening. They merely told me that tonight I was going to spend the night at Jack Goldman's house. Jack took me there immediately after the show. Meantime, Ralph and Lennie went to our house where, sure enough, they saw a squad car sitting quietly, lights out, just waiting for me to come home and thus violate the segregation law of this little suburb. Ralph and Lennie threw some things in a suitcase for me and brought them to Goldman's house. And that was that. The cops never followed and we, of course, did not return together to the house. Jack Goldman fired the waiter who had rented to us. Incidents like that can make you think very seriously about leaving home for good.

So can blacklisting. I was listed, along with many others, in *Red Channels*, and I was unable, during the early fifties,

to get on any television programs. Tex McCrary and Jinx
Falkenburg had a daytime local show in New York, mostly
interviews and talk, and they were absolutely the only ones
who would let me on their show. Tex tried to interest other
people in hiring me and discovered that it was not a question of my ability or even of color, in many instances. It
was my so-called political past—mostly, my friendship with
Paul Robeson and my interest, developed through him, in
the Council for African Affairs, which got named as a front.
Then there had been HICCASP in Hollywood, which got
on some lists, and through the years, I had done literally
hundreds of benefits for this committee and that, some of
which, I was informed were "tainted," at least in the minds
of the super-patriots. Listed in the pamphlets and publica-
tions of the blacklisters, my accumulated political misde-
meanors looked pretty impressive. I was never officially in-
vestigated by any government agency—at least as far as I
know—and, of course, the blacklist never reached out and
touched the cabaret business, so I could still make a living,
unlike many other performers.

Still you get a little teed off. For the second time in less
than a decade, some force outside myself had reached out
and arbitrarily, whimsically, stopped my career just at a
moment when it might have gone on to something new.
First there had been M-G-M curtailing my stage and movie
activities, now there was this blacklist business, just in time
to hold me back in television.

Everyone who went through blacklisting has a couple of
anecdotes that seem to sum up the absurdity of it. The one
I always think of first involved an Army colonel who happened to sit next to Ralph Harris on a plane from San
Francisco to Los Angeles. I had been working at the Fairmont in San Francisco, which is owned by the Swig family,
whose record on Civil Rights is absolutely wonderful. The
Fairmont was one of the first fine hotels in San Francisco

that admitted Negroes. The Army colonel had seen me working there and, not knowing who Ralph was started talking about me.

"She certainly is a fine entertainer," he said, "but you notice how these Communists work, the propaganda they get into their songs."

"No, I didn't notice," Ralph said, all innocent.

"That second song she sings—pure propaganda."

"What do you mean?" Ralph asked.

"Didn't you hear that line, 'Don't save your kisses, pass 'em around?'"

"Yes."

"Typical. Those Communists. Always talking about free love."

Well Ralph didn't know whether to argue or to laugh out loud. He didn't do either. It's just plain foolish to accept debate on terms as mad as those. How do you explain to some kook that the song was over twenty years old, had been written by Victor Young, who was about as far from being Communistic as it's possible to be and that—no kidding—it was really a light love song, not a political piece.

III

In the middle of the 1950s my situation was this: I had no place I could really call home. Lennie and I were living out of suitcases all over the world. My career was successfully in a rut at home and, although Europe could be fun, for some reason I did not want to cut my ties and go there for good. It seemed that there was nothing ahead but an endless repetition of what I had already accomplished.

And then, suddenly, things began to unravel themselves. The first good break was finding a New York apartment. That occurred in 1956. We were in Paris, and Ralph was approached by José Iturbi's manager. Mr. Iturbi wondered if I would appear, the following fall, on a benefit program for the symphony orchestra he conducted in Rochester, New York. Sometimes artists get more requests to do benefits than there is time to do. There is, first of all, the matter of ones schedule, to consider. Then there is the question of not wanting to overexpose yourself, so that you ruin your potential to raise money for the charities that are closest to your heart. It did not seem to me, or to Ralph, that Mr. Iturbi's symphony orchestra was the sort of thing that would be very high on my list. In fact, I remember saying at just about that time, that I was ready for somebody to run a charity of some kind for me, to find me a place to live.

Well, Ralph turned down the request, but the guy was persistent. Couldn't they get together for a drink, talk this thing over? Ralph decided he ought to do that much and so they met. Somehow, in the course of the conversation, it came out that Iturbi's manager was having all kinds of trouble with his New York apartment. He was on the road a good deal and the place was too big for him and he had not been able to get rid of it, as it was a fairly expensive co-op. The more he talked the more it seemed to Ralph that this was the very place we had been looking for these many years. By this time Ralph knew our specifications by heart.

If I did the benefit for Iturbi would this man be willing to let me take over the lease on his apartment? He leaped at the chance, as it solved two problems at once for him. Lennie and I leaped, too.

Now, finally, we began a home. We put down roots in New York and I became, again, a New Yorker as I had in 1941 when I worked at Café Society. We took an interest in New York things and institutions in a way I had not been able to do before. Now when I contributed my services to a charity I felt, for the first time, a sense of community, a sense of personal involvement that I had not felt in the past.

At about the same time, I also learned a way out of the blacklist. It was Lennie's agent who showed me the way. He said you had to go to see a man who was head of one of the theatrical unions who could, in turn, steer you to one of the informal clearance groups, which would, in *its* turn, get the word out that you might be hired again. Some people, of course, had to go before a Congressional Committee to clear themselves, but some could clear themselves through this more informal process. They could have cleared us without meeting us, but they enjoyed the spectacle of us having to come and ask nicely, please, couldn't we work again?

I talked by phone to the union man, who was vague about me and about the next step I should take. Somehow, though, it was arranged that I go to see George Sokolsky, the political columnist who apparently was in a position to act as a sort of broker in these matters. I think it's possible that both Ed Sullivan, who was very sympathetic and who wanted me to be on his show, and Tex McCrary, had something to do with my seeing Sokolsky. My impression is that they both vouched for me, but I am necessarily vague on the details of how my confrontation with Sokolsky was arranged. These things just quietly happened in due course, and the whole incident had a dream-like quality to it— Kafkaesque, as everybody so easily says these days.

Going to see him I felt very much as I did when I had gone to see Louis B. Mayer to straighten out my M-G-M problems. I must say, however, that Sokolsky did not act like Mayer. The first thing he said to me was, "I understand your difficulties completely—I once even had a Chinese wife." Now that to me, sounded like the "some of my best friends" and it always makes me angry and, besides, it took me a minute to make the connection between the fact that Chinese are colored people and so was I. Then it came to me that he was trying to put me at my ease. All he had succeeded in doing, of course, was to make me more uncomfortable.

But as he continued to talk he overcame my hostility. He did not make me feel like a supplicant and he did not make me feel I had been dumb to do what I had done in the past. For my part, I played it cool. I knew I was innocent, but I also knew that like a lot of people, both more and less prominent than I, I had occasionally allowed myself to be used for what, at the time, seemed a mutual advantage. I tried to discuss everything with him realistically, and he took a paternalistic tone with me in the end, in effect absolving me of the sins of my wayward youth.

I assumed that he talked to Sullivan and that they, together, prevailed upon the man who was running *Red Channels* to cease his objections to me. About the mechanics of this I know very little. All I do know is that shortly thereafter Sullivan was able to use me on his show. Steve Allen, then hosting the old "Tonight" show in New York, hired me a few times and thereafter I was able to work on variety shows.

My favorite among them has always been Perry Como's. In many ways he is in real life the same quiet, relaxed guy he appears to be on the air. But he also has a quiet temper, a quiet intensity about his work and a tremendous, sure professionalism. Besides which, he is just a naturally decent fellow. All the little unwritten rules about whites and blacks working together on camera (don't touch) are ignored by him, and he treats me like an equal. The result is that I feel free and natural when I work with Perry. I very much value the atmosphere he creates around him when he works.

So, by 1957 things were beginning to seem a little better to me. I was still anxious to gain some respite from the cabaret circuit and although television helped somewhat in this way, I could not really make a living from it. For that, you needed a show of your own, and no one would give me a show. If it had been a question of my talent I would not have minded. But I don't believe it was. It was a question of my being a Negro.

I was also anxious to do a Broadway show, but that presented another set of problems.

My payroll was still high, and one was rarely tempted to take a chance on a script, stop working, go into rehearsal, keep the musicians on the payroll so you could get them back and head back for the road if the show flopped. Also include the worry about the other people, the manager, the housekeeper and dressing room boss (by now, my wonderful friend Irene Lane). There was also the tax man to keep placated, and there were the growing family expenses. (Gail entered Radcliffe in 1956 and a little later, Teddy went to college and then had a year at the Sorbonne.) So one yielded not to temptation, one kept on in the damned rut.

We could have soundproofed a couple of rooms with all the scripts we had received by this time. One room could have been done in scripts about how the beautiful, exotic native girls in their simple way could teach the white man a thing or two about true civilization. The other room could have been done in scripts about beautiful, sophisticated, talented Negro girls who couldn't make it in America, went to Paris, became the rage and nobly gave up a nobleman. Well, I was the same broad who decided I wasn't going to pass for Spanish in 1940, so the first cliché didn't appeal to me. As for the second, Lennie and I thought the script of our own life was funnier.

I was offered revues, which at least didn't have book problems. But they did not have song material that was as good as the great songs I was free to do in the clubs, or as

good as the fine special material I was now paying to have
written for me. The only show that tempted me was *House
of Flowers*. It had Harold Arlen's beautiful, beautiful score
and there was a great part in it—that of a madam—but
unfortunately I was offered the role of the ingenue. But I
told him I hadn't felt like an ingenue since I was sixteen,
so I regretfully declined.

I was playing at the Waldorf-Astoria in New York when
Harold and his partner-lyricist Yip Harburg came to see the
show. They said, We think we have something that would
be wonderful for you to hear. That I admired their work
tremendously had been shown by the huge number of their
songs I had been using in my repertoire for a long time.

But the bait that really hooked me when Yip cast it, was
"We have a show for you which will show you as you
really are—not the sleek, sophisticated lady of the cabarets,
but a really basic, earthy, human being." Hot dog, I
thought, maybe at last the true "Lena" will finally emerge
and that'll show them—and me.

Now I didn't know that *Jamaica* had been written originally as a vehicle for Harry Belafonte, during the height
of the first calypso craze. What with one commitment or
another, he had been unable to accept the script. So when
I went to Harold's house and heard Fred Saidy, the co-
author of the book, Yip and Harold read the book, and
heard the songs as only Harold can sing them, I sat with
tears in my eyes thinking, "What a lovely show and what
a great part the leading man has, and who am I going to
be?"

The story was about a wonderful fisherman on one of
those lovely islands, who had the only brains in the place.
He believed that nature and innocence and goodness were
more to be desired than all the facilities of civilization, including especially, the bomb. The only lack of brains he
displayed was loving a stupid broad who has somewhere

gotten hold of a TV set and believes that the only place where things are really happening is New York—and besides she hates fish! I thought they must have called in the wrong person. We had agreed that the real me was earthy and basic, and that certainly did not describe Savanna, the part I was to play. It was the man's part that had all the earthy qualities they wanted revealed in me, and which I wanted to project. As things stood that afternoon, the part played so brilliantly in the show by Josephine Premice— that of Savanna's hip, wise-cracking friend—was superior to that of Savanna.

I think it was one of the most difficult afternoons of my life. I adored these giants of my profession, I wanted desperately to do a show, and this one seemed to be closer to being a real possibility than anything that had previously come up. Now I saw, or thought I saw, that the real me was no more to them than my box-office potential, someone to save a project in which they had already invested a great deal of themselves.

I allowed myself to believe them when they said, "Don't worry, we'll change Savanna so the part will be great," forced myself not to think that in the context of this script that was something like putting a straight seam down the front of a bias-cut dress. Hell, I said to myself, the real me *is* how much business I can do. So, still with tears in my eyes, I said, "Thank you, gentlemen. The answer is I'll do it."

And so began another exactly the same, just like you read about it, backstage, out front, out of town, terrible, funny, mean drama of life on the stage. You become the enemy of your closest show-biz cohorts, you make up again, you find yourself being used to ban respectable, creative, temperamental people connected with the show from the theater, to keep them from upsetting other respectable, creative, temperamental people, who are also connected with the show. You listen to someone telling you about the theory of acting, but you can't quite catch the key word that tells you what to do. You find yourself happy to be surrounded by people on a stage, for a change, learning how really comforting it is, when you *feel* and *see* them there with you. You learn to cope when you realize your leading man is finding it difficult to see you as a tender, loving ingenue which is, despite all the promises, what the role remained, since the new part that was going to fit me never did quite arrive.

I had worshiped at the shrine of the theater from the lowly depths of cabarets for so long that I was in shock when I actually walked out on a stage and began, in my awed way, to work with actors. I forgot every damn thing I knew. How could I have deluded myself into thinking that all those years of doing four or five shows a day in vaudeville or two or three shows a night in cabarets had anything to do with theater? What the hell did that naked, flesh-peddling, dirty title of cabaret artiste have to do with theater? You're damn right—it had everything to do with it. But it took me a long time to realize it.

All I could do was live those rehearsal days by reflex alone. I was aware of exhaustion, an aching body, and endless arguments among the bigger minds—management, directors, composers, designers; of straining to comprehend what all the talk was about and straining to absorb, too, all their advice on the art of acting, which was difficult for all concerned, since the part they were trying to get me up in was really never well written.

Even in all this confusion, though, there were compensations. I learned to drink up the tremendous vitality of the gypsies, the dancers. When we worked together I had the sensation of being a part of their bodies, that we were almost physically touching one another. I was so impressed with their dedication, their ability to go without something in order to pay for a dancing lesson—the Negro kids and the white kids in an association of creativity, unable to afford prejudice since they were all sharing the same problem, the difficulty of getting work in the theater. They sustained me.

And so did my family, making me feel safe and loved in my own little world.

Their patience was unshaken; all the questions and hysteria I carefully controlled in front of the cast, were cried out at home. There was Irene ready with warm food, Gail able to tell me so many helpful things, Lennie steady as a rock, and Ralph, whose fierce protection of me earned him the sobriquet "that gangster Harris" from various important people dealing with outside problems. Dear friend, Jimmy Wall, coached me in dialogue incessantly, and also taught me little niceties of protocol backstage. Josephine Premice and I managed to have a good healthy relationship, mainly because we liked each other. She had been in a couple of other fine shows (*House of Flowers* and *Mr. Johnson*) and was a brilliant performer with great European and Latin-American successes behind her. She had a marvelous biting wit, was brainy, beautifully educated, and Haitian. I was so busy being a "novice" in the theater I didn't have time to be jealous of her on stage—offstage, our personalities meshed very well. She had tremendous tact and sensitivity, and yielded to none of the feminine temptations of being sweetly solicitous with that kind of "do-you-mind-my-being-frank" remark that would have been disastrous at the time.

The cast, having been casually advised by Bobby Lewis, the director, to refrain from paying attention to and discussing the out-of-town reviews, never let on that I was obviously not too hot when we opened in Boston.

Meanwhile, a new love song never got written, various

costumes were never made, all the simple horrible things that happened to Ruby Keeler and Joan Crawford before opening nights in the movies—happened.

We came to New York with a huge advance ticket sale. We played two nights of previews in New York to charity audiences that were disastrous. There is something deadly about working in front of people who have spent $50 or $100 for their tickets and crowded into a theater to see a show. Something strange and perverse attacks them, and they hate everything they see. And I remember Jack Entratter saying, "What the hell are you trying to prove? You can make more in a month in Vegas than you can make in a year in that damn show."

Everyone was very discouraged by their reactions, me included. And yet, in a funny way, they helped me. I decided I probably couldn't be any worse than I was those two nights, and I hadn't yet killed myself when I got home. I was able to shrug it off and say, "Forget it." I was numb now, I had done my worst and the sky had not fallen.

Opening night was December 31, 1957. I had stumbled through the afternoon rehearsal and as curtain time approached I was sitting in my dressing room at the Imperial Theatre thinking just one dumb thought ("God, my feet are killing me") when I heard a knock at the door, and there appeared a huge, really enormous basket of flowers, propelled by Big Mike and Charlie Blackwell, our stage manager. On the card was written, "*Savanna, we love you, The Crew.*" Well, that did it. The last thing Bobby had said to me that afternoon finally penetrated. He had said, "When you make your entrance tonight, make it like you belong there and stand still." Just like in the movies, people do say things like that—when it seems to be necessary, I suppose. So standing inside the little shack, on stage, where Savanna lived, peeping calmly through the shutters at Marlene, Walter, Dorothy, Harold, Arlene, John, Carol, Richard,

Diane, family, friends—*tout* New York—I waited to enter
like I belonged. The entrance music stopped, I flung those
shutters open hard and spoke clearly—like my grandmama
taught me—barged down the steps, and stood still like
Bobby had advised me—and New York treated me like a
home-town girl. That sound was like warm summer rain.
My spine got straighter and my heart beat faster and I became so aware of everybody on stage, and I became aware
they were liking it and that we like each other, and I felt
for the first time as if it were really me living on the Island,
that I had been there always and that I did want to go to
New York desperately. And so we all worked together at
last.

Then it was over. Suddenly there were hundreds of
beautifully dressed, famous people on stage, in the dressing
room doorway. I was sitting in front of the dressing table—
sweaty, smelly, relaxed, being kissed first by Gail and Lennie, hugged by Ralph. Then photographed by the *Post*, I
think—all the while wondering if the Waldorf had prepared
enough food for the party I was giving us all—the cast and
crew—since no one up above had thought to tell us they
were giving one. Of course, we invited the bosses also. I
was so relieved that I had felt normal and natural on stage
that I forgot to worry about the reviews. After my first
drink at the Waldorf, I quite seriously thanked the kids and
said let's get drunk and enjoy ourselves. Mothers and
fathers and wives of crew and cast all beamed and I was
table hopping madly—when in walked David Merrick, the
producer, and various other big shots—with the first tele-
phoned report of the reviews. They were good, and Mr.
Merrick kissed my cheek and paid me a rather sportsman-
like compliment: "Well, I always said you were a money
runner." I wish he had told me that before.

Jamaica was heaven for a year-and-a-half. I was home.
After all those years of traveling back and forth and up and
down this continent, after all those trips to Europe searching for work that might be more pleasant, after all those
years, I was home—in New York.

We had two Christmases in our home in succession. I
can't remember when that happened before. And on Saturdays—after the last performance—we would throw a party
at our apartment. I loved the cast in the show, and it made
me feel good that they could accept me, even though my
life had been so different from the lives many of them had
led.

Those young, modern kids from the show, both black and
white, had a kind of dedication to their art that simply
amazed me. I couldn't help but compare their way of life to
the life I had led at their age. There had been so few open-
ings in the theater then that it would never had occurred
to us at the Cotton Club to scrimp and save and do without in order to take singing or dancing or acting lessons.
Consequently, we missed a whole experience of ambition or
involvement in our work that these youngsters had. Now
they struggled and trained, undaunted by the usual lack
of jobs. The opportunities in the arts, for Negroes in particular, have not expanded very much. Still, those among

them who were Negro were trying, and ready to offer psychological support to one another. They brought a thing to
my life that had been missing, that I had never seen as a
child and that I certainly never experienced in cabarets. I
recall that once, on the West Coast, finding some time on
my hands I actually enrolled in an acting class, just as these
kids do. I had done very well in improvisations, but I
could never bring myself to do the formal scenes. I remember having a go at Noel Coward's little one-act play, *Red
Peppers,* and how absurd I felt trying to do an English
music-hall performer. The corny jokes seemed to me just
that—corny—and not charming at all. Acting in scenes that
had a dramatic or social meaning, I could feel myself re-
treat inside, hide myself away from the students playing
the scenes with me, refusing to let them connect emotionally with me. The improvisations were different, because in
them I was working alone, with no need to connect, and I
could draw on so many memories I had tucked away inside
my head. Still, I had decided to quit the class rather
quickly, not wanting to continue the personal torture involved.

Now I saw *Jamaica* people devoting themselves to this
kind of preparation for their careers and, far from finding
it embarrassing, finding new strength in it. I knew how
tough their lives were, and I'm certain many of them faced
personal problems as difficult as any I'd faced. Yet they had
found new techniques for dealing with these problems, a
spirit, a dedication which sustained them, and which I
could only wish had been a part of my life when I had been
their age.

I also got a chance, at this time, to meet some Negro
youngsters who were not a part of show business, and I
found the same spirit, manifested in different ways, in them.
These were the daughters of my friend Marietta Dockery
and their friends—teen-agers who were in college in the

South. The first of the sit-ins began in these years, and some of them had participated. Some of them had even been jailed. From them, too, I learned something about the new ways this new generation was thinking.

I can't claim that any of these new friendships and experiences immediately transformed me or my life, but I think they started something.

For one thing, I finally screwed up my courage and went for a little while to a dance class that some of the kids in the show were taking, and there I felt none of the embarrassment I had felt in my previous classroom venture.

I think, too, that the activism I sensed in the young people had something to do with my response to an invitation to become an honorary member of Delta Sigma Theta, a Negro sorority. While I was working in *Jamaica* they pursued me for some time without me knowing it. They wrote me and they wired me and I paid no attention, did not even know why they wanted to get in touch with me. Through the years I had fallen into the habit of paying no attention to my correspondence, knowing how vicious much of it was. Thus, by mistake, the correspondence from Delta Sigma Theta was cast aside. But it had a group of officers who were real go-getters, and they tracked me down at the theater. Jean Noble, who was to become my close friend, was the president of the sorority, and she explained to me how Delta was different from the social sororities I had encountered when I was a band singer. Delta is a service organization with more than 35,000 members, all Negro college graduates. They donate scholarships. They have the country's oldest job opportunities program for young Negro women—and they are involved in international projects, especially the training of African women in this country for voluntary organization work in their own countries.

They work on voter registration, and try to be useful in

every possible way in building up social service organizations within the Negro community. The members themselves are doctors, lawyers, teachers, beauticians, houseworkers, seamstresses—the best of Negro womanhood; many of them, against tremendous odds, had accomplished fantastic things. They didn't spend much time on social activities. They had a tremendous, quiet pride in the tangible things they accomplished as individuals and as a group. They made me feel that my own suspicion of the ability of the middle class to accomplish good works was rather narrow and superficial. Through them I revived my work with the National Council of Negro Women, whose founder, Mary McLeod Bethune, was a close friend of my grandmother's.

Anyway, after becoming an honorary member I began to see them in cities outside New York. They became a kind of rallying point for me. I was very proud to be with them. I suppose they reminded me a little bit of my grandmother in their taste for hard work. In 1963 they even gave me a chance to see the direct link they formed with my grandmother's generation. In the March on Washington some of the Delta members who had been a part of the first suffragette parade there turned out to march again with us for civil rights. Somehow, that made me feel in touch with my own history, as well as with the history of the race, in a way that I had not been for many years.

II

I wish I could have experienced that feeling a little earlier, because after *Jamaica* closed in the spring of 1959 I fell into a deep apathy, the like of which I had never previously felt. Part of this was a natural let-down. I had wanted a Broadway show very badly. Now I had had it and

it was no longer a driving ambition, a hope to keep me going. Suddenly I was back in my old life again, shuttling
around from club to club. Nothing, it seemed, was changed
after all. A kind of inertia, born of melancholy, came over
me. I didn't believe anything I sang, I took no pleasure now
in professionalism, in polishing my work to a high degree.
I wanted to sing songs that hurl more meaning, more social
relevance, but my background as I've said did not even prepare me to sing the blues. So I felt incapable of doing any
serious songs.

Even Barney Josephson had seen the gimmick of my singing "My Man Done Left Me"—Billie's song—because it was
just that—an amusing trick—but hard to really believe. I
had been taught that you don't cry publicly about your private self, and besides, in the early days I was not actress
enough to act "the blues." But in 1960, the unreality of
"moon, June, penthouses, nostalgia for ocean liners"—pop in
general—began to stick in my craw. Songs of dying for love
and dedication to a man, airy-fairy songs, began to be difficult to sing. I was listening more and more to "folk music,"
which, I realized, seemed to speak about the "times" and to
be truly contemporary. Yet I felt that it would be completely dishonest of me to pull a switch in midstream and
sing folk music because it was popular. Besides, by the time
it left the lunch counters in the South and was recorded in
New York, it was "popular." I began to think there was nothing I could sing honestly anymore. I was beginning to question myself and my lack of compassion seriously.

In general, I could feel nothing except a lack of love
coming out of me toward anybody or anything; I was aware
of this lack in my dealings with family and friends. Now,
I'm certain I was not, at first, aware of what was happening
to me. I don't think anyone is totally aware of it when her
spirit starts to die.

It was at this point that a kind of racial anger began to

grow in me. I had to ask myself if I were merely attaching private feelings, disappointments and resentments to a larger, more critical, crisis. Perhaps. I don't really know. But I felt it painfully one afternoon after *Jamaica* had closed. I had managed to keep in touch with some of the young people who had appeared in the show. On this particular afternoon one of the young men dropped in for a drink. He was brilliant. He had had practically no work since the show closed, and then some white manager had got a group of Negro dancers together to appear in Puerto Rico, and they had all gone down there and worked and had not been paid all they were entitled to. Suddenly, I was angry. Suddenly, I saw again all the white bosses of my early days who had exploited us at the Cotton Club, who had treated Noble Sissle's band badly on the road, and I thought: "Nothing has changed, damn it, nothing is ever going to change." I didn't see, any more, the interracial solidarity of the dancers in the show. I saw that this boy, being Negro, was going to have a tougher time than his white contemporaries, no matter how many hardships they seemed to share.

He talked too, about the fact that one or two Negroes were being let on to the network musical programs and he knew and I knew that was just tokenism, a sop to the spirit of the times—no real breakthrough.

And I started crying—and bitching everyone out.

I began to think, What an ass I've been all these years. Back in the days when I had gone to Hollywood for the first time, people like Walter White had spent a lot of time telling me to be on my best behavior, to remember that I was the first of my race to be given such an opportunity in the movies. And I had, mostly, been a good little symbol. I had tried not to step out of line, not to make a fuss. And now it seemed to me that Walter had been wrong and I had been wrong, too. I had been a false symbol—and somehow I sensed, indirectly, I had let this young man down. I just felt like he was my flesh and blood, and I suffered with him in a new way.

When chance seems to single you out to act as a symbol, you are made to feel (or I should say *I* was made to feel) that you are being granted this big favor. It takes no talent, nothing unique, to be a symbol. (As a matter of fact, it's better if you're not too special.) Anybody could take your place was, implicitly, what was said to me. So, watch your step, be grateful, be modest. I never liked the role, but I had gone with it. And now it seemed, it was all a lie. All of us who had been symbols of Negro aspirations for the past couple of decades, had minded our manners, been the responsible, reasonable people we were supposed to be, and nothing had come of it. Down South very few more Negroes could vote now than had been able to then. Most Negro kids still get poor educations, were denied equal opportunities in employment, in housing, in everything else (and, of course, I thought mainly of show biz). So what had it all been for?

A new generation was taking over. And they were not interested in being symbols. They knew the symbol was obsolete—before I did. They were not interested in appeasing the white man, in cajoling favors from him. They were demanding their rights and not getting them yet. They knew my generation had been sold a bill of goods—and I was just learning it.

I also sensed another kind of separation, a separation from my race. I had lived a long time now in the white man's world and in a part of it that was far removed from Chitlin' Switch, Alabama, or from the streets of Harlem. What did I know, from current knowledge, of what life was like for most Negroes? I knew what I could remember from my childhood, but what did I know about here and now? I was an alien in the world of the average Negro. Financially and socially my role as a symbol had certainly paid off. In that way, at least, the favor that had been done me was something of value. I did not have to suffer the same stresses most of my race had to suffer. They had left me just one little old question, a minor point, nothing serious: "Who the hell am I?" and what did it prove?

I did not live like most Negroes, and for a long time had not thought like a Negro. The only thing was, my skin was still black. I thought I ought to come to grips with that fact.

III

My membership in Delta helped me in this. It's activities seemed to me ones that I could, given my age and the sort of life I lived, appropriately take part in. I really felt I belonged with them—and I had a tremendous admiration for them. It did not seem right for me to suddenly burst forth with a lot of fiery statements on civil rights, or to become a militant leader, taking to the streets of the South or North to lead protests. That was not in my character, and more important, I thought that the average Negro would be quite right to reject me, or at least to suspect my motives. Who was I to come around and start telling them what to do or how to behave? But I did feel that a service organization was quite a different matter.

It was great to release at least some of the anger, some of the raw feeling that I had bottled up in me for so long. I let some of it loose in 1960 in my famous—or infamous—unscheduled performance in the Luau in Beverly Hills. Lennie and I were supposed to meet Kay Thompson there for a drink. She was late, and Lennie went to call her to see what was holding her up. I was left alone at the table, which was on the upper level of the dimly-lit restaurant. Directly below it, on the main floor, some drunk started demanding immediate service. The waiter explained that he would be with him shortly, but that he was in the process of serving "Miss Horne's table."

"So what?" the drunk yelled. "She's just another nigger. Where is she?"

I reacted. Boy, did I react! I jumped up and held the table lamp to my face. "Here I am, you bastard, I'm the nigger you couldn't see." Then I started throwing things. The lamp, glasses, an ashtray. I'm an excellent thrower—as Lennie will testify—and I hit the man with something. He got a cut over his eye and he was bleeding, as they say, profusely. The waiters and management hustled up and led him away. Then I felt Lennie grab me from behind. "For God's sake, what happened?"

I explained, and he just nodded. "Did you hit him?" was all he asked. "Hell yes," I said. He nodded again, pleased. Then I noticed I was still clutching an ashtray, ready to let fly again.

We never did have that drink with Kay Thompson, and she's always been furious that she was late for our date.

It was, for sure, a minor incident, but it made all the papers. I got a bundle of mail, mostly from Negroes, praising me for what I had done. I was surprised at that. I always thought they knew that I would respond this way to a provocation of this kind. But apparently they had not really known that. In the early days, my name was not big enough to make headlines, and later I never made it a point of announcement. The mail made me feel that they wanted to identify with me, as I wanted to identify with them. I realized, as I read their letters, that this was something I had wanted more than I had ever admitted to myself, and that I had always been afraid that they would not believe me if I did something militant or just plain angry. I thought they would put it down as a cheap publicity stunt. How wrong I was! They didn't think that at all. In fact, they were genuinely pleased, I think, to see a famous symbol reacting as an outraged Negro person. Shortly thereafter Lennie and I went to the Caribbean on vacation, and I was amazed to have all sorts of Negroes come up and congratulate me personally on what I had done, just as if I had committed some act of heroism. There was, of course, nothing heroic in the incident. It was merely an expression of the mood I was often in, a temporary and unsatisfying (except in the immediate sense) resolution of the inner conflict I had been suffering.

That conflict continued to fester for almost three years. I wanted to re-identify myself with the Negro people. And yet I did not want to be forced into it, by some organization, by some external pressure. I wanted it to be an act of my own choosing. Involvement of this kind implies the right to choose non-involvement sometimes, too. You can call that selfish. I call it selfish myself. But I thought I had earned that right. I had allowed myself to be used, through the years, for all kinds of causes and benefits and charities, and I had gone passively along with those demands. I had also, in my preoccupation with my own life and career, allowed myself to be carried in an opposite direction as well sometimes—allowing myself to be "too busy" to respond to some requests for the use of the symbolic me.

Now, I was determined not to be a symbol. I wanted my responses to be determined not by the symbolic me—and the protection of same—but by the real me. Unconsciously, I think I wanted to act now as I knew my grandmother would have acted. I wanted, at last, to be my own woman, to be as sure of my motives, my place in society, my rights and privileges, as she had been.

IV

In the spring of 1963, I was presented with a situation in which I could make a clear-cut choice of behavior. Lennie and I were at the little home we had bought in Palm Springs in the late fifties. The situation in Birmingham was worsening. Martin Luther King's activities were beginning to be met with brutality and police repression that was to shock the world. I had stayed glued to the television set all day, watching and hearing the reports of the police dogs turned loose on Negro children, of fire-hoses knocking down Negro women as they marched in protest. I was in agony—and also feeling completely impotent to do anything.

I had planned to go to Birmingham myself, before the violence had started. Jean Noble and some other ladies from Delta had wanted me to go and join the marchers there. The special contribution they wanted me to make was to sing on the steps of a church there on Mother's Day. Jean had asked me to fly East to join them. But I had refused to go because I am afraid to fly. In the war years and in the fifties I had been involved in many near-miss plane accidents and I had simply refused to get on a plane since. There was no time for me to take a train to join them. So, combined with my sense of outrage and impotence there was one of anger with myself. I could have been there and I was not.

That evening James Baldwin called. We had met casually a few times—the first time when he came backstage at *Jamaica* to visit some of his friends in the cast—and I had once even written him a fan letter, something I practically never do. He's a strange, distant, brilliant man whom I don't suppose I will ever know very well. But I did respect him enormously. So when he told me that Attorney General

Robert Kennedy wanted to arrange a meeting of a number of prominent Negroes to discuss the crisis, and that he, Baldwin, wanted me to be one of them, I was naturally predisposed to going. But I did want to think about it. I wanted to make sure of my motives, make sure that I was simply not allowing myself to be trotted out as a symbol again.

Less than an hour after Jim's call, Jean Noble called. Her group had not been allowed to make its march. The night before, the Negro hotel where Dr. Shuttlesworth, Dr. King's assistant, was staying, had been bombed. The situation was so tense that those responsible for the demonstrations had turned Jean and her group away and they had come back to New York. I told Jean about the invitation to the Kennedy meeting and she advised me to come East. She agreed with me that Mr. Kennedy had always seemed to be someone Negroes could at least approach for a sympathetic hearing. That he had approached us, or rather this small group who really could speak for no one but themselves, was an added benefit. But I told Jean what I told him, that I would have to think about it a little longer.

I had begun to convince myself that all of us "firsts"— first glamour girl, first baseball player, first this-that-and-the-other—had reached the end of our usefulness. We were not symbols of the approaching rapprochement between the races. We were sops, tokens, buy-offs for the white race's conscience. Now millions of Negro people were reaching out, as a mass, to take what had been so long denied them. I did not want to be used to remind them of the old days. I wanted to join this movement not as a tired symbol but simply as me, as a private Negro person. I wondered if I still had that right.

It was Lennie who helped me make the decision to fly to Mr. Kennedy's meeting. He made me feel it was natural for me to go and contribute what I could. He made me real-

ize that I had a right to go, no matter what I had been or
how far I had drifted away from militancy or direct involvement through the years. It was, he led me to think, a
simple basic right that I still had as a Negro. The clincher
to his argument was this: "If you don't go, maybe you won't
love *me* any more . . ."

I think that what he was saying was if I didn't go then
I would lose respect for myself completely. If I did that I
would lose respect for our marriage, and finally, for him.
Perhaps he would, suddenly, become a white man in my
eyes.

And so I flew to New York. I arrived early at the address
Jimmy had given me. It turned out to be a big modern
apartment building. The doorman said no one was home in
the apartment I was supposed to go to (I think it belonged
to one of the Kennedys). So I sat down in the lobby on a
ledge. The next person to arrive was Rip Torn, the actor.
He is a Southerner and was a friend of Baldwin's, who had
invited him. He came over and introduced himself and we
chatted until the others all arrived. Among them were Baldwin, of course, the late playwright, Lorraine Hansbury,
Harry Belafonte, Kenneth Clark, the sociologist, a man
named Berry, from Chicago, and Jerome Smith, a young
man from SNCC (who turned out to be the heart and soul
of the meeting) and, finally, Mr. Kennedy, accompanied by
his aide, Burke Marshall.

The character of the meeting was symbolized by the seat-
ing arrangements. Somehow, all the white people were on
one side of the room, all the Negro people on the other.
The meeting began rather dryly. Dr. Clark and Dr. Berry
had come prepared with a large number of statistics showing the lack of opportunities for education, for employment,
for decent housing, for all the human necessities; really, I
think someone even had statistics on how many FBI men
were Southerners, because that agency's lack of real enthu-

siasm—as it seemed to us—for Civil Rights cases was on everyone's mind.

Mr. Kennedy's reactions were essentially defensive. I think he had called the meeting in hopes of persuading us that he and his brother were doing all that could be done to help the Negroes, and more than any other administration had ever done before. The funny thing was that no one there disputed that. It was just that it did not seem enough, especially in light of all the history that had gone before. We all wanted more. Many of us told him that we were grateful for the strong stand the government had just taken on getting James Meredith into the University of Mississippi. It was accepted as evidence of good faith—otherwise none of us would have been there—but he didn't realize how much we expected of him and how much more we felt had to be done, and quickly.

Mr. Kennedy seemed a proud man. He had the pride of the important offspring who had seen his family grow to power and greatness in a short period of time. He said something about his family and the kinds of discrimination it had had to fight. He also said he thought a Negro would be president within 40 years. He seemed to feel that this would establish some sort of identification, some sort of rapport, between us. It did not. In fact, it had the opposite effect. I wondered afterward whether he had read any of James Baldwin's books or been briefed on them. If he had, he would have realized that the emotions of Negroes are running so differently from those of white men these days that the comparison between a white man's experience and a Negro's just doesn't work. I don't even think logic works any more. What has made the Negro mood of the moment is not logic. You can't think about his condition or his demands these days in a purely logical way. There is no logic in the way the Negro has been treated and so, to suddenly start asking the Negro to be logical and reasonable and patient in his demands, which is what Mr. Kennedy was trying to do, was ridiculous to me.

These logical people have not treated the Negro logically, which is to say that he has not been treated as a human being. We should be properly grateful that Mr. Kennedy's brother was the first president since Lincoln to have paid some attention to the Negroes. But we were past accepting that sort of thing easily, just as we were past hearing the reasonable explanation for why the FBI assigns Southerners to their bureaus in Southern cities. All we knew was that they were part of the system that was oppressing the people in the South. In that moment, with the situation in Birmingham the way it was, none of us wanted to hear figures and percentages and all that stuff. Nobody even cared about expressions of good will.

Rip Torn had been sitting on an ottoman on the Negro side of the room, and after Kennedy had been placed on the defensive, Rip stood up and started talking about his own attitudes and the history that had formed them, trying to bridge the gap, I suppose, between the reasonableness of the white people and the emotions of the Negroes. He said he had been born in a little town in Texas so small its name wasn't even on the map and had gone to high school with kids who had gone coon-hunting (that is, baiting Negroes) at night for kicks, and that his own family had been bigoted. He said that he had learned how stupid that was and finally had to learn to take his own stand for what he thought was right. But neither side of the room listened to him. They didn't care that he was making, really, a marvelous sound. It didn't matter that Rip had salvaged his own soul. I think the white people thought he was just another one of those kooky actors, while the Negroes were past taking any joy in a single salvation.

They might have, and they might have appreciated Mr. Kennedy's efforts more and his explanations of them, if

Jerome Smith of SNCC had not been there. This young man cut through the fog of statistical arguments, through the expression of this personal attitude and that one.

His story was just thrown out on the floor for all to see. It was very simple. He had been in the South, working for voter registration. His wife and children had to be sent away for their own protection. He had been jailed and beaten and he was still physically ill from what had been done to him. You could not encompass his anger, his fury, in a set of statistics, nor could Mr. Belafonte and Dr. Clark and Miss Horne, the fortunate Negroes, who had never been in a Southern jail, keep up the pretense of being the mature, responsible spokesmen for the race any more. All of a sudden the fancy phrases like "depressed area" and "power structure" and all the rest were nothing. It seemed to me that this boy just put it like it was. He communicated the plain, basic suffering of being a Negro. The primeval memory of everyone in that room went to work after that. We all went back to nitty-gritty with that kid who was out there in a cotton patch trying to get poor, miserable Negro people not to be scared to sign their names to a piece of paper saying they'd vote. We were back at the level where a man just wants to be a man, living and breathing, where unless he has that right all the rest is only talk.

That's what I mean about that young man being the soul of the meeting. He took us back to the common dirt of our existence and rubbed our noses in it. Mr. Kennedy was taken aback by the naked fury of the boy and also, I think, at the response it drew from us. He was even made angry by it, I think. Baldwin sensed this and it was he, I think, who asked the boy if, feeling the way he did, he would fight for his country. The boy said he wouldn't. And Mr. Kennedy just could not understand that. The whole thing had gone beyond the give and take of politics, beyond the possibility of rational adjustments between people of good will. Mr.

Kennedy had worked hard to do what he had done. So had the President. But there was no gratitude, no willingness to take half a loaf. There was only an alienation from the system, so deep that a young man could risk his life in Mississippi but would not risk it in Viet Nam—so long as the country tolerated Mississippi.

After that, the Negroes there took a very hard line. The basic question we asked, in a lot of different ways, was why the government continued to promote the economy of a region that treated its Negro citizens the way the South did. We also wondered why pressure could not be brought to bear on Northern-controlled industry whose Southern branches (for example, the Northern-owned steel mills in Birmingham) went along with the Southern style of discrimination. There was much talk, but no conclusions. If the meeting had any real value, I suppose it was to impress on Mr. Kennedy the depth of the feelings that Negroes not directly involved in the movement brought to a Civil Rights discussion. The only surprise to me was that he didn't know in advance.

I went home to mull. And I mulled for several days. During that period I called the NAACP and told them I wanted to go South. I was told that I could sing at a rally in Jackson, Mississippi. I wanted to. Now the idea of flying gave me no pause. But I wondered whether Southern Negroes could possibly accept someone like me, a Northerner, not a notable militant, a rather worn-out symbol of another era of racial struggles. But I did want to go, I had to go. I felt something inexplicable drawing me South. I had just about made up my mind when a very angry Negro journalist came to interview me. He started chiding me, saying that I was too scared to go South. If I needed anything to confirm my decision, it was that man. In his voice I heard again that orchestra leader telling me how "his people would never accept me." I thought "Hell, I better find out." I invited

Jean Noble to come with me and rounded up Billy Strayhorn to play for me and off we went.

Medgar Evers was head of the NAACP in Jackson and as I look back on it, meeting him was the great thing that happened to me on that trip. He was a strong, vital, active, modern man and he had an incredibly difficult job. Jackson is not a town where it is easy to apply economic pressure on the segregationists. It has very little industry susceptible to outside pressure. The Negroes there work in the white kitchens, or in menial jobs, or teach in the segregated schools. But a schoolteacher who speaks out in favor of voter registration is going to lose her job. So the only hope of improving conditions in Jackson is to use moral persuasion on the whites there. And who gives a damn about morality? But Medgar was trying, and trying under the most difficult circumstances. He was an NAACP field representative, which means he was an organization man. He had to fit his plans into the over-all plans of the national organization, make his responses to local situations within the patterns it laid down. At the same time, he had to remain an inspiration to the people with whom he worked, and keep up his own inspiration. The remarkable thing was that he managed it. And managed, as well, to be a warm, sympathetic human being, too. I'll never forget that this man, with all he had on his mind, came out to the airport to meet us when we flew in. We could not stay at his house because it had been recently bombed and it was not fixed up yet. But he saw to it that we were comfortably settled.

I thought then—and I think now—that it is harder to be that kind of soldier in the battle than it is to be an inspirational leader. Until he was killed, Medgar Evers was an anonymous man, with none of the protections given to a celebrity. I saw how unprotected Medgar was, how easy it would be to kill him. In Jackson he had no big administrative organization to protect him, not even the sanction of religion. Medgar and his family just lived their lives the same as any other Negro down there.

I had a chance to see the contrast between his position and that of an outsider while I was in Jackson. Dick Gregory was also down for the rally, and he led the faction there who wanted to go out in the streets afterward to make a more militant protest. Now Dick is a fantastic human being. He was flying in and out of the South all during this summer, accepting the risks of jail and injury and abuse on the same level as everyone else. And he did all this at the time his wife had just lost their second baby in childbirth. In Jackson, he and Medgar came into conflict. The NAACP had decided that there should be no street protest in connection with the rally and Medgar, whatever his real feelings, had to go along with that. Dick was angry and even claimed that the reason for the ban was that the NAACP was trying to protect me. I don't believe the NAACP grinds to a halt just to protect the likes of me. I hated being caught between these two men, because I had tremendous respect for both of them. Each was doing something I was incapable of doing, Medgar as a tactical officer—a sort of first lieutenant at the front—Dick as an emotional rallying point. I don't know who was right, strategically, in this instance, but my sympathies were with Medgar, if only because he had to live there and, therefore, knew best what suited the local situation. In any case, there was a rally, but no protest beyond that.

I was scared to death, but not of the white Southerners. I was afraid of the Negroes, afraid that they might reject me. Who the hell was I to go to Jackson, Mississippi, to give those people the benefit of my worldly wisdom? I can't help thinking that if that rally had been held in Harlem they probably would have thrown eggs at me.

However, I had underestimated the natural kindness and gentleness of the southern Negro people and they were wonderful to me, although I certainly did not inspire them in any way. They don't need "celebrities" to come down and inspire them. To use an old-fashioned phrase, theirs is a people's revolution and they have their own leaders who, like Medgar Evers, lead every day by example. But they were good to me.

They gave me much more than I could possibly give them. Basically, I am an urban Northern Negro. We, as a group, are a lot more cynical than the Southern Negroes, which may be why we have not produced more idealistic leaders like Medgar or Martin Luther King. This Northern cynicism is the result of all the half-promises that are made to us and then so frequently broken. Southern Negroes are promised nothing, so their idealism and their aspirations are untainted by the kind of suspicion that the Northern Negroes come to feel. The Southern Negro Revolution, I think, is expressing a very pure thing.

To be in touch with that kind of purity, just for a moment, was a very great thing for me, after all the years I had wandered in the wilderness of my career, my personal preoccupations. I remembered what Paul Robeson had said years before. He said that we could not win through anger and bitterness, but through pride and belief that our cause was just. I saw that pride and that belief in Jackson.

A few days after I returned I was scheduled to go on the "Today" show on NBC. There was nothing special about the invitation. Hugh Downs and I had met and talked several times and he said he wanted me to come on the show and talk about this and that. Our schedules had never worked out before, but now, coincidentally, they did. I was glad because I was so keyed up emotionally by Jackson that I thought I would have more to talk about than I might otherwise have had. But I was exhausted. I had had very little sleep since coming from Palm Springs and when I did have time for it, I couldn't really rest. So, knowing that I would have to be up at five in the morning to be at the studio, I went to bed at 6 P.M. the night before. Irene brought me dinner there and Jean Noble sat and talked with me for a while and then I went to sleep, shutting off TV, radio, and telephones. The next morning it was the same thing. I got up at 5 A.M., had my coffee, put on my make-up, and went down to the studio.

As I guess everyone knows, the "Today" show is done in the Florida showcase, a shop in the RCA Building with a large window facing 49th Street. It's very cramped for doing a TV show, and guests are usually asked to wait in a little storeroom until it's their turn to go on. I was sitting there, having another cup of coffee, watching some girl demonstrate judo exercises for the TV audience, when a floor manager came up and said: "We're sorry to hold you up like this Miss Horne, but we want you to be on the second section of the program, when the full network is carrying it. Besides, Mr. Wilkins hasn't come yet."

Roy is the head of the NAACP, of course, and I hadn't known that he was to appear and so I said, "I'd be happy to see him."

"I suppose he's been held up," the man said, "considering what's happened."

"What's happened?" I asked.

"Don't you know? They murdered Medgar Evers last night."

And that's how I heard about it. This was less than a week after I had been with Medgar in Jackson. I was so shocked and incoherent that I did not think I could go on the show at all. But I had a few minutes to pull myself together. I hardly knew what to say to Roy when he arrived or he to me. We were both numb. And I knew he and Medgar had been very close. I don't really remember what I said on that show, except that the girl who had been demonstrating judo reminded me of a class I had attended in Jackson in which they had been teaching little nine-to-twelve-year-olds self protection, how to protect their bodies, how to cover their heads if they were knocked down and someone started to kick them.

Medgar's death had so filled me with horror that all I could see were miles and miles of little Negro children lying in the knee-chest position, protecting themselves from white people. I talked about that. And I talked about the terrible loneliness of the Negro child when his mother first explains to him what it is to be a "Nigger" and he knows that he is, from that day forward, forever set apart.

I think my heart broke that day.

I had made a commitment to go, that same day, to a luncheon put on by the Gandhi Society to honor Dr. Martin Luther King. I forced myself to go. Of course, Medgar Evers' death dominated the meeting and there were many beautiful eulogies to him. I can't pretend to know the thoughts in everyone's mind that afternoon, but I know many of them saw him as a martyr of the large cause, which he was, certainly. But all I could think of was something a teacher had said to me in Jackson:

"You know, this town is really tough. Bad. Hard. We work at the jobs we're allowed. We teachers say only what we're allowed. We cannot feed our children unless we're allowed. By the white man. Medgar is our courage. He inspires us to be a little less afraid."

So my thought that afternoon was: That's what the whites tried to kill—the meaning Medgar had for those people, not for the larger cause. God, make it too late for his murderers to do this. I believe they were too late.

After the meeting I went up to Dr. King and met him for the first time. He then asked me if I would go to Atlanta to sing at a rally that was being staged by the Southern Christian Leadership Conference. I said I would. Mercer Ellington, Duke's son, whom I love very much, agreed to conduct for me and George Kirby, the comic, was to be on the program, and the rally was supposed to be much bigger than the one we had staged in the church in Jackson.

But somehow it was not as inspiring. There were empty seats, and the usual arguing between committees about who had and who hadn't sold enough tickets. The irony of the situation really hit me when I found great interest in the big reception they were to attend to meet the performers after the show. I resented the champagne and flowers at that reception. They must have cost as much as three or four hundred of the unsold tickets to the rally. For an instant there I felt as if I was back in my old symbolic role again, and I felt separated from the spirit I found in Jackson, though I knew, of course, that none of this was the fault of Dr. King and his associates. Just life's little round of formal hang-ups.

V

The long, hot summer of 1963 enabled me to get a new perspective on myself. I saw now that the experiences that had made me what I was had to be accepted by me without guilt and without shame. I was different from many Negroes because my life had been different from theirs. It would be false for me, now, to learn to type and become a secretary for CORE or SNCC or the NAACP. It would be equally false for me to attempt a role like Jimmy Baldwin's on the one hand or Dick Gregory's on the other. I had to go on being me. And that meant that I must find ways to contribute to life as it was happening now—to the cause—without losing myself in it, without being false either to it or to me. I've said the thing that struck me most about the people I met in the South was the purity of their devotion to their revolution. I could not be any less pure in the contributions I made to it, however modest they were.

Late that summer *Show* magazine asked me to write a piece about myself and about being a Negro in America. I had been asked many times to do such articles—and books, too—but had always refused. This time I accepted. I wanted to see if I could figure out, in the course of writing, who I was as of 1963, when I was forty-six. I wanted to face my past honestly and see if it could tell me anything about my future. I did not know it then, but it was the beginning of a long period of re-evaluation that is still going on.

The piece had one immediate benefit for me. In it, I wrote:

"I don't want to sing the same old songs or act in the same stereotyped musicals. There is a great problem for me as a performer in all this. I am not about to get a guitar and start singing revolt songs. I know fifty-two other singers who can sing them better than me, including Peggy Lee. And I'd look pretty silly at the Waldorf in a Balmain dress describing the feelings of small children attacked by dogs and hoses—then they really *should* throw eggs. But there has to be some way for a sophisticated urban adult to express the movement. How can I go on singing a song about a penthouse way up in the sky when, with housing restrictions the way they are, most of us still couldn't rent the place.

"The great protest songs are coming from the Southern students. I can't sing *these* songs, but I think that songs can be written and plays and musicals produced which simply put the Negro in the context of the world—not necessarily as youth in protest and certainly not as something 'special'—but just as people who are around and alive. I think it is the great chance of my generation to try and express this. I would like the songs I sing in the future to be more realistic, to sound the way this new generation sounds."

Now, I didn't expect any direct result from that statement of mine, but after the *Show* piece had been out for a
few days I got a call, out of the blue, from Harold Arlen.
He said: "I've thought about it a lot, and, you know, you're
right. I started reviewing all the stuff I've written and we
should all get involved in this new awakening—and I remembered this piece I originally wrote with Ira Gershwin.
I think if we changed the lyric a little bit it could be the
song you were asking for." I went over to his house to talk
about it, and the upshot was that Yip Harburg put new lyrics
to it, and we did have the sort of piece I could sing and
which did have contemporary meaning. It was called
"Silent Spring" and it was dedicated to the four children
murdered in the bombing of the church in Birmingham.

At almost the same time, Jule Styne came over to the
house and played the score for *Funny Girl.* I loved the
score but I told him: "Goddamit, I'm sick of you coming
up here and playing scores for other broads on my piano."
We laughed, because we had tried to work together on a
couple of things but they had never quite come off.

By this time I had committed myself to do a benefit at
Carnegie Hall for SNCC. Frank Sinatra and I were to be
the two stars. The proceeds for the second night were to
go for a favorite charity of his, the proceeds from the first
night to SNCC, which was my choice. So I asked Jule if
he could do something special for that concert. He mulled
it over and said, "Hey—how about putting some lyrics—
just the way you talk and the things you talk about—to the
Jewish song called 'Hava Nagillah.'" He got Betty Comden
and Adolph Green to do the lyrics and the song was called
"Now" and it became a *cause célèbre,* when the networks
refused to allow the recording I made of it to be played.

But I got my wish. I got the kind of protest songs that
I could sing, sing in a way that was true to me and yet
also, I felt, true to the movement.

I also got a wonderful fringe benefit, because I was able to recruit Harold Arlen to accompany me in a medley of his songs at the concert, ending with "Silent Spring."

That concert was a tremendous event in my life. It started out badly. Frank had not had time to rehearse any duets as I had hoped we could, since the people were being asked to pay a lot of money and I thought we ought to give them our fullest potential.

And then we had a great deal of trouble selling tickets for the night SNCC was to receive the money. You see, in that year SNCC was controversial, whereas Frank's charity was not. The two-dollar and five-dollar seats went fast enough, but the $100 seats and $800 boxes just weren't moving. I went out and browbeat my friends and slung my name around in a way I'd never done before. I got on the phone, and wrote letters to everyone I could think of, making demands on them and through them on people I didn't even know. My friends rose to the occasion and we finally sold all the expensive tickets. It was the hardest work of my life.

But the result was a spirit on the SNCC night that was just fantastic. Everybody in the audience felt that he was a part of something big and good. I was so thrilled that I had to say something. "I don't make speeches," I said, "but tonight I have this overwhelming feeling of gratitude and pride that I am a New Yorker." Everybody yelled and clapped and clapped—for themselves, I thought, because they were all participating in something bigger than itself.

It was a real peak in my life. For once I felt the symbol had been useful. It had made something wonderful of the spirit happening. This wasn't the usual charity, where you could write a check and send it off and forget it. A lot of people had had to think hard about committing themselves publicly to this cause. Much examination of the soul went on and some good people who didn't come found out,

I guess, that they weren't as good as they thought they were. But some others, who did come, found out they were a little better than they thought they were. And when I sang "Now" I knew I had the privilege of singing out loud the sentiments of everyone there. Sometimes it is thrilling to be an artist!

That night I felt I was really home at last. Home to the city of my birth, home to myself and maybe getting home to my race and my people.

EPILOGUE

But I was not home free. Perhaps I never will be, for I still have not finished sorting out all the implications of the personal reawakening that took place for me in the midst of the Negro Revolution, which I think should be retitled "The Second American Revolution." I am not certain that I ever will completely understand what happened to me during the summer of 1963.

Nor will I ever completely forgive myself for allowing that ennui, that malaise of the spirit, that shutting off from life to take over in me. Nor should I have blamed everything on "the system." Nor will I forgive myself my inability to love—my family, my work, my race, myself, as fully as I might have in the long, dead years.

I can see now that my trouble was that a laziness of spirit made me unable to create for myself a strong identity. I was forever living up to someone else's idea of what I should be, who I should be. My mother wanted me to be a star and I worked hard for her goal, though I hated it so much that when later I achieved what she wanted for me I could really not enjoy it, and neither could she, so deep was our alienation.

The influential Negroes who advised me and helped me early in my career wanted me to be a symbol of Negro aspirations, and I accepted that role unwillingly and came, in time, to hate it, too. I was not strong enough to maintain myself inviolate beneath the symbol. Nor, knowing myself, did I ever think that I was a good enough person to be a worthy symbol. As a result I found only guilt and shame in my symbolic role. As for the white man, he either advised me to forget the basic fact of my color and to pass or he urged me to exploit it, to be an exotic sexual symbol. Rarely did he try to find out who I was, what my talents and desires were. He, too, was the prisoner of his preconceived ideas about what a Negro woman should be. As a result of this I spent most of my life being pulled in this direction and that, never finding my own true path, until at last I gave up and played dead for a while, sinking deep into spiritual indolence and self-hatred.

I look at Irene—my friend, my housekeeper, my dresser whom I mentioned earlier—a beautiful, dark brown woman, born in Pennsylvania Dutch country. Her grandmother walked over the Alleghenies to find her husband, who had fought on the Northern side in the Civil War. She has a Bible which traces her ancestry back to the French Revolutionary time. She is of a large, loving family, one of thirty Negro families in the town where she was born. When she came I said, "I'm so happy because I've found it difficult to find a Negro to work for me." And she said, "But I only work for ladies and gentlemen." And I looked at her with envy because she seemed so completely sure of who she is and why she is. Her judgment of a person is just simply whether he is worthy of her friendship or not. I find her so much like my grandmother.

I sometimes think that if I had been able to spend all of my childhood with my grandmother, I would have been able to develop a character strong enough to resist all these pulls and able to assert itself without fear, or hesitation, right or wrong. That strong, sure woman! If only I could really have tested myself against her. I would have ended up hating her, perhaps, but I would have ended up stronger, and as my own person, too.

The title of the article I wrote for *Show* in the summer of 1963 was, "I Just Want to Be Myself" and that summed up my desires then and now. But it seems significant that I could not express that desire until that summer when the entire Negro race, in effect, expressed that same desire for all the world to see. In the moment when they definitely rejected all the white man's clichés and images, all the half-kept and unkept promises that had prevented them from being truly themselves, then and only then could I openly say that I, too, wanted to be myself. I took my strength from them, and I'm beginning to feel less and less guilty that I take more from the revolution that I can possibly give it. I know it's selfish, but I also know that most Negroes do not resent me for doing it. They too, are drawing individual strength from the collective strength of the many. And I am more grateful than I can say for their allowing me the same right, for granting me my right to act for myself and not as a symbolic figure.

It is a real drag to be of the interim generation, or so I've often thought. But the political pressures are beginning to be reversed now because we Negroes are emerging politically powerful. World War II and the Korean War have made great changes in the pattern of Negro life in this country. So has Africa and its catalytic mood. Now, I feel as if I had been buried in that interim period like a body in an iceberg, but that the ice is beginning to melt and crack and I'm emerging still alive.

I've lived through all the deadly "firsts"—the years of the white impresarios looking for the white hope Lena Horne, and, more recently, some of those same impresarios looking for the black Lena Horne (talk about divide and conquer). I'm so glad that no Negro girl has to accept any yardstick but her own ability now. I like to think that if any comparison is made to me and my career, she will not be embarrassed by me "the person" even if the stereotype "me" is distasteful.

I have lived through a fifteen-year period when I desperately wanted a TV show of my own and I finally had to go to England last year to get someone to pick up the tab and help me sell it. When I was asked how it felt to have my own show I found I had outlasted the bitterness and overcome the apathy. I was just glad it was a damn good show which made me anxious to do more. I want to work —I want to live. I have met and worked for and with Presidents and even curtsied to Queens. I have felt pain for Medgar Evers' murder and for John F. Kennedy's murder. I know the great and have frequently met the infamous— for that is part of the experience in a life like mine. The interim period is over.

So the end of this book is the writing of this book. The decision to face my past and the self which existed in and was formed by it could not have been made before this time. I had many times rejected the idea of writing an autobiography. Before this time, I could not bear the idea of exposing myself again, even in memory, to the forces that shaped me and to the person I have been. The guilts I bore for the things I had left undone, for the empty symbol I then thought I was, were too heavy for me to contemplate.

But now I am free. The Negroes no longer need a handful of successful people to symbolize their hopes. They no longer need to live vicariously through us, for they are reaching out to take, *en masse,* what we were "given," in order to keep *them* still. History has passed us by—the generation of the celebrity symbols. We are free merely to be human, free to speak, frankly as individuals, not as examples, not as "credits" to our race. And so I do not have to measure myself against an impossible ideal of Negro womanhood and feel shame over my failure to meet the standards. I can, at last, try to be myself.

I confess that I felt lonely and strange when I realized that the need for the symbolic me was over. However unhappy it made me, it was an identity and sometimes a protection. For a brief time I resented, I think, the younger generation which has made this revolution and, now has, perhaps, a certain contempt for the way people like me were bilked by the previous generation's lies.

But that feeling has passed also. Not so long ago I found myself at three o'clock on a Sunday afternoon climbing on to a revolving stage about to be transported by it before a matinee audience in a theater-in-the-round. There was nothing terribly glamorous about that huge, coldly modern place and the atmosphere was not really right, I thought, for my kind of performance. But I went on and entertained that audience. I worked and felt a kind of pride that I had rarely felt in my professional ability. There was nothing special about this crowd—no chi-chi. They were just people. And I was just doing my job. But I did it well. I did not feel the contempt for the medium that I have so often felt in show business. Neither did I feel they had come to see a freak—the Negro who doesn't sing like a Negro. They had come to see Lena Horne, who may not be the world's greatest entertainer, but who sure gives you your money's worth. Lena Horne, the professional. How I used to hate the critics who reluctantly praised me with that term. Now I could feel what they meant and I could accept it.

One day when I was working on this book I felt an overwhelming need to telephone my father. He manages a small motel in Las Vegas that I own, but we had drifted into that "Horne silence" through the years and had not been really close for a long time. I reached him immediately and the first thing he said was: "What's wrong?"

"I just had to call you," I said. "I've been thinking of you so much lately and I realized I've been identifying with you all my life without knowing it."

"And now you feel bad because you've been accused of coldness and hardness, huh?"

His instantaneous understanding made me burst into tears. I began to apologize—for my whole life, I guess—but he would have none of it.

"Ask for no mercy and give less," he had always said and now he said it again. "You've got nothing to apologize for," he added. He has never defended his course. He simply ran it. "Trust no bush that quivers," is another of his oft-repeated mottoes, and that's the way he has gone through life—suspicious of favors, independent, proud, astringent. It has made him a distant and forbidding, if glamorous, figure to me.

Now as I listened to him talk I could understand that independent spirit of his for the first time, and I had to say, "Daddy, I love you." And the saying of those words felt so good, because I know now that the strength and hardness I had used to help me live for so long had, until then, not permitted love. For I had always thought that to admit love was to admit weakness. I had always taken. I had never been able to give back as I was now able to, just for an instant, with my father.

I don't think I've been searching for a father all these years. It's so corny I wouldn't admit it if it were true. But I did want, I'm sure, to be able to accept him simply for what he was, because to accept Teddy Horne is to accept all the perils and all the pleasures of freedom. And it is to accept a large part of myself as well.

I still do not accept everything. My mother and I will probably be working at understanding one another until we die. And then there's my son, Teddy, proud, sensitive, tremendously brilliant, mystic, poet, writer, loyal to two parents under difficult situations——I know I love him for himself, not because he is mine. He and I are still not as close as I wish we could be. I hope these things will change. But if they do not, I hope I will have the grace not to torture them about it. Or myself. I hope I will at least be able to set them free of the pose we share and in the process, allow myself to be completely free, too.

In 1963, my daughter married Sidney Lumet, the director, and of course, I acted like a typical mother. I did not want my daughter to leave me and start a life of her own. We had been apart so much when she was growing up that it seemed especially cruel, now that we were living together in New York, to have to let her go so soon.

"You're a good friend, Mother, but I don't think you really love me," she said to me one time. Now she was leaving. How could I prove to her that she was wrong—that I did love her, even if I had not let her see it? I was afraid she would never know. And so, secretly, I resented her marriage.

But then in the fall of 1964 it came time for her to have her first child and I went to London to be with her. It was a difficult birth and for two days her life and the baby's life hung in balance. And yet, strangely, it was a beautiful time, too. I saw the uncomplicated honesty of the way her husband loved her and I saw that they had something going there that could survive anything and I saw something bigger and grander than my life. So I gave up my Gail. I knew there was no promise I could make to anyone that would help her. I knew there was no punishment I could agree to accept that would help her. Nor did I think her pain was somehow a punishment being inflicted on me for my past sins and errors. And when all that came clear to me I knew—I just absolutely knew—that Gail was going to be all right and that the baby was going to be fine. And it was so. When it was all over I walked out of that hospital feeling freer than I had ever been, because I knew my child and my grandchild were going to be free in a way that I had not been until that moment.

I will be freer still. Of that I'm sure. Sometimes when Sidney and Gail don't even realize I'm there, I've been welcomed by the housekeeper and I've crept up the stairs to the nursery to sit alone with Amy and look at her and talk to her. Sometimes, then, I think of a phrase I heard down South when I was a child: "Ain't 'bliged to love you."

I hope little Amy never feels obliged to do anything she does not want to. In fact, I hope she never has to feel obliged to anyone *for* anything. I hope, though, that free of obligations she will be able to love and to give of herself in a way that I have not always found it easy to do. That's why I like to be alone with her sometimes, without people around to make her feel she owes me something. I hope, some day, when she's old enough, she will offer her love freely, without constraint. Tiny as she is, I look for a sign. I know the times are better than they were for me. I know, too, that her house is full of love, as many of my houses were not. And so I wait in hope as the afternoon shadows lengthen and Gail's little Amy lies sleeping.